HOT TOWNS

OTHER BOOKS BY PETER WOLF

Land in America: Its Value, Use, and Control (1981)

The Future of the City: New Directions in Urban Planning (1974)

The Evolving City (1974)

Eugène Hénard and the Beginning of Urbanism in Paris 1900–1914 (1969)

HOT
TOWNS

*The Future of the
Fastest Growing
Communities
in America*

PETER WOLF

RUTGERS UNIVERSITY PRESS
New Brunswick, New Jersey, and London

Wolf, Peter M.

Hot towns : the future of the fastest growing communities in America / Peter Wolf.

p. cm.

Includes bibliographical references and index.

ISBN 0-8135-2696-5 (alk. paper)

1. Urban-rural migration—United States. 2. Cities and towns—United States—Ratings.

3. United States—Rural conditions.

I. Title.

HT381.W65 1999

307.2'4'0973—dc21   99-11942
                                        CIP

British Cataloging-in-Publication data for this book are available from the British Library.

Manufactured in the United States of America.

CONTENTS

TABLES

Acknowledgments

Much appreciated support from the Graham Foundation for Advanced Studies in the Fine Arts liberated time for me to get started on this book. There are also individuals I want to thank for help all along the way. My children, Phelan and Alexis, endured innumerable conversations and contributed ideas early on, as did Cristina Wysocki, Calvin and Alice Trillin, Glen Hartley, and Lynn Chu. Imaginative initial research was commendably executed by Brian Williams. Rick Adams completed more detailed probing. Tuesday Fonville held to demanding schedules as she worked with much appreciated skill retyping drafts. For realistic advice and editorial guidance I am grateful to Barbara Plumb, Jean Strouse, Shannon Gifford, and Sarah Gold. Marlie Wasserman, director of Rutgers University Press, exhibited early interest and confidence in this project and so gave it a home; her later critique of the rough draft helped to better organize the manuscript. Pamela Fischer's patient, skillful, and deeply appreciated editing shortened and enhanced this book.

HOT TOWNS

THE NEW MIGRATION
Perils and Promises

For those cities that were great in earlier times must have now be-
come small, and those that were great in my time were small in the
time before. . . . Man's good fortune never abides in the same place.
HERODOTUS

IN A NEW AND VAST migration, each year a million of the most successful, accomplished, and well-off Americans are moving to the nation's most desirable communities. The wealth and cash flow that transfer with them each year is greater than the entire market value of all Manhattan real estate. This book is about that migration and also about those communities—today's hot towns—and how they may be harmed by their new inhabitants. Those growth towns scattered all across the country that learn to incorporate newcomers wisely will survive and prosper. Those that grow rapidly without new guiding precepts are already losing their appeal.

In the twenty-first century, I believe, wise inhabitants of growing places will come to a new conclusion: rather than promote growth at any cost, as in the past, they will exert every effort to preserve the qualities that attract people in the first place. Desirable consequences for all will follow. Today, residents and managers of these communities have the option, as described in this book, of acting responsibly to encourage wise, spawl-free growth while simultaneously preserving and even enhancing community quality—an option not exercised in any of the four previous mass relocations of people to and within America.

Today's voluntary movement of people of all ages out of older cities and suburbs to generally smaller, more remote, more physically attractive locales, and back into the most desirable locations in some cities, is the fifth national migration and is unlike any that preceded it.[1] The previous four overlapping surges of people on the move, each of which was based on need or was involuntary, shaped the settlement map of America. Discontented Europeans and enslaved Africans created the first coastal communities (1600-1785). The poorest Americans pushed across the continent during the westward settlement of the interior (1750-1890). Urban concentration followed as millions of job seekers moved into industrial cities (1820-1920). And, finally, between 1930 and 1990, suburban disbursement occurred when one hundred million people in young households drove out of town.[2] The fifth migration, which began about 1970, is and will continue to be every bit as influential.

Today participants in the fifth migration are streaming into highly desirable communities across the country—places distinguished by fine climate, awesome physical beauty, abundant recreation opportunities, pristine air, pure drinking water, relatively few social problems, and low crime—and they are also returning to the best locations in the most interesting older cities. They bring with them, or help to create, over $150 billion of assets in these new places, each year.

Fifth-migration growth towns cannot be defined by location, size, history, or economic profile. But the population in each has increased by 30 percent or more in fifteen years. The areas considered growth towns may thus change from time to time; but within them population is accelerating at two to four times the national average. Growth towns are as varied in location and character as Bozeman, Montana; Orlando, Florida; Charlotte, North Carolina; and Aspen, Colorado. Tables in this book single out specific hot towns for detailed examination. Many are the sort of place a traditional family stuck in its daily routine thinks of visiting on vacation. Others are new centers of work and commerce. They may be rural counties, country villages, exurban communities, or even cities. A growth town includes both the named place and its immediate outlying areas or suburbs. It may be smaller than one county or, in metropolitan areas, may include one or several socially and economically interrelated counties. The term *growth town* is thus an inexact catchall. But growth towns do have one thing in common: by luck or by design they have become principal destinations for participants in the fifth migration. Indeed, some are under siege, inundated by new people, new businesses, new jobs, and more traffic. These are the boom towns of the next fifty years.

Today's redistribution of people contrasts vividly with the four previous migrations. A new species of American migrant is on the move: not, as in the past, the needy, but the comfortable, well-educated, and well-trained; not the job seekers and risk takers, but those with leisure, choices, and the wherewithal to seek out the best. This privileged group, a small fraction of the forty-five million Americans who change address annually, is composed of well-trained recent graduates, influential professionals, highly skilled workers, and well-off retired citizens. Many fifth-migration participants think of themselves as individual adventurers rather than as part of a broad national movement. They will find themselves, and plenty of company, in this book. I not only present a profile of those moving but also explain why they are on the move and what they are looking for.

There are, of course, people everywhere who elect not to move, although they are qualified by income and job skills to participate in the fifth migration. These fifth wavers share the values and the priorities of fifth-migration participants but have not changed primary residence. The *fifth wave* thus refers to both those who are moving and those who could if they wished to do so.

I began the research for this book in the early 1980s. Once I recognized the general shape and some of the consequences of the fifth migration, I wanted to know more. How do demographics, new values, new ideas about health and leisure, and new technologies drive the fifth migration? What are the big issues in growth towns, and what do these towns look like? How do both established residents and newcomers react to rapid growth and change? How is the fifth migration different from others? How decisive is the impact of this massive relocation and wealth transfer, and are the results positive or negative? And then perhaps the most problematic issue of all: can a fifth-migration growth town become a sound, well-managed, sensibly evolving place?

To some extent, the influence of the fifth migration is already being felt. Polls reveal considerable anxiety. In western states over 20 percent of residents feel negatively affected by recent growth. In many growth towns, 80 percent of residents are concerned. In seasonal resorts forced into becoming year-round hubs, the changing status of the town is a constant preoccupation. Many residents living in communities under intense growth pressure wish their town would retain its special quality of life and character of place. But in many of these most desirable places the warning signs of deterioration are already flashing: overbuilding, inadequate land-use controls, traffic congestion, increasing crime, depleted natural resources, rising taxes, uninspired public-private collaboration, and, often, underprepared town management.

In this book I do not address the problems found in deteriorating parts of older cities and decomposing suburbs. But these troubling, stubborn issues, created in part by the fifth migration, have in a variety of ways stimulated my thinking. The regrettable decline of these previous destinations of Americans on the move has been under way for many decades. Perhaps it will prove reversible with the institution of wise policies, financial sacrifices by residents and businesses, and the extensive dedication of public, private, and semipublic resources. But that is another though related story, one outside the bounds of this book and already addressed by many others. There are, however, instructive parallels. Today, as in the early stages of urban and suburban decline, significant numbers of growth towns are in the process of becoming the victims of their own attractiveness. Without an insightful approach to future development, another destructive cycle of boom and bust can be expected, a cycle experienced over and over as the four previous national migrations exerted their inexorable impact on the physical, social, and environmental resources of America.

In response to the concerns raised nationwide by the fifth migration, I pay special attention to the question of whether another round of boom and bust is inevitable. Looking at what we have already experienced, I conclude that the energy and capital transfers of the fifth migration can be converted into a positive force. Attaining this admittedly optimistic goal depends on growth towns doing most things right for years to come. In Part III, I present information and ideas any town can adopt if it wants to avoid sprawl and grow in a smart way. Part IV summarizes sixteen strategic initiatives that constitute the basic building blocks of wise growth-town planning and development. These initiatives cut across traditional professional boundaries. They incorporate physical planning precepts for new development, preservation and conservation priorities, engineering and technological objectives, public-sector policies, and collaborative public-private interventions. Rather than rely on more bureaucracy and additional costly layers of government, communities can achieve these objectives largely through the skillful use of existing regulations, attainable market dynamics, and readily available human energy. Taking my suggestions will set a community on a low-cost, high-return path to quality and longevity—a path based on the feasible and the ordinary. Utopian dreams exert a strong appeal, but the expectations they produce are not consistent with the slow, organic way in which communities actually move along toward the next day.

In any desirable community that does take charge of its own destiny, the quality of life will improve substantially, and the threat of diminution and decline will recede. Educational and cultural institutions will improve. Collaboration among traditionally competing factions will increase. Emphasis on preservation, conservation, open space, and attractive public areas will slowly transform the physical environment. Wise government policies mixed with strong reliance on public-private partnerships and local entrepreneurship will relieve the pressure on municipal finances. Private initiatives will provide housing, jobs, and institutional growth. Investment in such a fifth-migration growth town will be well rewarded.

This book is intended as an impressionistic sketch and a wake-up call. In it I hope fifth-migration participants will find themselves and their situation portrayed in a new way that will inspire them to become advocates for and to work toward wise community growth. This set of sketched ideas, sent forward for discussion and debate, may also alert public officials and professional groups to the gathering storm. I hope to provide a fresh glimpse of powerful, long-term national trends sure to shape settlement patterns, community growth, and real estate values in America deep into the twenty-first century. I believe that the balanced approach I propose to our physical, natural, and cultural infrastructure will profoundly and positively affect the quality of all our lives—and the lives of those not yet here.

This book extends an exploration of issues that have long interested me. For over twenty-five years as an investment advisor and planning consultant I have been engaged with the fifth migration. I first examined some topics discussed here during the early 1970s in *The Future of the City* and then mulled them over in other ways during the late 1970s and early 1980s, as summarized in various sections of *Land in America*. In my professional practice, research, and writing I have been on the track of a stunning event without understanding just what it was. I was seeing, thinking about, and reporting fragments without recognizing the whole—the rumblings of the fifth migration.

Then, after *Hot Towns* was complete, I discovered an entirely unintentional and previously unrecognized autobiographical investigation beneath this project. I was searching for myself. A member of a successful family settled for seven generations in New Orleans, I moved in the 1960s to New York to pursue a career. I thus left a charming but stagnant first-migration town and arrived in one of the great confections of the third migration. Quite by chance, in search of an open and beautiful place, I started at the beginning of my working life in New York to visit East Hampton, which has since become a quintessential fifth-migration growth town.

All three places have shaped my views and contributed to the proposals I make in this book. A long and affectionate attachment to New Orleans explains my emphasis on historic preservation and the benefits of community boundaries. After all, New Orleans began as a protected outpost, walled in by ramparts, canals, and the Mississippi River. When I lived there, it was still surrounded by natural barriers—a set of watercourses composed of "The River," Lake Ponchartrain, impenetrable and incomparably beautiful swamps to the west, and to the east low, soggy terrain made up of marshes, spillways, and mosquito-infested muck. Like so many other places, New Orleans jumped all those barriers with causeways, bridges, and highways as the fourth migration took its inevitable toll on the once compact, conveniently organized community. New York too was economically stagnant and beset with its own seemingly insuperable social and physical problems when I arrived in the 1960s. And since my original, part-time immigration to East Hampton, it has been transformed, compromised, and now threatened by the fifth migration.

My personal journey was conducted without an intentional plan. I operated out of instinct in search of opportunity, challenge, and optimal living conditions. I suspect that my story is not very different from those of many others who now find themselves either completely or partially engaged in the fifth migration. By writing this book, as it turns out, I have discovered what my own impulses were based on, what I was reacting to and also what I was seeking: a way of life based on new options never before available to individuals in America.

I

The Fifth Migration

CHAPTER ONE

The Fifth Migration Begins

ALL OVER THE UNITED STATES people are on the move, driven by new fears, new technology, and new goals. They are migrating to entirely new destinations. The fifth migration, which began around 1970, will continue for at least the next fifty years. Like the migrations before it, it is dictating the destiny of communities and the settlement map of America as it influences the economic fate of millions of people. Wealth and cash flow are being transferred at a rate and in quantities never before experienced. As a result America is once again witnessing a continentwide struggle for community survival. Only this time the consequences are even more serious. The overall population is no longer growing rapidly; as fifth-migration growth towns thrive, older places are depleted.

Previous Migrations

America is the site of four previous mass movements of people. The earlier migrations, like the fifth, were distinct reflections of changing social and economic priorities. Each produced dramatic changes in the location of financial capital and human talent. And each reshaped the settlement pattern of the country.

The First Migration

The first migration was in effect a massive immigration from Europe. Most participants, driven by social dissatisfaction, religious persecution, or economic need, left their homes across the Atlantic. Over a period of nearly two hundred years, these newcomers created the thriving, compact coastal settlements of North America, the places where great careers were launched and the first American fortunes were earned. New York, Boston, Baltimore, Charleston, New Orleans emerged out of woodlands, swamps, and riverbanks as new cities on the edge of the continent. This was a movement of the young, the unsettled, and often the desperate to a tough, raw, but seemingly promising new world.

No one is entirely certain of the scale of the first migration. Sample figures are available for 1760-1775, the period roughly between the end of the Seven Years' War and the American Revolution. During that time, from Britain alone, over 55,000 Protestant Irish emigrated to North America, as well as over 40,000 Scots and over 30,000 English. They were augmented by at least 12,000 from the German states and Switzerland. Another 84,500 enslaved Africans were brought to the southern mainland colonies. This total of about 221,500 arrivals in a fifteen-year period, or some 15,000 per year, is thought to represent approximately 10 percent of the entire nonnative population of mainland America in 1775.

The Second Migration

Private land-speculation schemes in the West and new federal policies triggered the second migration, which extended for about one hundred years—from the Ordinance of 1787, the beginning of the survey of the continent, to roughly 1890. It also coincided with the depression of the 1780s. Hard times encouraged young, able people to venture out of the most populous states, especially Massachusetts, New York, Pennsylvania, and Virginia.

Joined by ever-arriving newcomers, estimated at about 120,000 a year, principally from Europe, second-migration participants settled the valleys and highlands near the coast and then moved beyond the Ohio River valley into the vast interior of the United States. By 1890 thriving settlements dotted trails and rivers all the way to the western coast. Most of the population remained in valleys and plains, where field crops would grow without irrigation. Vast tracts of land were devoted to farming and cattle ranching and related supply, sales, and storage industries. The railroads, overland trails, and interior watercourses determined where growth would occur and commerce thrive.

During this prolonged transnational movement, the young and inexperienced U.S. government instituted policies such as the 1862 Homestead Act to provide the nation's generally poor but growing population with inexpensive land on which to settle. Through railroad land grants and other give-away programs the new federal government encouraged town building and land speculation on a vast scale, underwriting the settlement of new communities across the continent.

THE THIRD MIGRATION

Beginning as early as 1820, a new form of industrial entrepreneurship, enabled by new technologies, began to challenge the dominance of agrarian life. By the end of the nineteenth century industrialization had taken full command, as rapid improvements in mechanics and machines of every imaginable kind facilitated the onset of the industrial revolution. Steam power and electricity rearranged settlement patterns throughout the world. People migrated to wherever the factories and mines and machinery were set up. In those locales towns grew rapidly into cities. Late nineteenth-century factory and trading centers such as Chicago, Minneapolis, San Francisco, Portland, and Seattle attracted millions of rural families and small-town residents. Cities such as Chicago, Pittsburgh, Newark, and Brooklyn, located near mines, ports, rivers, and rail lines—all essential to industry—grew rapidly.

The large-scale manufacture of shoes, textiles, and somewhat later of steel and carriages introduced new forms of work that offered higher pay and more reliable employment than agriculture. This type of manufacturing activity depended on large concentrations of low-skilled workers. By the end of the third migration, at its most powerful from 1870 to 1920, unprecedented numbers of people lived in newly congested cities. The 1920 census counted 106 million U.S. residents and found, for the first time, that a majority lived in urban areas. As a consequence of the great population redistribution caused by the third migration, in the early part of the twentieth century cities began to dominate the federal politics of the United States.

Generally located within ten miles of the city center, the first suburbs were built adjacent to a number of third-migration cities. These were intricately linked to the city core by public transport—rail lines and a world-class network of electric streetcars. No other country had anything like it. Berlin's streetcar system, the largest in Europe at the turn of the century, would have ranked twenty-second in America. Los Angeles, for instance, generally thought to be a product of the automobile and its freeway system, can be understood most fundamentally by tracing the lines of the Pacific Electric Railway Company, founded by Henry Huntington. Land development and urbanization followed the tracks of the "Big Red Cars." But these routes were not intended as a comprehensive system of public transportation; their purpose was to make Huntington's land accessible for development.

Between 1940 and 1970, as a late phase of residential resettlement in industrial locales, a great wave of southern blacks migrated out of the Dixie countryside and out of troubled southern communities. Although the relocation of liberated blacks began after the Civil War, the greatest thrust of their participation in the third migration occurred during the middle decades of the twentieth century, when five million blacks moved to northern and midwestern cities. These workers and their families had suffered through the Depression, many losing jobs to advanced types of mechanization including cotton-picking machines introduced in the 1940s. As jobs opened up in northern factories during World War II, many moved. Economic inducements on top of social hope triggered this last wave of the third migration.

The Fourth Migration

The automobile, perhaps the most notable product of industrialization, literally set in motion the fourth migration. In 1900 there were only eight thousand motorcars in America; by 1920 there were eight million, and that was only the beginning. The automobile proved to be enormously popular with a wide variety of Americans, thus disproving Woodrow Wilson's prediction in 1906 that the automobile would turn the country toward socialism by making the poor envy the rich. From the Federal Aid Road Acts of 1916 to the forty-four thousand-mile Interstate Highway System provided through the Federal-Aid Highway Acts of 1944 and 1956, the federal stimulus to road building prompted the most costly public-works project in history.

It also created the ultimate avenue out of the cities for people driving their increasingly affordable cars. The Ford Motor Company's first Model T was released to the market on October 1, 1908, at $850. By 1916 mass-production advances had reduced its cost to about $350, with over three hundred thousand vehicles produced that year compared with ten thousand in 1908. By 1929 annual production of all motor vehicles in America reached 5.3 million—ten times the combined output elsewhere worldwide.

Once the private automobile became a reliable and relatively affordable means of transport, and once government road-building assistance was firmly in place, the parkway, the highway, then the Interstate Highway System were imprinted on the land, lavishly financed by state and federal governments. As each link was built, new real estate development followed. Formerly remote open land and small towns became accessible by auto to major job centers. Retail stores and services, schools, recreation opportunities, and civic amenities followed in proportion to the demand created by new housing. Land speculation along the highway routes was as intense as it had ever been along the rail lines. To assure continuation of this trend and the popularity of automobiles, starting in the 1930s a company known as National City Lines—backed by General Motors, Standard Oil, Phillips Petroleum, Firestone Tire and Rubber, Mack Truck, and other auto interests—bought up and then closed down more than one hundred electric trolley lines serving forty-five cities. In 1949, too late to make any difference, a federal jury convicted some of the backers of National City of conspiring to replace electric transportation systems with road-based transport. As late as 1947, 40 percent of U.S. workers went to work on public transportation; today fewer than 5 percent do.

During the half century from 1920 to 1970, jobs to some extent, and families in 'great numbers, drove right out of the cities. People seeking better real estate values and a private home selected sites twenty miles and eventually fifty miles beyond the city's edge. By 1970, the United States had become the only nation in the world with more suburbanites than city residents. By 1980 more than one hundred million Americans, nearly half the population, had moved into fourth-migration suburbs scattered along highways surrounding third-migration cities. By then all but one of the fifteen largest metropolitan areas in the country had suburban populations greater than central-city populations. The fourth migration, unlike the previous ones and unlike the fifth, was not geared to amenities found in the natural landscape. Any place would do—farm, woods, river delta, marsh, prairie, desert—as long the roads came through and the job center wasn't too far away.

With the advent of the car and the highway, the pattern of land settlement also changed dramatically. Unpaved roads were inexpensively thrust into new areas, and the remarkably versatile automobile followed. Thus, whereas throughout the first three migrations travel by boat, foot, horse, wagon, and rail had created communities clustered around transportation stops, the automobile and the highway promoted a new pattern of human habitation, one that is now characterized as sprawl.

Besides the cars and the roads, a great enabler of this massive movement of people into single-family suburban homes was the founding of the Federal Housing Administration (FHA) in 1934. Established to salvage the collapsed private housing market during the Depression, the FHA insured mortgages for privately owned, bank-financed houses. By reducing lender risk, these mortgages brought down the cost of new house construction. The government's willingness to make loans for up to thirty years and sometimes longer further reduced the monthly cost of owning a new home. In addition, property-tax and real estate interest deductions for owned homes were a boon to new development, as no parallel offsets were offered to renters.

The security provided by government-backed mortgages encouraged banks to lend for home construction. Large projects became possible, whereas prior to the FHA program credit worthiness was difficult for a private person to establish, and most builders were unable to finance large-scale projects. As a result of the program, the FHA became a more powerful influence on home building in America than any planning agency or other agency of government. By 1959, FHA mortgage insurance had assisted 60 percent of all the American families who had purchased a home since its inception, and it had helped repair or improve twenty-two million properties.

The early suburbs enjoyed many advantages. Large properties and assured privacy attracted the rich. Members of the working and middle classes were drawn by lower taxes and less entrenched and often less corrupt governments in communities that were generally safe, clean, and free of congestion. A property with a yard and a garden and a small house could be purchased for less than it cost to live in the city. In 1904 writer William Dix set out the idyllic suburban vision harbored by many others in the years following: "Imagine a healthier race of working men, toiling in cheerful and sanitary factories, . . . who, in the late afternoon, glide away in their own comfortable vehicles to their little farms or houses in the country or by the sea twenty or thirty miles distant. They will be healthier, happier, more intelligent and self-respecting citizens because of the chance to live among meadows and flowers of the country instead of in crowded city streets."[1]

Nor is the fourth migration over. Today some fourth-migration participants settle fifty to seventy-five miles beyond a central city and commute there to work. Outside New York City, for example, developers are at work building commuter housing in Duchess County, sixty-five miles from the city center. As a yardstick for measuring continuing fourth-migration activity, from the mid-1980s to the mid-1990s the number of peak-hour, long-trip commuters on the New York City regional rails nearly doubled.

Just as black migration into the cities from the South signaled the tail end of the third migration, so black migration into the suburbs is evident as a late development of the fourth. By 1990, 32 percent of all black Americans in metropolitan areas lived in suburban neighborhoods, a record 6 percent increase from 1980 and way up from 1960.

Characteristics of the Fifth Migration

Migrations always overlap. The fourth is surely not over. But it has been replaced as the major event in American resettlement. Today, over a million people a year are relocating, not to suburbs but to communities considered even more desirable.

How Is the Fifth Migration Different?

The fifth migration is distinct from the previous four in a number of revealing ways. And it is taking place under very different circumstances. Government policy is not a direct stimulant. Destinations are no longer primarily centers of employment, and their attractiveness does not depend on easy highway access or government credit.

Unlike their predecessors, fifth-wave migrants are skilled, well-educated, and relatively affluent people who are voluntarily relocating to promising towns and rural areas. In the first three migrations, those moving on tended to be the disadvantaged seeking unskilled jobs and increased earnings. Most participants in the fourth migration wanted to improve their residential life while keeping their jobs in the city. Today's migrants, for the first time ever, have as the highest priorities leisure, health, and personal safety.

All prior migrations were led by the young. Today, retirees, the fastest growing segment of the population, are significant participants, and their impact is just beginning to be felt. The greatest explosion of seniors in the population will occur around 2010. The size of the elderly population is expected to double between 1990 and 2030. Besides experiencing the most dramatic growth in sheer numbers of any age group, older Americans have the greatest disposable income and the fewest restraints on moving elsewhere. Rather than relocating entirely, retirees may shift their primary residence to a second home they have long used and enjoyed. The result is depletion in the older place and increased use and impact in the new one. In such cases, a tiny undulation has occurred in the fifth wave, and a moving van isn't necessarily needed.

SIZE OF THE FIFTH MIGRATION

I have tried in a number of ways to compute the size of the fifth migration. In late 1997 the U.S. population was about 268.6 million. According to the U.S. Census Bureau, each year about 17 percent of all Americans change residence—nearly 46 million people in 1997. For 1994, a further breakdown in overall mobility statistics is available. That year, when the U.S. population was 260.4 million, the Census Bureau estimated that over 6.7 million moved to a different state and 8.2 million moved to a different area in the same state. Within these two groups, a total of almost 15 million people, can be found most of the potential participants in the fifth migration—a pool of roughly 6 percent of all the people in the country. That same percentage applied to the 1997 U.S. population would include over 16 million people. If only 10 percent of this group qualifies by income, inclination, education, and skill level to be part of the fifth migration, then some 1.6 million people would be involved annually. I regard this figure as the high end of the range for participants in the fifth migration.

The scale of the fifth migration can be derived another way by arbitrarily restricting the potential group to the approximately 5 million American households that earned at least $100,000 in 1997. With each household averaging 2.63 people, about 13.2 million people are part of the fifth wave. However, if only 6 percent of this well-off group move to a different state or different area in the same state, the low end of the fifth-migration range is around 750,000 to 800,000 people a year.

It may be unreasonable to establish an income bar as high as $100,000 per household in defining the fifth wave because this limit excludes many younger individuals and families as well as students. In 1997 approximately 73.6 million people were in "affluent" households, those with incomes of $50,000 or more. Subtracting the 13.2 million with incomes over $100,000 leaves about 60.4 million people with incomes between $50,000 and $100,000. Within this group are potential fifth wavers—for example, students and young professionals, who may earn even less. I take these groups into account by reaching below the $100,000 income bar and adding some 250,000 to 300,000 out of this group who are likely to be fifth-migration participants.

Thus, after all the figures are evaluated, I believe that a good working number for the fifth migration is about 1 million people a year, with a low limit of 750,000 and a high of 1.6 million. Members of this group are far more flexible and far more mobile than the average American.

Implications of Slowing Birth and Death Rates

For the first time ever the population in America is no longer growing rapidly, so movement to new places causes significant depletion elsewhere. In the late nineteenth century, as a result of strong immigration and a high birthrate, the U.S. population grew 25 to 30 percent each year. Since then the trend has been down, with especially big dips during the Depression and World War II, and population growth is still slowing. In 1960 the U.S. birthrate was 23.7 per 1,000 population. In a short time, this rate is expected to wither to approximately 14.2, or about a 1 percent gain a year, a 40 percent decline in forty years. Between 1995 and 2001 American women will have fewer than 4 million babies a year. Countering the roughly 4 million births a year are some 2.2 million deaths.[2] Net immigration is estimated at about 720,000 per year. Thus, total population growth per year is about 2.5 million. Responsible forecasters expect this overall growth rate of less than 1 percent per year to continue until at least 2020.

These rather nominal population-growth figures suggest the enormous

TABLE 1.1.
NET POPULATION MIGRATION BY STATE, 1980-1994
(IN THOUSANDS)

Biggest Gainers		Biggest Losers	
State	Gain	State	Loss
Florida	3,626	New York	816
California	3,079	Michigan	795
Texas	2,318	Ohio	692
Georgia	915	Illinois	659
Arizona	864	Pennsylvania	290
North Carolina	619	Iowa	271
Virginia	501	Indiana	234
Washington	493	Massachusetts	189
Colorado	445	Louisiana	156
Nevada	414	West Virginia	120

SOURCE: Cognetics, Inc., 1996.

relative importance of migration decisions made each year by the approximately one million people who are members of the fifth migration. One million people is about equivalent to 40 percent of the size of the annual population growth in America. In a slow-growth nation whose population is increasing at less than 1 percent each year, those who move out of town are not easily replaced by newcomers, as they were when the population was increasing 20 or 30 percent each year. Table 1.1 lists the ten states with the largest net gains and the ten with the largest net losses in population between 1980 and 1994. The three largest gainers were Florida, California, and Texas; the biggest losers were New York, Michigan, and Ohio. The regions of fast growth, where the fifth migration is becoming concentrated, were primarily in the South and West. Table 1.2 lists the nation's twenty fastest growing counties between 1990 and 1994; almost all of them are in the South and West. Of the one hundred fastest growing counties between 1980 and 1994, forty-nine were in the South and forty-two in the West, leaving only nine distributed throughout the rest of the country.

Because of a slowdown in births and advances in medicine, the population is aging. In 1960 children under the age of eighteen made up more than 36 percent of the nation's population. By 2001 this group will be whittled down to less than 26 percent. In the 1980s the age profile began to bulge with Americans sixty-five and older. Because of increased individual longevity, the elderly population has become a more significant force than ever before. The 1990 census reported 31.2 million Americans age sixty-five or older, the so-called elderly, a potent 22 percent increase since 1980. This group now constitutes 13 percent of the population, up from 11 percent in 1980. Of these, about 57.7 percent, or 18 million people, are between sixty-five and seventy-four, and the remaining 13 million are

TABLE 1.2.
TWENTY FASTEST GROWING U.S. COUNTIES, 1990-1994

Rank	County	Population, 1990	Population, 1994	Increase (%)
1	Douglas, Colo.	60,391	88,078	45.8
2	Summit, Utah	15,518	21,526	38.7
3	Camden, Ga.	30,167	41,662	38.1
4	Washington, Utah	48,560	66,124	36.2
5	Elbert, Colo.	9,646	13,016	34.9
6	Henry, Ga.	58,741	78,814	34.2
7	Paulding, Ga.	41,611	55,718	33.9
8	Flagler, Fla.	28,701	38,048	32.6
9	Park, Colo.	7,174	9,450	31.7
10	San Miguel, Colo.	3,653	4,796	31.3
11	Edwards, Tex.	2,266	2,934	29.5
12	Teller, Colo.	12,468	16,125	29.3
13	Bryan, Ga.	15,438	19,942	29.2
14	Forsyth, Ga.	44,083	56,827	28.9
15	Custer, Colo.	1,926	2,481	28.8
16	Boise, Idaho	3,509	4,498	28.2
17	Hinsdale, Colo.	467	598	28.1
18	Loving, Tex.	107	137	28.0
19	Pike, Pa.	27,966	35,489	26.9
20	Kendall, Tex.	14,589	18,485	26.7

SOURCE: Population Division, U.S. Census Bureau, 1995.

TABLE 1.3.
STATES RECEIVING THE LARGEST PERCENTAGE OF ALL INMIGRANTS
AGE SIXTY AND OVER, 1985–1990

Rank	State	% Received	Rank	State	% Received
1	Florida	23.8	6	Pennsylvania	3.0
2	California	6.9	7	New Jersey	2.6
3	Arizona	5.2	8	Washington	2.5
4	Texas	4.1	9	Virginia	2.4
5	North Carolina	3.4	10	Georgia	2.3

SOURCE: Charles F. Longino, Jr., "From Sunbelt to Sunspots," *American Demographics*, November 1994, p. 24.

over seventy-five. Within the younger group, over half are married, in good health, financially comfortable, and mentally alert; many are fifth-migration participants.

Considering the special objectives of the elderly who do migrate, it is understandable that a limited number of states and within those states a limited number of places attract the lion's share of them. As indicated in Table 1.3, Florida, California, and Arizona receive the largest percentage of interstate migrants over sixty, with Florida way ahead of all the others. A look at the states that people age sixty and over are leaving illustrates the fluidity and dynamics of this migration. As indicated in Table 1.4, be-

TABLE 1.4.
STATES CONTRIBUTING THE LARGEST PERCENTAGE OF ALL
OUTMIGRANTS AGE SIXTY AND OVER, 1985–1990

Rank	State	% Contributed	Rank	State	% Contributed
1	New York	11.7	6	Pennsylvania	4.2
2	California	9.9	7	Michigan	3.9
3	Florida	6.8	8	Ohio	3.9
4	Illinois	5.6	9	Texas	3.7
5	New Jersey	5.6	10	Massachusetts	3.0

SOURCE: Charles F. Longino, Jr., "From Sunbelt to Sunspots," *American Demographics*, November 1994, p. 25.

tween 1985 and 1990, New York, California, and Florida were the three largest losers of people age sixty and over. Thus, Florida and California appear in the top echelon of both the winner and loser lists, but overall California registers as a net loser and Florida as a strong net gainer. Nor do retirees stop migrating once the first move is over. As healthy, active bodies turn into dependent ones, the "older elderly," those over seventy-five, often journey back to desirable communities in the Northeast and Midwest, from states such as Florida, California, and Arizona, to be near children and grandchildren.

Although most retirees prefer to remain at home, about 20 percent move within their home state and another 4 percent move out of state. Both groups generally relocate to vacation and tourist destinations, often spots discovered and enjoyed prior to retirement. Table 1.5 lists the twenty counties nationwide with the largest increase of people sixty-five and older; most are clustered in the coastal regions of the Southeast, in the Rocky Mountains, and in Alaska. Only about 1 percent of retirees elect to live in planned adult communities in sunbelt states. The 20 percent of elderly people who move within their own state are a formidable force. They come from everywhere but concentrate in a relatively few especially appealing communities. As a result, places far out of the sunbelt such as southern Ocean County, New Jersey, home of over eighty thousand retirees living in at least sixty adult communities, experience rapid growth and often have a healthier economy than the places left behind.

Indeed, places with fast-growing, active elderly populations tend to be healthier markets for a wide range of products and services than those that house decreasing, stable, or slow-growing elderly populations. The presence of retirees in concentrated force creates jobs, consumer demand, and bank assets. It also ensures a supply of capable part-time workers whose skills are proven. Experts estimate that each new elderly resident migrant creates demand for one-third to one full-time job, and each average resident retiree household pours into the local economy over $70,000 per year.

And then there is "aging in place," which is what most people do. People who stay put but who have other options tend to be living in a desirable community. Many who age in place are fifth wavers. Growth towns of the fifth migration are more likely to retain their older people than places with less to offer.

TABLE 1.5.
TWENTY U.S. COUNTIES WITH THE LARGEST PERCENTAGE INCREASE
OF PEOPLE AGE SIXTY-FIVE AND OLDER, 1980–1990

Rank	County (Metropolitan Area)	Number Added	Increase (%)
1	Flagler, Fla.	7,345	266.7
2	Hernando, Fla. (Tampa–		
	St. Petersburg–Clearwater)	31,048	186.1
3	Nye, Nev.	2,179	166.4
4	Fayette, Ga. (Atlanta)	4,468	159.5
5	Matanuska-Susitna, Alaska	1,866	155.6
6	Summit, Colo.	300	145.9
7	Kenai Peninsula, Alaska	2,015	143.7
8	Anchorage, Alaska	8,258	134.6
9	Los Alamos, N. Mex. (Santa Fe)	1,668	131.0
10	Washington, Utah	7,898	127.0
11	Mohave, Ariz.	19,272	125.5
12	Clark, Nev. (Las Vegas)	77,678	121.2
13	Douglas, Nev.	3,352	116.3
14	Douglas, Colo. (Denver)	2,524	115.7
15	St. Lucie, Fla. (Fort Pierce)	31,534	113.1
16	Collier, Fla. (Naples)	34,583	111.0
17	Okaloosa, Fla. (Fort Walton)	13,319	109.0
18	Marion, Fla. (Ocala)	43,189	106.7
19	Indian River, Fla.	24,592	101.9
2o	Beaufort, S.C.	10,664	101.1
	U.S. average		22.3

SOURCE: U.S. Census Bureau, 1980, 1990.
Note: Includes only counties with ten thousand or more people in 1990.

BABY-BOOMER POWER

In addition to the elderly, the much-tracked baby-boom generation is a
potent source of fifth wavers. This group is generally defined as people
who were twenty-five to forty-four in 1990. Although only two decades
are represented, the demographic bulge of the baby boomers accounts for

TABLE 1.6.

METROPOLITAN AREAS WITH THE FASTEST GROWTH AND HIGHEST PERCENTAGE OF BABY-BOOMER POPULATION, 1980–1990

Rank	Metropolitan Area	Growth in Boomer Population (%), 1980–1990	Boomers as Percentage of Area Total, 1990
1	Orlando, Fla.	51.6	35.1
2	Fort Worth–Arlington, Tex.	34.5	36.1
3	Atlanta, Ga.	33.0	37.7
4	Santa Rosa–Petaluma, Calif.	30.2	35.1
5	Vallejo-Fairfield-Napa, Calif.	29.1	35.3
6	Dallas, Tex.	28.3	37.5
7	Manchester-Nashua, N.H.	24.2	36.3
8	Reno, Nev.	23.4	36.3
9	Portsmouth-Dover-Rochester, N.H.	23.3	36.4
10	Seattle, Wash.	22.1	37.6

SOURCE: William H. Frey, "Boomer Magnets," *American Demographics*, March 1992, p. 36.

about 31 percent of the country's population. This group is also the most economically powerful in the United States and will remain so into the first several decades of the twenty-first century. According to a study by economists at Cornell University, baby boomers are in line to inherit over $10 trillion in stock-market and real estate assets now in the possession of their elderly parents. Within this group, most of the preretirement migration has already occurred. One-third of Americans in their twenties move every year, but the share drops to one-fifth of adults in their early thirties and one-tenth of adults aged forty-five and older. Those baby boomers who have strong educations or work skills (or both) are asserting fifth-wave values in their wish to improve their lifestyle.

Where have those with a choice within this important group elected to live? The answer is primarily in the newer and more distant suburbs, within smaller communities at the edge of metropolitan areas, and, increasingly, in more remote smaller cities and towns that offer environmental advantages. Many prime baby-boom destinations support quality educational systems and diverse cultural institutions. Table 1.6 lists the

TABLE 1.7.
METROPOLITAN AREAS WITH THE GREATEST LOSS OF
BABY-BOOMER POPULATION, 1980–1990

Rank	Metropolitan Area	Decline in Boomer Population (%)
1	Provo-Orem, Utah	27.7
2	Davenport–Rock Island–Moline, Iowa-Ill.	20.2
3	Peoria, Ill.	20.1
4	Huntington-Ashland, W. Va.–Ky.–Ohio	17.4
5	Gary-Hammond, Ind.	16.9
6	Youngstown-Warren, Ohio	16.8
7	Erie, Pa.	15.8
8	Beaumont–Port Arthur, Tex.	15.5
9	Pittsburgh, Pa.	13.1
10	Buffalo, N.Y.	12.4

SOURCE: William H. Frey, "Boomer Magnets," *American Demographics*, March 1992, p. 36.

ten metropolitan areas that were most successful in attracting members of the boomer generation between 1980 and 1990. All ten places increased their boomer population during the decade by more than 20 percent and up to over 50 percent, while harboring a residential population of boomers that exceeds the national average by 4 to 7 percent. As illustrated in Table 1.7, half the places that sustained the heaviest losses of baby-boomer population were in the Midwest. Many of these communities share a mix of geographic isolation, poor economic performance, and unappealing climate.

POPULATION SURGES IN GROWTH TOWNS

As the fifth wave has hit, population surges in growth towns (which may include areas of varying size, as described in the previous chapter) have been particularly powerful. While the national population between 1980 and 1995 increased by approximately 0.98 percent per year, growth towns were attracting people at two to four times that rate. Towns whose population has grown by 30 percent or more in fifteen years are by definition growth towns.

To vividly capture the difference growth can make over a period of thirty years, let's review a few projected statistics from typical growing communities and from representative stable or declining communities for the interval from 1970 to 2000. For the representative growth towns I select Santa Fe, Las Vegas, and West Palm Beach–Boca Raton. I examine Los Angeles, New York City, and New Orleans as nongrowth communities, although the situation may turn around in New York and Los Angeles. In population and jobs, each of these nongrowth communities increased or decreased less than 1 percent per year from 1970 to 1994, and I expect similar results to the year 2000. During the same thirty years, the growth towns are expected to show increases in jobs and population of 2.5 to 5.0 percent per year. On a comparative basis, as illustrated in Table 1.8, the growth towns' annual rate of population change is almost ten times the rate of slow-growing communities, while jobs increase nearly

TABLE 1.8.
PROJECTED AVERAGE ANNUAL RATE OF CHANGE IN POPULATION AND NUMBER OF JOBS IN SELECTED STABLE AND GROWTH TOWNS, 1970–2000

Place	Population Growth (Decline) (%)	Job Growth (Decline) (%)
Stable Towns		
New York City	(0.08)	(0.25)
New Orleans	0.34	0.91
Los Angeles	0.86	0.95
Average	0.37	0.54
Growth Towns		
Santa Fe	2.48	3.68
Las Vegas	4.66	5.00
West Palm Beach–Boca Raton	3.54	3.83
Average	3.56	4.17
Growth vs. Stable	+9.62	+7.72

TABLE 1.9.
PROJECTED TWENTY HIGHEST ANNUAL POPULATION GROWTH
RATES, METROPOLITAN AREAS, 1995–2005

Rank	Metropolitan Area	Annual Rate (%)
1	Naples, Fla.	3.83
2	Myrtle Beach, S.C.	3.77
3	Punta Gorda, Fla.	3.44
4	Fort Myers–Cape Coral, Fla.	3.18
5	Provo-Orem, Utah	3.02
6	Laredo, Tex.	3.01
7	Orlando, Fla.	3.00
8	Greenville, N.C.	2.92
9	Yolo, Calif.	2.81
10	Las Vegas, Nev.	2.79
11	West Palm Beach–Boca Raton, Fla.	2.56
12	Raleigh–Durham–Chapel Hill, N.C.	2.53
13	Fort Worth–Arlington, Tex.	2.44
14	McAllen-Edinburg-Mission, Tex.	2.42
15	Tucson, Ariz.	2.34
16	Fort Pierce–Port St. Lucie, Fla.	2.28
17	Santa Fe, N. Mex.	2.27
18	Tacoma, Wash.	2.17
19	Austin–San Marcos, Tex.	2.16
20	Houston, Tex.	2.11
	U.S. total	0.86

SOURCE: Woods, Poole Economics, Inc., 1997.
NOTE: Growth rates are annual compounded rates. All metropolitan areas are
defined by the Office of Management and Budget as of July 5, 1994.

eight times faster. This enormous and characteristic difference engenders
consequences of every sort.

By the year 2020 I estimate that the average city, suburb, and town in
America will be experiencing population changes of plus or minus 1 percent per year. But I expect each of the twenty fastest growing metropolitan areas to expand its population by 2 to 4 percent per year through the

year 2020. And, in addition, numerous nonmetropolitan communities in exurban and rural parts of America will sustain equivalent or even greater growth surges. At this rate, a typical growth town will double in population in less than twenty-five years.

As indicated in Table 1.9, which projects population growth rates between 1995 and 2005 for the twenty fastest growing metropolitan areas in the country, high population growth will continue to be clustered particularly in Florida, Texas, and California. Altogether, the top twenty metropolitan areas for projected population gains should expand by 8.5 million people between 1995 and 2005. They will account for 36 percent of the U.S. population gain during this period.

REAL ESTATE VALUES IN GROWTH TOWNS

Fifth wavers are attracted by value, and they create it. In their early stages, growth towns tend to be recognized as places that deliver value. For example, a house in such a town may be relatively expensive but so well built and in such a desirable location that the price seems reasonable. Fifth wavers may perceive the community as relatively affordable, especially compared with the place being abandoned. Young fifth-migration families want inexpensive housing in a quality environment. Businesses seek reasonably priced office space and competent, educated employees in an attractive community. As time goes on, high appeal tends to induce higher prices, as demand for housing and for work spaces outstrips supply. Eventually land and built-out property are accorded an extra premium just because of the perceived desirability of the growth town itself.

During periods of rapid growth, the value of well-located vacant land tends to escalate sharply. By assessing changes in the value of well-situated raw land, it is possible to pinpoint the location of a community on the arc of growth and decline. Communities in decline, as one would expect, are located on the downward portion of the arc. In the average American community, since the mid-1980s, land values have fluctuated on the order of plus or minus 2 percent per year. But in growth towns the figures tell an entirely different story. There, in the same time period, I estimate that raw-land prices have climbed on the order of 4 to 10 percent per year and more. In ten years these increases equaled at least 40 percent and, in the most exceptional circumstances and locations, well over 100 percent.

A similar increase can be found in the median cost of houses in growth towns. I estimate that these values have advanced within a range of 4 to 10 percent per year with 4 to 6 percent typical. In some growth towns real estate prices have appreciated rapidly in the wake of the fifth migration because of restrictions on new land development. In Seaside, Florida, for example, with all first-offering house-site lots sold out, local brokers estimate annual lot price increases at around 25 percent a year since 1982, compared with roughly a 5 percent annual increase elsewhere in the Florida panhandle during the same period. Near the top of the list of places with escalating home prices is the fifth-migration high-tech magnet Salt Lake City, where, even without stringent land rationing to constrain supply, median housing prices advanced 92 percent between 1992 and 1997. During the same period, the price of the average home in Los Angeles and in southern California declined by 4 percent. By way of contrast, between 1975 and 1998, the average median advance in housing prices in America was closer to 3 percent, or about in keeping with the rate of inflation.

As detailed in Table 1.10, during 1998 the median rise in U.S. home prices in the largest metropolitan areas is expected to be approximately 3.2 percent. Home prices in twenty-five of these areas are expected to exceed this gain; of these areas fourteen are in the West. Most of the top areas are strong fifth-migration destinations.

Within any given community or area, of course, price changes that occur over one to five years do not necessarily reveal the full picture. Local events such as the opening of an important plant, the closing of a major government installation, or even a regional recession may dictate sharp, temporary fluctuations in land and housing prices. But in growth towns price increases in the most sought-out locations over five to ten years will be much higher than in nearby communities or than national medians.

Growth towns inevitably sustain enormous increases in the construction of houses. Las Vegas, with the nation's fastest growing employment base, also has the nation's fastest growing housing base: more than 110,000 new units were built between 1993 and 1996, or the equivalent of 92 new units per 1,000 residents. More typical for growth towns was Raleigh-Durham, which added 52 new housing units for every 1,000 residents during the period. Not far behind, places like Austin, Charlotte, and Salt Lake City showed increases of between 44 and 100 percent in new housing units during the period. On the other side of the coin are places

TABLE 1.10.
PROJECTED GAINS IN MEDIAN HOME PRICES, FIFTY LARGEST
METROPOLITAN AREAS, 1998

Rank	Metropolitan Area	Increase in 1998 (%)	Median Price, 1998
1	San Jose	5.7	$318,800
2	Seattle	5.6	182,600
3	Salt Lake City	5.4	134,300
4	Orange County, Calif.	5.0	238,400
5	San Diego	5.0	192,700
6	Las Vegas	4.9	128,300
7	Phoenix	4.9	119,400
8	Dallas	4.4	114,700
9	Boston	4.3	199,100
10	San Francisco	4.3	296,100
11	Los Angeles	4.2	181,000
12	Washington, D.C.	4.1	176,000
13	Newark	4.1	200,600
14	Oakland	4.0	282,500
15	San Antonio	3.9	90,100
16	Sacramento	3.8	120,700
17	Houston	3.8	93,700
18	Atlanta	3.8	110,900
19	Fort Worth–Arlington	3.8	88,800
20	Portland, Ore.	3.8	156,700
21	Denver	3.4	144,400
22	New Haven	3.4	139,100
23	Riverside, Calif.	3.4	117,800
24	Chicago	3.3	164,800
25	Charlotte, N.C.	3.3	126,200
	U.S. median	3.2	126,600

(*Continued*)

TABLE 1.10. (CONT.)
PROJECTED GAINS IN MEDIAN HOME PRICES, FIFTY LARGEST
METROPOLITAN AREAS, 1998

Rank	Metropolitan Area	Increase in 1998 (%)	Median Price, 1998
26	St. Louis	3.2	99,700
27	Detroit	3.2	121,100
28	Kansas City	2.9	107,900
29	Tampa–St. Petersburg	2.9	86,700
30	Miami	2.8	121,500
31	Columbus, Ohio	2.8	119,400
32	Philadelphia	2.8	128,100
33	Cincinnati	2.7	111,800
34	Buffalo–Niagara Falls	2.6	84,800
35	Nashville	2.6	116,100
36	Fort Lauderdale	2.6	125,200
37	Greensboro–Winston-Salem, N.C.	2.5	119,400
38	New York City	2.5	181,800
39	Minneapolis–St. Paul	2.5	119,000
40	Pittsburgh	2.3	88,500
41	Long Island, N.Y.	2.2	166,000
42	Milwaukee	2.2	125,900
43	Hartford	2.1	138,800
44	Cleveland	2.1	118,100
45	Norfolk–Virginia Beach	2.0	108,100
46	Baltimore	1.8	119,500
47	Orlando	1.8	95,300
48	Indianapolis	1.4	103,600
49	Bergen-Passaic, N.J.	1.4	208,800
50	New Orleans	1.1	90,400

SOURCE: Regional Financial Associates, January 1998.

struggling to sustain themselves, like the New York City metropolitan area, where only 149,000 privately owned units were built between 1993 and 1996, or just 7.6 new units per 1,000 residents.

In growth towns, houses are generally larger than the national average, even when built by older couples and retired people. After the children are gone and tuitions are paid, fifth-migration participants are likely to opt for the space and luxury they could not previously afford. And there are extra accommodations for grown children and grandchildren who might visit occasionally.

As a consequence of rapid development, the amount of open land that a growth town loses annually is roughly three times the amount that an average mature community loses. (The issues and problems this rapid loss of open space generates are discussed later.) A population increase of 38 percent in the Seattle area between 1970 and 1990, for example, triggered an 87 percent increase in the amount of land committed to development. Developed land in the Denver area in 1992 consumed 350 square miles. By 2012, if sprawl is unabated, the built-up area is expected to triple to 1,000 square miles, while Denver's population is projected to increase by only a third.

Wealth Transfer

New real estate demand is only one of the ways the fifth migration brings new assets into a growth town. In order to make a rough stab at quantifying the asset and cash-flow transfer involved in the fifth migration, I have considered, in addition to the acquisition of a new house, additional local jobs generated, bank-account transfers from elsewhere, local purchases and contributions, and local taxes. Although this estimate includes a mixture of revenue items, expenditures, and assets, and therefore is not strictly quantifiable as an annual wealth transfer, each of these items, it seems to me, represents a direct and obvious financial gain brought to a growth town when a new household moves in. My guess is that these items alone, for a given year of the fifth migration, add up to over $150 billion, as detailed and summarized in Table 1.11. The enormous significance of the annual magnitude of these transfers becomes apparent when one recognizes that the entire assessed real-property value of all of New York City for fiscal year 2000 is expected to be approximately $87.56

TABLE 1.11.
ESTIMATED ANNUAL WEALTH TRANSFER INTO FIFTH-MIGRATION
GROWTH TOWNS

Item	$/Household
House purchase	$350,000
New job creation[a]	18,000
Savings/bank-account transfer	10,000
Purchasing power locally spent	15,000
Property taxes/local government fees	3,000
Local sales taxes/charitable giving	1,000
Subtotal per household	$397,000
All households per year[b]	$151 billion

[a]Based on approximately 0.5 to 1.5 new jobs created locally per household.

[b]Based on 2.63 people per household and 1 million people moving per year as the fifth migration, or 380,228 households.

billion; and the entire market value of all of Manhattan real estate that year is expected to come in at around $127 billion.[3]

In subsequent years, locally, there will of course be a multiplier effect. As new households continue to move in, those in place continue to spend locally. As illustrated in Table 1.12, which uses the estimates proposed in Table 1.11 for expenses that recur annually, the financial impact of the fifth migration quickly escalates.

DISSATISFACTION WITH PREVIOUS DESTINATIONS

Given a choice many people now at home in a city or suburb would rather live somewhere else—not abroad, not necessarily in a specific town, but just in a different sort of place, one more rural, less congested, and safer. The feeling is broad-based. A 1989 Gallup poll asked people all over the country what kind of place they would like to live in: 34 percent chose a small town; 24 percent, a suburb; 22 percent, a farm; and only 19 percent, a city. Taken together, preferences for small towns and farms were expressed by 56 percent of the country's population, or approximately 136 million people.

TABLE 1.12.
COMPOUNDING FINANCIAL IMPACT OF THE ANNUAL WEALTH
TRANSFER INTO A FIFTH-MIGRATION GROWTH TOWN

	Year 1	Year 2	Year 3	...and so forth
Household 1	$397,000	$ 47,000	$ 47,000	
Household 2	0	397,000	47,000	
Household 3	0	0	397,000	
...and so forth				
Total	$397,000	$444,000	$491,000	

In 1985 a Gallup survey asked, "Would you move away from your community if you could?" Over 40 percent of people living in cities with more than one million inhabitants said they would. In smaller cities of fifty thousand to five hundred thousand people, 30 percent declared they would prefer to go. More recently, a 1995 national poll revealed that half the people living in the most populous metropolitan counties were "dissatisfied" or "somewhat dissatisfied" with their place of residence. In the New York–New Jersey–Connecticut area, 42 percent said "they would move away immediately if they had the opportunity." The same feeling was expressed by residents in the metropolitan areas of Los Angeles (41 percent), Dallas (36 percent), Atlanta (35 percent), and Seattle (31 percent). In fact, among the metropolitan areas sampled all across the country, even in those that are growing rapidly, one-third or more of all residents want to move out.[4]

Although there are different conventions of reporting, and available accounts in some places probably undermeasure actual events, crime statistics are an increasingly recognized measure of community health and well-being. Many people who reveal their motives for leaving older cities and suburbs report a wish to flee crime—although "crime" in many instances is also a thinly veiled way of saying social problems and racial mixing. Analysis indicates that the incidence of crime is not higher in older places than in growth towns. But the fear of crime is justifiably greater in older places in the midst of decline because the crimes being committed are more serious. In many older large cities and increasingly in smaller cities and towns, the impact of drugs on the incidence, level, and cost of crime is enormous. Experienced police departments report that in most communities 25 to 50 percent of killings are linked to drugs. Fear penetrates a drug-infested community as residents quickly learn, through intimidation and worse, to be afraid. In many of the largest cities crime rates associated with drugs have stabilized or even fallen since 1994; but they are on the rise in nearby suburbs, mid-size cities, and smaller towns. Since the early 1990s drug dealers in large cities have run into both stiffened law enforcement and market saturation. So they look to nearby places where operations are easier and the market more promising. In many suburbs and in mid-size cities such as Louisville, Fort Wayne, Chattanooga, and Nashville, for example, growing drug markets have sparked turf wars between dealers and provoked associated serious crime including murder. As a consequence, all over the country fast-growing, desirable places are attracting businesses and families looking for relief from crime and also from the congestion, expensive housing, and poor schools endemic to cities and now encroaching on the suburbs. Many also want to escape seemingly endless increases in local property taxes accompanied by ever more degraded municipal services.

CHAPTER TWO

Forces Driving the Fifth Migration

C LEARLY, AS DISCUSSED IN CHAPTER 1, strong forces—high rates of crime, high property taxes, poor schools, degraded environments, loss of jobs—are driving Americans from the cities and suburbs that appealed in previous migrations. But what forces attract them to the new growth towns? And what trends in the economy and in the culture facilitate their move to fifth-migration destinations?

What Are Fifth Wavers Looking for?

Not long ago most individuals were satisfied if they had an affordable place to live and a job that made it possible to continue living there, to educate their children, to feed and clothe their household, and to take a few weeks of vacation. For members of the fifth migration, the wish list is different.

People with options have new priorities. They want opportunities for outdoor and indoor recreation near home. They insist that environmental quality not be compromised: clear air and clean water are primary. They have as overt or covert top goals security, safety, and insulation from crime. Whereas they have long considered access to medical facilities desirable, they also now want to be near colleges, museums, and other cultural institutions. They demand intellectual recreation, including adult education—an altogether new ingredient in the mix of criteria. Capable retired or semiretired people look for the availability of challenging, income-supplementing work that can be undertaken on a flexible schedule. Other fifth wavers seek places far enough away to avoid the social and economic troubles of the towns they are leaving but near enough to go back for top-quality entertainment, cultural events, and convenient visits to family and friends. Still others want to live where it seems economically wise and safe to own a business or home, often the largest single investment made in a lifetime.

As an indication of how pervasive these fifth-wave objectives have become, back in 1977 Partners for Livable Communities, an influential, Washington-based, nonprofit, urban information-exchange organization, considered "livability" to refer exclusively to physical design. By the spring of 1993, it declared in its annual report, "Today it is clear that livability is more than just a matter of physical design, more than a matter of amenities. It is a matter of essentials—safety, health, jobs, justice, environmental concerns, education—that build a sense of community and of individual worth within the community."

Efforts have been made to define what the vague term *quality of life* means to most people living in metropolitan areas. The New York Regional Plan Association and the Quinnipiac College Polling Institute in Hamden, Connecticut, in 1995 undertook a public-opinion research study to obtain statistical data about the meaning of the term. They interviewed fifteen hundred people from the New York metropolitan area and four hundred individuals in each of the metropolitan regions of Atlanta, Dallas, Los Angeles, and Seattle. Instead of obtaining a clear and direct definition, the research team found out what quality of life does not mean. Nationwide, the quality of contemporary metropolitan life was blemished first of all by crime (27 percent) and second by the "lack of a sense of community" (25 percent). These were followed by unpromising economic factors (24 percent), the low quality of public schools (15 percent), traffic congestion, and poor public transportation. The survey also discovered that people would pay more for improved access to open space, for clean air and water, and to reduce traffic congestion.[1]

Media and marketing polls try to discover every year where people with a choice want to live. The criteria they choose to rank answers reveal much of what people are looking for. *Money* magazine's 1996 survey of the

"The Best Places to Live in America," for instance, graded the economy, healthfulness, crime, housing, educational quality, weather, transit, leisure opportunities, and availability of the arts. Readers gave their highest priority to "safety," followed by clean water and clean air. In the 1998 poll, the top five concerns were clean water, low crime, clean air, good public schools, and low property taxes. Of all these criteria, I doubt that any but low property taxes would have counted during the fourth migration, and probably none but economy and transit (access) during the third, second, and first.

Low property taxes can be an important attraction. At least in the early years of expansion, the local property tax as a percentage of the value of property owned is generally lower in most growth towns than in the locales from which fifth-wave migrants depart. Fewer social services are required, lower crime rates and smaller police departments prevail, and a less extensive social-service network is generally in place. In transferring, for instance, from the New York metropolitan area to a suburb of Albuquerque, and into a house of about the same size and value, a family recently found that its first-year property taxes declined from $4,000 to $1,500. Declines of as much as 50 percent or more are common.

Many corporate managers and entrepreneurs are attracted to small cities and to rural locales as places to live, and they bring their businesses with them. They especially like towns that give them special tax breaks and that have inexperienced and often pandering local governments, a weak labor movement, and comparably feeble environmental controls, even though eventually these attractions spell trouble for the growth town and for the fifth-migration participants as well. Companies that are reorganizing and downsizing often also seek to relocate to less expensive and more appealing remote places. And they encourage their most desirable workers to move along with them.

I can sum up the eleven community attributes most sought by fifth wavers. These are in no particular order; different ones will be most important for different people. For example, retirees may care more about recreation; corporations may care more about taxes.

1. Nearby recreation

2. Upgraded environmental quality, including clean water and clean air

3. Security and safety

4. Reduced living costs, including affordable housing and work space

5. Reduced local real estate taxes and business taxes

6. Easy access to family members remaining in nearby cities or suburbs

7. High-quality cultural, medical, and educational institutions

8. Real estate that is safe and profitable to invest in

9. A skilled labor pool (businesses) and available jobs (individuals)

10. A high-quality, safe public school system

11. An easily accessible regional airport

A glance at some trends in American culture and the economy reveal how they have facilitated the development and attractiveness of the kinds of destinations fifth wavers are seeking.

Job Markets

Many fifth-migration participants—the young baby boomers and even many older people—are in the work force. Since 1988 job growth in non-metropolitan areas has been faster than job growth in metropolitan areas. Three out of five new jobs are now being created by enterprising new companies located in nonurban areas beyond traditional suburbs. As a result, the stream of capable, skilled, employable people is flowing to new places. Qualified people living in cities and suburbs are finding employment out of town. Young people living in many rural areas have less incentive to move to cities, suburbs, and edge cities.

Table 2.1 lists the twenty fastest growing job markets among metropolitan areas for the period 1985–1990. The list is topped by Las Vegas, which boomed in tourism and gambling, and Orlando, which, in spite of about a year of recession, captured jobs related to tourism and construction because of the expansion of Disney World, Universal Studios Florida, and related attractions. In these job-attracting fifth-migration growth towns, jobs increased annually between 3 and 8 percent.

Table 2.2 projects job increases in metropolitan areas between 1995 and 2005. By 2005, it is expected that these top twenty areas for employment gains will add 4.7 million workers, representing 32 percent of the total U.S. gain. These gains, as projected in 1994, were expected to be

TABLE 2.1.
TWENTY FASTEST GROWING JOB MARKETS, METROPOLITAN AREAS,
1985–1990

Rank	Metropolitan Area	Increase in Nonfarm Jobs (%)	
		Total	Annual
1	Las Vegas	48.9	8.2
2	Orlando	37.8	6.3
3	Seattle	30.8	5.1
4	Sacramento	28.1	4.7
5	San Diego	27.3	4.6
6	West Palm Beach	26.4	4.4
7	Portland, Ore.	22.9	3.8
8	Raleigh, N.C.	22.1	3.7
9	Grand Rapids, Mich.	21.9	3.6
10	Charlotte, N.C.	21.8	3.6
11	Fresno	21.2	3.5
12	Tampa	21.2	3.5
13	Indianapolis	21.1	3.5
14	Charleston, S.C.	20.6	3.4
15	Honolulu	20.1	3.3
16	Columbus, Ohio	19.2	3.2
17	Richmond, Va.	18.7	3.1
18	Cincinnati	18.4	3.1
19	Greenville, N.C.	18.4	3.1
20	Jacksonville	18.3	3.0

Thomas G. Scott, *Where to Make Money: A Rating Guide to Opportunities in America's Metro Areas* (Buffalo, N.Y.: Prometheus, 1993).

approximately 2 to 4 percent annually, way above the national average of approximately 1 percent. They may, in fact, be understated because of the exceptional strength of the national economy from 1995 to 1998.

A growth town will generally exhibit sustainable job growth rates of 1.5 to 3.0 percent per year. The fastest growing job markets may expand at 4 to 6 percent annually, but this rate is not sustainable. In Boise, for instance, a top-ranking small metropolitan area, job growth was running at

TABLE 2.2.

PROJECTED TWENTY HIGHEST ANNUAL EMPLOYMENT GROWTH
RATES, METROPOLITAN AREAS, 1995–2005

Rank	Metropolitan Area	Annual Rate (%)
1	Laredo, Tex.	3.51
2	Myrtle Beach, S.C.	2.51
3	Orlando, Fla.	2.50
4	Punta Gorda, Fla.	2.37
5	Fort Myers–Cape Coral, Fla.	2.28
6	Las Vegas, Nev.	2.28
7	Greenville, N.C.	2.27
8	Naples, Fla.	2.19
9	Bryan–College Station, Tex.	2.14
10	Raleigh–Durham–Chapel Hill, N.C.	2.11
11	Tucson, Ariz.	2.06
12	Atlantic–Cape May, N.J.	2.03
13	Yolo, Calif.	2.03
14	Brazoria, Tex.	1.99
15	Sarasota-Bradenton, Fla.	1.96
16	San Diego, Calif.	1.89
17	Sacramento, Calif.	1.89
18	Augusta-Aiken, Ga.-S.C.	1.89
19	St. Cloud, Minn.	1.88
20	Phoenix-Mesa, Ariz.	1.88
	U.S. total	0.97

SOURCE: Woods, Poole Economics, Inc., 1994.
NOTE: Growth rates are annual compounded rates. All metropolitan areas are defined by the Office of Management and Budget as of July 5, 1994.

5.8 percent per year in 1995 but is expected to settle closer to the national average for a growth town. In the Rocky Mountains, one of the fastest growing areas, employment has been increasing at nearly five times the national average. In all growth towns, job growth is off the charts compared with the stagnant or declining number of jobs in a great number of other places.

Cybernation and Globalization

Cybernation and globalization, two factors of great importance to the fifth migration, have emerged as dominant determinants of job and population growth. Cybernation, the rapid spread of computer systems, particularly the Internet, requires new and updated equipment and people with updated skills. When a community possesses the human and physical infrastructure that drives rapid advances in computer and telecommunication technologies, then it is attractive to both working and retired fifth wavers.

Because of the capabilities of computer networks, America is in the midst of a profound change in the organization of business—a change that is enabling new places to become growth towns. The old, well-known information and decision-making model, in which reporting flows upward and control flows downward, is giving way to a "networked" format. Modern organizations increasingly disperse decision making to a confederation of flexible centers, with managerial control arranged horizontally along a network rather than concentrated at a single center. In this format, many middle-level analysis and reporting positions are eliminated, productivity is enhanced, and dependence on central headquarters is reduced. As long as the quality of the technological link is maintained, this organizational pattern enables highly efficient interlinked work to occur in dispersed locations connected via private, high-speed communications. This new paradigm is sometimes called "the virtual firm." Its strength and efficiency are based on the ability to be organizationally flexible, unburdened by fixed overheads, opportunistic with respect to trends, and responsive to competition.

This increasing fragmentation of the traditional organization of work in part explains the recent and rapid movement into growth towns and is connected to the expansion of telecommuting as a way of work life. When a town possesses many of the sought-out natural, social, and environmental attributes, the cybernation of work enables fifth wavers to move in.

New York City provides a pertinent example of the dynamic changes going on in modern business structures and the consequences of these changes. On the job-loss side of the ledger, many traditional space- and labor-intensive operations have moved away because of high costs. Third-migration manufacturing has been leaving for a long time; more recently, so has telecommunications-based service work. Citibank moved its on-line banking support to Austin and its credit-card processing to North Dakota. Metropolitan Life moved its claims processing to Ireland. And many Wall Street firms have moved their "back-office" activities to other states. Simultaneously, New York spawned "Silicon Alley" in lower Manhattan, a concentration of more than a thousand entrepreneurial companies engaged in creating multimedia software targeted generally at four thriving New York market sectors: finance, publishing, television and radio, and advertising. These new technology and information firms, which require up-to-date skills, entrepreneurial flair, and risk capital, are a product of and a reflection of the fifth migration. Many are single-person firms inhabited by young fifth wavers. So although New York is certainly not a fifth-migration growth town in overall population and job growth, it does reveal aspects of the fifth migration in selected industries (as well as in certain residential locations).

Cybernation has also opened up locations all across the country to the global economy. Towns that have the attributes sought by fifth-migration participants but were never before attractive to internationally oriented companies now are alert to the incentives they can offer. The more than three thousand high-technology companies in landlocked Colorado, for example, now earn over 10 percent of their annual revenue from foreign trade. In this global environment, those places that are the complacent benefactors of long-term, seemingly stable local employers display a dangerous attitude.

Since the late 1970s, the demise of international communism and the ascendance of democratic capitalism as a worldwide standard have accelerated Americans' participation in the international economy. Changes in the composition of the Gross National Product (GNP) reflect trends that have stimulated fifth-migration settlement. In 1955, which marked the middle, approximately, of both the postwar boom and the fourth migration, imports and exports of goods and services each accounted for little more than 5 percent of GNP. By 1970 imports accounted for 7.3 percent and exports for 8.6 percent; by 1988 imports accounted for 13.1 percent and exports for 15 percent. By 1996 exports and imports, as a percentage of GNP, had more than doubled since 1970. The overall impact of foreign trade on economic life is expected to increase even more dramatically in the years ahead.

Contrary to common belief, the prominent role of exports in the

American economy is not driven by large multinational corporations. Most of these enormous companies build or acquire their own production facilities around the world. Rather, smaller, aggressive, often quite new, and sometimes remotely located companies account for the lion's share of current exports. Today, over 90 percent of all exports come from companies with fewer than five hundred employees. Even more pertinent for the fifth migration, almost 60 percent of all exports come from firms with fewer than twenty employees.

Today, as long as adequate air links and communications are available, an enterprise focused on the export market may locate where it pleases, based on the attraction of the place itself. Air access and access over the airwaves are as basic a requirement as rail lines were to the third migration and highways to the fourth.

Technology

Through most of the long history of American migrations, people settled along major access arteries. Trail intersections grew into villages. Natural ports became big cities. Railway stops mushroomed into towns. State and interstate highways created the suburb, just before airport hubs established new marketing and distribution centers all across the country. Until recently, then, most investment by both businesses and communities was focused on enabling centralization. The factory and all the changes brought about by industrialization induced workers to live reasonably nearby. Office centers and retail centers had the same effect. Even suburbs, which we generally think of as dispersed, and surely they are compared with earlier centralized villages, towns, and cities, are located along major highway systems. But today's technology, and tomorrow's, does not dictate centralization. Although other forces in the culture may keep people living in reasonably tight clusters, the location of these clusters is no longer as dependent on traditional forms of access. The access arteries of today are telephone wires, fiber-optic cable, and impulses beamed through space.

It is difficult to exaggerate the role of technology in modern life; its impact on the fifth migration is no exception. For an investment in equipment within the means of fifth wavers, and with a few weeks of simple training, an individual almost anywhere in the country can be intimately and interactively in contact with the office, with a network of dispersed businesses, with vast libraries and data sources, with educational and medical institutions, and with sources of current news, financial information, and an ever-expanding array of other knowledge and data—the matrix within which productive work and successful investment are carried out. The Internet offers millions of people worldwide the ability to communicate and interact across national borders and oceans. The U.S. Commerce Department estimates that 12 to 14 percent of Americans are linked to the Internet, amounting to as many as thirty-five million people. And the number is growing dramatically as are the potential uses of this invisible system.

New technologies are making it easier than ever before to move and to move far. Information-linking technologies, including the Internet, modem, and fax, have untied workers and retirees from old moorings. As Calvin Beale, a senior demographer at the U.S. Department of Agriculture, says of developing towns, "If you wire them, they will come." With satellites, you don't even have to wire them.

A sea change in communications has revolutionized the way money is distributed and how and where it is spent. As a result of the buildup of the computer-assisted postal economy, millions of people receive their income and merchandise through the mail. It is now convenient to live in places remote from the central office or the government agency writing the check—or from the store housing merchandise. Some merchants don't even bother with the store anymore; they send out a catalogue or put their wares on television and the Internet. An 800 call or computer click will send goods anywhere. Because of the boom in overnight shipping services, merchandise of any type, right down to the kitchen sink, is delivered to the front door the next day. Salary and savings and retirement-plan distributions are routinely, instantly, and automatically transferred by computer to mutual funds, money-market accounts, and remote banks. Cash is extracted from street-corner vending machines. These innovations allow millions of people of all ages to live conveniently in the most desirable enclaves.

Aware of the importance of advanced technology to the growth of rural areas, representatives in Washington from these places are mounting offensives reminiscent of earlier drives to obtain electricity, telephone service, and highway funding. Rick Boucher, a Democratic member of the House of Representatives, argues with characteristic political hyperbole that "rural America will gain enormously from advances in telecommunications. We have a low-cost business environment, an excellent work force, and a superb quality of life. What we're lacking is telecommunications services." Rural legislators in both the House and the Senate continue to press for extension of high-speed transmission lines to small towns, as well as for clarification of Internet protocols related to obtaining and freely using information available over wires and by satellite. Many legislators from rural areas are convinced that the information revolution is the best hope for economically developing their remote districts. And they are probably right.

In addition, an increasing number of full-time employees are telecommuting—working for large firms from home offices.[2] Telecommuters are a significant and growing segment of the working population. Independent market studies and the Bureau of Labor Statistics estimated the number of telecommuters, defined as those who work from their homes on a regular basis at least two days a week for an outside company, to be somewhere between nine and fourteen million people in 1997. These same observers estimate another ten to twelve million people are home-based workers, or those who run a business from their homes. One additional subgroup is broken out: independent contractors who work for multiple companies, estimated at twelve to sixteen million. Taken together, some thirty-one to forty-two million people are taking advantage of new technologies to perform home-based work, at least part of the time; and the number, especially of independent contractors, is growing rapidly. Approximately one of every eight U.S. households has at least one adult working full-time from home, for himself or herself or for an employer, a number expected to rise to one out of every five households by 2002.[3]

In 1997, about 42 percent of companies, up from 33 percent in 1995, offered some form of telecommuting arrangement for workers, including giant corporations such as Hewlett-Packard, IBM, and AT&T. Surveys indicate that about 7 percent of employees in these companies take advantage of the option. The fastest growing segment of home-based workers, full-time corporate telecommuters, is expected to increase by 14 percent a year through 2020.

Some people abandon telecommuting because they are lonely, feel as though they need more direction, or worry about losing out in political and economic ways as a result of their absence from the office. But more are installing increasingly inexpensive, user-friendly, easily networked home-scale technology that allows them to perform almost any task imaginable either through the Internet or by being networked into closed proprietary systems. The personal freedom allowed is changing the nature of work, liberating schedules for millions of competent people, and—most important for the fifth migration—permitting settlement in desirable places. It also allows children to see more of their parents, reduces commuter traffic, and fosters strong neighborhoods.

An exhaustive analysis of the migration habits of people with home-based businesses was completed in 1993 by the Information Access Co., a division of Ziff Communications Co. The surveyors consulted moving companies, evaluated National Association of Home Builders data, and analyzed Census Bureau statistics as well as a vast array of other material. Out of it all came a list of the top ten locales for home-based work. The attributes of these places are just what we would expect of any fifth-migration growth town: "relatively affordable housing, permissible zoning regulations, good-quality public schools, an educated or skilled workforce, easy access to a major city, leading colleges and universities, and business opportunities."

The impact of technology on settlement patterns is just beginning to be studied by social and economic researchers and by business organizations. As an example, Bill Rogers, writing in the *Wall Street Journal* in late 1994, quotes John Allen, a rural sociologist at the University of Nebraska: "We are right on the edge of a new form of social and economic organization. We are rapidly approaching the point where technology empowers people to change their living patterns. In the U.S. people will be able to take their family and their skills and settle somewhere based on the quality of life, not on how close they'll be to the big city job market. That's a departure from the traditional form of social organization in this country."[4]

The mass production of the automobile was easily and quickly recognized as a breakthrough applicable to the manufacture of many different products. But it was not recognized at the outset that the introduction of relatively inexpensive, reliable, mass-produced cars would trigger the physical reorganization of the United States. Communications technology and all its associated changes are having an equally potent impact on American settlement patterns.

The location of businesses, too, is being transformed by technology. At a time when industry must be more competitive than ever to survive, firms fully exploit information-based options. Companies burdened with large plants and large payrolls escape from expensive urban and suburban communities in decline. Enhanced telecommunication and computer connectivity, overnight delivery services, and regional airports make it practical to set up in totally new locations, some of them very small towns. For instance, fifth-migration towns now include Bolivar, Missouri (population 6,845), where there is a software design company; North Sioux City, South Dakota (population 2,019), home of a big computer maker; and Dodgeville, Wisconsin (population 3,882), base for a major catalogue retailer. All attract workers who want to live where the landscape is emptier and life is simpler. A variety of companies can now migrate to wherever the boss wants to live. Janus Worldwide and Overseas, a mutual-fund group with a combined market value of $10 billion, has its major operations in Denver.

Interrelated advanced-telecommunication and computer-technology companies tend to locate together near established research universities in high-quality environments, just as steel companies clustered near their needed resources, coal mines and rail depots. So entirely new fifth-migration settlement regions now thrive, such as Silicon Valley south of San Francisco, the Raleigh–Durham–Chapel Hill entrepreneurial zones of North Carolina, and the Digital Coast of greater Los Angeles. Another and less-known territory is also forming from Baltimore down through northern Virginia, where more than a thousand Internet-related start-up companies are domiciled. This cluster of start-ups is joined by every major technology company that must have a presence in or around Washington, D.C., because of government regulatory involvement and because of their desire to sell digital services to the federal government, the largest customer of all.

Changes in the Nature of Work

As the economy changes and as the nature of profitable activity evolves, a major shift has occurred in what most working people are doing. As recently as 1970, about one-third of all jobs in America were in goods-producing industries such as farming and construction and manufacturing—activities that produced a tangible product. By 2000, this sort of activity is expected to account for no more than 15 percent of all employment, a drop of more than 50 percent. Today, more than eight out of every ten U.S. workers are occupied in the service economy, broadly defined as any activity whose product is not a material good. Service jobs, the sort of work that appeals to fifth wavers, are the fastest growing in the nation.

For the first time in American history, the majority of all new jobs require postsecondary education. The increment of value added by brawn and reliability, the mainstays of the assembly-line worker, is diminishing. In the new service jobs being created, income is more directly related to education and skills, to continuing education, to constant retraining, and to flexibility of mind and schedule. In many respects, this new service economy is building within the older one. Previously, value was added by converting raw materials into manufactured products. In what has come to be called the "knowledge-value" economy, value is added when knowledge and up-to-date skills are utilized by continuously retrainable and constantly learning participants to produce services and data.[5]

Table 2.3 lists the twenty metropolitan areas with the highest projected increase in service employment to the year 2010. Understandably, this list overlaps considerably with the list of locales enjoying the fastest total job growth in Table 2.2. As might be expected, given the nature of service work, places attracting service employers include many of the destinations found attractive by fifth wavers. Table 2.3 reveals places where they can use their skills. The appeal of academic institutions explains the appearance on the list of places such as Champaign-Urbana, Provo-Orem, and Raleigh–Durham–Chapel Hill. Wherever entertainment venues and tourist attractions are numerous, there is likely to be fast growth in both service jobs and new residents, as in Orlando and Las Vegas. Concentrated health care and medical centers create service jobs as well as a high concentration of professionals, so places in Florida such as Sarasota, Naples, Punta Gorda, Tampa, and West Palm Beach will continue to surge.

The Special Role of the University

Universities are magnets for fifth-wave migrants. They offer employment to skilled, highly educated, and often risk-taking, iconoclastic individuals. They are creators of, as well as shelters for, fifth wavers. The university

TABLE 2.3.
PROJECTED TWENTY HIGHEST SERVICE-JOB GROWTH RATES,
METROPOLITAN AREAS, 1996–2010

Rank	Metropolitan Area	Increase (%), 1996–2010	Service Jobs in 2010 (in thousands)
1	Orlando, Fla.	59.4	339
2	Laredo, Tex.	57.5	16
3	Sarasota-Bradenton, Fla.	48.6	132
4	Naples, Fla.	45.5	36
5	Middlesex-Somerset-Hunterdon, N.J.	43.7	205
6	Champaign-Urbana, Ill.	43.5	33
7	Ventura, Calif.	42.3	119
8	Tacoma, Wash.	41.7	87
9	Punta Gorda, Fla.	41.6	16
10	Tampa–St. Petersburg–Clearwater, Fla.	41.2	452
11	San Diego, Calif.	40.0	480
12	Waterloo–Cedar Falls, Iowa	39.8	22
13	Raleigh–Durham–Chapel Hill, N.C.	39.7	219
14	Provo-Orem, Utah	39.3	63
15	Olympia, Wash.	39.3	25
16	Springfield, Mo.	39.3	62
17	Las Vegas, Nev.	39.2	290
18	Des Moines, Iowa	38.9	92
19	West Palm Beach–Boca Raton, Fla.	38.5	199
20	Tucson, Ariz.	38.5	131
	All metropolitan areas	22.1	46,988

SOURCE: Woods, Poole Economics, Inc., 1996.

campus is frequently the place where one's innate talents are honed into the skills needed for success in modern life. Graduates are often attracted to their university community as a place to live and work because there they have an already-formed network of friends, mentor relationships, and professional options. New business formations and growth in service jobs around universities in Boston, Seattle, San Francisco, Dallas, Austin, Atlanta, Provo, and Chicago are stunning.

Although some might argue that distance learning will diminish the role and impact of the university, I believe just the opposite. The more the information generated by the university reaches out through advanced technologies, the greater the appeal will be of gaining direct, intimate exposure to professors, laboratories, seminars. No substitute will be found for the dynamics of direct learning, the thrill of seminar debate, the charisma of a superb lecturer right in the room, the insights available from an authority in the laboratory. To those with a choice, at-home learning, even when supplemented with satellite study groups, will only enhance the appeal of the university setting.

Technical schools and specialized apprentice programs are also increasingly sought out and are important to the fifth migration. Jobs that were once based on strength and endurance now require much more: truck drivers operate in a world of computer-controlled scheduling; workers on the assembly line are just as likely to monitor robotically controlled machines as to be fastening nuts and bolts. Office workers, always participants in the service economy, can no longer get by with the simple skills of arithmetic, filing, typing, and answering the phone. The telephone is answered by a computer; typing requires knowledge of constantly changing writing, printing, and publishing software and databases; and computations require mastering separate software that operates on different principles, platforms, and protocols.

At universities across the country, continuing and adult education—more important than ever before—are growth sectors. Adults, often encouraged by their employers, update skills as well as explore new professional directions and new sources of enjoyment. At UC Berkeley Extension, for instance, between 1992 and 1997, adult enrollment climbed 40 percent; course offerings, 50 percent. On the East Coast, at New York University, where continuing-education attendance is growing at 5 to 7 percent a year, adult students are swelling classes in information technology and other types of applied knowledge. At Brown University courses in Japanese and Chinese offered to nonmatriculated students are booming. Many part-time students at Boston College are in search of a way out of low-level jobs. Adult-education courses in the liberal arts and boutique courses in subjects as alphabetically and conceptually dispersed as yoga and ancestor research are also gaining students. UC Berkeley, for instance, reports lively interest in Shakespeare, opera, and the arts of India. All across the country adult education is becoming not simply a ticket to job survival and income upgrading but a widely appreciated and sought-out form of recreation.

The success of an increasingly large roster of companies depends on their staying atop new technologies, processes, and ideas. They want to be where the idea factories are: the advanced technology departments, the science labs, and the astute faculty all conveniently concentrated at the university. Consider Raleigh–Durham–Chapel Hill in North Carolina as a prime example of this phenomenon. Duke is located in Durham, once best known as a tobacco town rather than a center of learning. The University of North Carolina is ten miles to the south in Chapel Hill. North Carolina State University is twenty miles to the east in Raleigh, the state capital. This cluster of institutions, with their joint emphasis on quality education and advanced research, has spawned a fifth-migration growth center of impressive magnitude. High-tech giants like IBM and Northern Telecom have established major research facilities in the area, as have big pharmaceutical companies such as Glaxo and Burroughs-Welcome. Dozens of smaller companies that rely on advanced knowledge start up in the area each year. In 1993 *Fortune* magazine rated Raleigh-Durham first in its annual assessment of "Best Cities for Business"; by the middle of the 1990s, Raleigh-Durham was generally considered one of the best locations, if not the best, for advanced-knowledge workers in America.

At the heart of the Raleigh-Durham success is the seven thousand–acre Research Triangle Park, located roughly midway between the area's three universities. This powerful high-tech center is home to more than thirty-five thousand scientists and researchers and over fifty organizations of various kinds specializing in microelectronics, telecommunications, chemicals, biotechnology, pharmaceuticals, and environmental and health sciences. What makes the park so potent is the mixture of communities it contains—academic, business, and government. The three universities oversee a central research institute within the park where university scientists and technicians are often engaged in research and development projects with government and corporate participants.

The fifteen thousand students who graduate from local universities and colleges in the Raleigh-Durham area every year not only strengthen the Raleigh-Durham economy while in school but, upon graduation, many become instantaneous, capable members of the fifth wave, remaining in the area, attracted by unusual business opportunities, educational institutions, relatively low living expenses, and fine recreation options. The ski slopes of the Great Smoky Mountains are three hours away; Atlantic Ocean beaches are a two-hour drive.

When surveys are conducted to determine the most desirable places to live, good weather and recreational amenities always rank as high priorities; but so too does the presence of good schools and especially high-quality universities. Many of the top ten places where Americans want to live, as surveyed by *Money* magazine in 1996, are home to a university. These desirable communities often are close to or the same as the entrepreneurial hot spots that will be discussed in Chapter 3. In 1998 *Money* magazine, using its own formulas, which are skewed toward business and investment opportunity, concluded on the basis of data from the three hundred largest metropolitan statistical areas and interviews with five hundred households that among the best places to live were Boulder, Charlottesville, Madison, and Washington, D.C.—all locations of major universities.

CHAPTER THREE

Where the Fifth Wave Is Going

T HE FIFTH MIGRATION IS obviously firmly under way, with multiple trends converging to impel this nationwide migration. Where are fifth wavers moving to? In what kinds of places are they most likely to be encountered?

Entrepreneurial Hot Spots

The places where new, small firms are now locating and where they are expected to locate over the next ten to twenty years are important destinations of the fifth migration. In general, entrepreneurial adventurers prefer the Mountain states, the South (the South Atlantic and West South Central in particular), and the Pacific West. As of 1996, the top states for job growth in small, entrepreneurial companies were, in order, Utah, Arizona, Nevada, Alabama, Virginia, Georgia, Colorado, Tennessee, Florida, and New Mexico. The next bracket of ten were, in order, North Carolina, Indiana, Minnesota, Texas, Maryland, Ohio, Wisconsin, California, Delaware, and Idaho.

The location of these fifth-migration companies can be traced more finely. The three lists below, derived from a nine million–company database, pinpoint the twenty-five top American entrepreneurial hot spots as of 1996 in three categories—large metropolitan, small metropolitan, and rural.[1]

Here, in order from the highest to the lowest ranked, are the top twenty-five large-metropolitan entrepreneurial hot spots:

Salt Lake City–Provo, Utah
Atlanta, Ga.
Birmingham-Tuscaloosa, Ala.
Phoenix, Ariz.
Washington, D.C. (Md.-Va.)
Orlando, Fla.
Raleigh-Durham, N.C.
Minneapolis–St. Paul, Minn. (Wisc.)
Indianapolis, Ind.
Nashville, Tenn.
Dallas–Ft. Worth, Tex.
Charlotte, N.C. (S.C.)
Denver-Boulder, Colo.
Memphis, Tenn. (Ark.-Miss.)
Columbus, Ohio
Miami–Ft. Lauderdale, Fla.
Milwaukee-Racine-Sheboygan, Wisc.
San Antonio, Tex.
Houston-Galveston, Tex.
Louisville, Ky. (Ind.)
Grand Rapids–Muskegon, Mich.
Richmond, Va.
Norfolk–Portsmith–Virginia Beach, Va.
Dayton-Springfield, Ohio
Kansas City, Mo.-Kans.

It is surely no accident that nine of the top ten are in the vicinity of busy hub airports, and over half contain one or several significant, established universities.

In the smaller metropolitan areas, the impact of the fifth migration is more obvious because the migrants are added to a smaller initial population base. In order of ranking, here are the top twenty-five small-metropolitan entrepreneurial hot spots:

Las Vegas, Nev.
Huntsville, Ala.
Austin, Tex.
Boise, Idaho
Albuquerque, N. Mex.
Sioux Falls, S. Dak.
Tucson, Ariz.
Pensacola, Fla.
Lincoln, Nebr.
Springfield, Mo.
El Paso, Tex.
Madison, Wisc.
Tallahassee, Fla.
Mobile, Ala.
Green Bay–Appleton, Wisc.
Manchester-Nashua, N.H.
Des Moines, Iowa
Hickory, N.C.
South Bend–Benton Harbor, Ind.-Mich.
Knoxville, Tenn.
Montgomery, Ala.
Evansville, Ind. (Ky.)
Jacksonville, Fla.
Chattanooga, Tenn. (Ga.)
Fort Wayne, Ind.

The twenty-five rural areas that had the strongest increases in fifth-migration worker population were these (in rank order):

Northern rural Alabama
Northern mountain region, Georgia
Rural Utah
Western New Mexico
Western Colorado
Rural Arizona
Rural South Florida
Outer islands of Hawaii
Central rural North Carolina

Mountain region, North Carolina
Rural Southeast Georgia
Tennessee River Valley, Tennessee
Western rural Tennessee
Northwestern rural Ohio
Southern Delaware
Eastern North Carolina
Mountain region, Virginia
Eastern rural South Carolina
Eastern rural Virginia
Southern rural Alabama
Rural Idaho
Southern rural Indiana
Eastern Maryland
Northern Mississippi
Southwestern Texas

Growth in rural entrepreneurial hot spots is enabled, as I discussed in Chapter 2, by a variety of technological advances. Many smaller, entrepreneur-driven companies are breaking metropolitan bounds and heading off to places where their president used to spend summer vacation.

Worker scarcity for high-level intelligence-based jobs is beginning to be a problem in many places as the fifth migration proceeds. The U.S. labor-force growth rate is expected to decline from an unusual high of about 2.5 percent per year in 1980 to perhaps 1.0 to 1.5 percent by the year 2000. In the strong economic surge of 1996–1998, when nearly anyone who really wanted to work could find a job in most places, the labor force continued to grow faster than expected, reaching a surprising rate of almost 2 percent per year. But this rate is not sustainable.

Most of the new jobs are for a relatively small group of people such as students, university graduates, and recently retired white-collar workers capable of handling complex, intelligence-based tasks. Many of the workers who accounted for the 2 percent growth rate of 1996–1998 were college students working part-time. Nationally, in 1997, college students in the work force totaled almost 5 million, up 6 percent from 4.7 million in 1994. When they are not on the payroll, college students are not included among the statistically unemployed. These potential fifth wavers, many already located in fifth-migration communities, swell the ranks of the employed but do not contribute to the unemployed statistics in these communities when work is unavailable. They are already getting ahead by virtue of education, flexibility of mind and schedule.

Capable people who consider themselves to be fully retired or semi-retired also increase the number of flexible fifth-migration workers capable of handling the advanced-knowledge jobs available in new growth towns. Many have already relocated to a fifth-migration destination. Once there, and willing to work as contract employees with no benefits on flexible, often uncertain schedules, they fulfill demands created by the burgeoning service and global economy. The loss by older communities and aging suburbs of capable, independent retirees and advanced students creates a genuine shortage of one of the basic resources needed by a community to thrive at century's end. And, conversely, the gain of these people through the fifth migration provides new destinations with one of the most basic ingredients for dynamic growth.

In the future, whether or not it is recognized today by town managers and influential citizens, competition for members of the fifth wave is sure to intensify. Because of shortages at the top, the most sought-out, best-educated workers—certain newly minted college graduates, advanced professionals, and technologically sophisticated workers—are able to move first and obtain a good job later.

The Ubiquitous Exurbs

When it's not the city and it's not the suburbs and it's not the rural country way out, what do you call it? Planners and demographers have agreed on "the exurbs." A transitional zone between the dense urban-suburban settlement and the very sparsely settled open countryside, exurbia is an important destination for fifth-migration participants.

Exurbia may contain suburban-looking subdivisions, edge cities (large, decentralized business, shopping, and residential complexes), large farms, small towns, factories or warehouses, miniranches, and hobby farms. This mixed bag is left undefined by the U.S. Census Bureau. In the language of the Census, whatever is not urban is rural; and whatever is not metropolitan is nonmetropolitan. Nevertheless, various demographers and planning experts have come up with a working definition of the exurbs. They classify all counties within the forty-eight contiguous states as urban, suburban, exurban, or rural. Exurban counties surround all metropolitan areas, extending up to seventy miles beyond the outermost circumferential highway. The exurban area covers about 30 percent of the forty-eight contiguous states, or 940,000 square miles.

The places in exurbia that contain desirable communities and attractive open spaces are prime destinations for a portion of the fifth migration. Between 1960 and 1990 exurban counties added more population than any other type of county, with population escalating from about forty million to nearly sixty million. Since the late 1960s, exurbs have been the sites of over 25 percent of all population growth and 60 percent of all new manufacturing jobs. At the time of the 1980 census, only 4 percent of the U.S. population lived in exurbs. In fact, many of the currently dynamic exurban areas were in decline for a good part of this century. Since 1980 many exurbs have been growing at twice the rate of the country as a whole, a reflection of fifth-wave choices, and I believe the migration to selected exurbs and small towns has only begun. People of all social and economic and educational backgrounds, not just fifth-wave migrants, have become exurban residents. Many exurban households have two wage earners. And many are living as they are and working as they are out of necessity rather than choice.

Although exurban terrain may defy precise characterization, new settlers arrive with a common expectation: a rural lifestyle laced with the advantages of being fairly close to a city. The blended and sometimes inconsistent wishes of the new exurban pioneers have been characterized as follows:

> While exurban households derive their incomes from urban jobs, their members may consider themselves primarily farmers purchasing farms of varying sizes to effect this desire. They may not feel the need for the social services offered in urban areas, but they do not wish to be too far away from them. They may want small-scale government and basic, low-cost government services such as police, fire protection, and education. They may value accessibility to outdoor recreational opportunities more highly than suburban households do. They may be very conscious of the environment. While rural households depend on resource exploitation for a living, exurban households flee the city to enjoy unexploited resources. Overall, exurban households may be more like rural households in sociocultural aspects, but more like urban households in economic and environmental aspects.[2]

A detailed study of the Portland, Oregon, exurban area and population revealed the primary factors that motivated former urban and suburban residents to move to the more rural exurbs. First on the list was the wish to have a large lot. Second was the determination to own rather than rent, and third was the perception that the rural exurb would be a good place to raise a family. So at the forefront is the desire for additional and affordable space, mixed with an unexpressed yearning for greater security plus a better quality of life—the same attractions that were originally sought in the suburbs.

Although jobs are growing in exurbia, exurbanites' places of work and ways of getting there are as diverse as the places they live. Most who work commute to urban or suburban jobs. Some undertake long commutes to cities. Others travel fast roads to nearby suburbs or edge cities. Some travel to work infrequently because of flexible schedules or telecommuting.

The exurban growth burst since 1970 has been both stimulated by the fifth migration and separate from it. Many participants are not fifth wavers. They are predominantly residents of and employees in the nearby urban-suburban area who are moving farther out. I estimate that about 30 percent of fifth wavers settle in the exurbs. Based on that assumption, between 1970 and 1990, a period during which there were some twenty million fifth-migration participants, roughly six million would have moved to the exurbs, or about three hundred thousand a year. This would represent roughly 45 percent of total migration to the exurbs between 1970 and 1990.

Micropolitan Areas within the Exurbs

The exurbs contain "micropolitan" areas—groups of small cities and their surrounding settlements. They vary in location and character as dramatically as Ames, Iowa, differs from Key West, Florida. Although the government does not have a definition for micropolitan areas, they are distinct and important to the fifth migration. A micropolitan area—which must be located in an exurb—has been defined by marketing specialists as having at least one central city with at least fifteen thousand residents located within a county containing at least forty thousand residents, including those who reside in the central city.

The 1994 official population estimates counted 193 micropolitan areas housing fourteen million people, or approximately 5 percent of the nation's population. In nearly all of them, population growth rates easily exceeded the rate in the nearest metropolitan area. As micropolitan growth rates are based on small initial population bases, percentage increases can be quite large when resettlement is sustained. To give some dramatic examples, between 1990 and 1994, Bend, perched on a high desert plateau near the geographic center of Oregon, grew by 21.5 percent, twice the rate of its nearest metropolitan area; during the same period the Mount Vernon population increased at twice nearby Seattle's rate. The fastest growing of all the micros, St. George, Utah, grew by over 34 percent during the four years, more than three times the rate of Salt Lake City or Provo-Orem and more than eight times the national average.

The growth in these areas is driven by appealing fundamentals. The most attractive micros offer urban benefits on a manageable scale, without the crush and stress of big-city life. They are large enough to attract jobs, restaurants, diversions, and community organizations, but small enough to avoid the traffic jams, high crime rates, crowded schools, and high property taxes often associated with heavily urbanized areas and older suburbs. More than half of micros are within fifty miles of a metropolitan city center; the median price of housing was about 70 percent of the national average in 1990; property taxes run around 60 percent of the national average; violent crime rates are 56 percent below the national norm; and the total crime rate is 25 percent of the national average.

The most vibrant micropolitan small cities, those especially attractive to fifth-migration participants, cluster in three categories: college towns, vacation spots, and specialized fast-growing areas. The twenty micros considered by the editors of *American Demographics* magazine in 1998 to be the most attractive in overall quality of life, taking into account economics, education, diversions, health care, housing, public safety, transportation, and urban proximity, are listed in order here:

Mount Vernon, Wash.
Ames, Iowa
Morgantown, W. Va.
Ithaca, N.Y.
Traverse City, Mich.
Sandusky, Ohio

Columbus, Ind.
Port Angeles, Wash.
Concord, N.H.
Mason City, Iowa
Rome, Ga.
Bozeman, Mont.
Longview, Wash.
Mankato, Minn.
Bend, Ore.
Wenatchee, Wash.
Frankfort, Ky.
Plattsburgh, N.Y.
Willmar, Minn.
Burlington, Iowa

College micros such as Ames, Ithaca, and Bozeman attract because of the unusually high levels of literacy and proportion of resident college graduates. In Ithaca, home of Cornell University and Ithaca College, 42 percent of adults have earned a college degree, twice the national average; in Bozeman, site of Montana State, 34 percent are college graduates; and in Ames, home of Iowa State, 38 percent of adults hold at least a college degree. These factors also attract employers eager to find a well-educated work force. In addition, the presence of a college or university increases community arts and educational offerings—visiting performers, art exhibits, live theater, lecturers, and other events.

Vacation spots high on the micro list such as Wenatchee, Traverse City, and Bozeman appeal because of their beaches, ski slopes, and other natural amenities. Vacationers tend to spend money on merchandise and entertainment, stimulating service-job growth while increasing demand for recreation and entertainment facilities. The special character of the natural environment in vacation spots and the vitality of community life created by well-off visitors attract affluent seasonal and year-round residents. In recreation-oriented micros, resident personal income tends to exceed the national average by at least 20 percent.

Specialized micropolitan cities are the third fast-growth category. Between 1990 and 1994, thirty-nine small cities grew at more than twice the national average, and of these eleven grew at more than three times the national average. Table 3.1 lists the ten fastest growing micropolitan cities between 1990 and 1994.

TABLE 3.1.
TEN FASTEST GROWING MICROPOLITAN CITIES, 1990–1994

Rank	City	Population Increase (%)
1	St. George, Utah	34.3
2	El Centro–Calexico–Brawley, Calif.	25.4
3	Coeur d'Alene, Idaho	25.1
4	Eagle Pass, Tex.	21.8
5	Bend, Ore.	21.5
6	Elko, Nev.	20.9
7	Prescott, Ariz.	18.8
8	Columbia, Tenn.	16.6
9	Mount Vernon, Wash.	15.4
10	Bozeman, Mont.	14.6
	U.S. average	4.4
	Micropolitan median	3.8

SOURCE: "Small Is Beautiful," *American Demographics*, January 1998, p. 45.

The Rural Resurgence

It is easy to become confused about the urban/rural and metropolitan/nonmetropolitan designations. Following standard U.S. Census Bureau practice, I use the terms *rural* and *nonmetropolitan* interchangeably, as I do the words *urban* and *metropolitan*. A nonmetropolitan county is defined by the Census Bureau as a county with no hub exceeding fifty thousand people. And nonmetropolitan, or rural, areas tend to be farther away from city or suburb than the exurban areas discussed above.

Beginning in the 1980s and accelerating in the 1990s, people with a choice began to trade in urban and suburban life for rural living. And more people in rural areas elected to stay put. As a result, rural America is again showing up on the charts as a growth domain, a reversal of the situation that prevailed through most of the third and fourth migrations. Three out of every five jobs created between 1963 and 1987 were located beyond exurbia. American Demographics, Inc., identified the twenty fastest growing counties of the 1980s and found that many were in rural areas, including Fayette, Georgia; Dakota, Minnesota; and Hamilton, Indiana.[3] In 1994 Peter Francese, the founder of American Demographics, Inc., predicted, "This is the growth edge of white-collar America, the power centers of tomorrow." "There's definitely something going on," says J. D. Delanger, publisher of *Country Magazine*, based in Withee, Wisconsin. "A couple of years ago," he notes, "our circulation sank to 4,000. Now, we're back up to 50,000."[4]

Rural America experienced a net inflow of 1.6 to 2.0 million people (or about 360,000 per year) in the first half of the 1990s, a gain of about 4 percent, compared with a loss of about 1.4 million people during the 1980s. Today over 52.5 million people, or approximately 20 percent of the population, live in rural America. Because of this new migration, after years of decline, approximately 75 percent of the nation's 2,304 rural counties are growing again. Many are growing at their fastest rate in a century, and almost all are growing at their fastest rate in more than two decades. Calvin Beale, senior demographer at the U.S. Department of Agriculture, believes, "Some are growing so fast they couldn't turn it off if they wanted to."[5]

Surveys indicate that over 40 percent of those arriving in small rural towns today are coming from nonrural areas. Beale has remarked, "The people living in these new homes are in the vanguard of a new trend, but the rural rebound is rooted in an old-fashioned American dream—the dream of a better life in a new land."[6] Unlike the middle-class fourth-migration exodus from multiethnic cities to the suburbs, this more recent resettlement is from both cities and increasingly crowded suburbs.

A generally unspoken motivation for moving out of certain older metropolitan areas and near-in suburbs, especially by some whites, is to avoid living in a racially diverse community. Demographers at the University of Michigan have discovered that virtually all the forty fastest growing rural counties are at least 70 percent white, and most are more than 85 percent white. Commenting on the role of race in the internal migration now going on in America, Beale said, "It's fairly clear to me that a certain amount of movement into rural areas can fairly be described as white flight. I have rarely heard anyone mention race in the context of talking about this." Then he added, "They talk about getting away from urban crime, drugs, congestion and school problems. But it also means getting away from areas that have significant percentages of blacks, Hispanics and Asians."[7]

A snapshot look at Connecticut between 1990 and 1994 tells a story repeated in nearly every state. During this period, the population of Connecticut's five largest cities—Bridgeport, Hartford, New Haven, Stamford, and Waterbury—dropped by 6.6 percent. Their inner-ring suburbs lost population as well. In contrast, the seventy-eight Connecticut towns with ten thousand or fewer people had a combined population growth of about 4.5 percent. And of all the 169 towns in the state, 133 grew, or nearly 80 percent.

Across the country, by the mid-1990s, the growth rate of rural counties had nearly caught up with that of metropolitan counties. It is my guess that by the end of the century, their rates of overall growth will be about even. I believe that the migrant stream to rural counties picked up during the second half of the 1990s, increasing to a rate as high as five hundred thousand people a year, many of them fifth-migration participants.

Two rural demographers, Kenneth Johnson, professor of sociology at Loyola University in Chicago, and Calvin Beale, completed in 1995 the most thorough recent statistical analysis of the rural resurgence.[8] Their research offers a detailed look at who is responsible for newly experienced growth in rural areas. Between 1990 and 1994, 56 percent of rural growth was caused by net gains in migration, or by the migration of roughly 1.1 million people. The other 44 percent, or about 875,000 people, was a net gain from "natural" increases—the dominance of births over deaths.

Based on the precise locations of growth and the profiles of the people moving, I estimate that of the new migrants to rural areas at least half are fifth-migration participants, or some 550,000 people between 1990 and 1994, about 110,000 a year. To this I would add 15 percent of the people gained from natural increases as genuine fifth wavers, people with a choice who elect not to move because they are able to satisfy their fifth-wave instincts right where they are. This group adds an additional 131,000 people over the 1990–1994 interval. (Of course, many other fifth-wave adults brought up in rural areas seek other destinations and become a part of the fifth migration.)

The fastest growing rural counties are ones that attract people in search of recreation. Of the 285 rural counties classified as "recreational," 85 percent gained migrants between 1990 and 1994, and this strong trend continues.[9] These counties are located predominantly in the western mountains, the upper Great Lakes, the Ozarks, parts of the South, and the coasts of Florida, North Carolina, South Carolina, Delaware, and Massachusetts.

In their analysis, Johnson and Beale found that America's 443 "retirement" counties show more growth than any other type of county except those that offer strong outdoor recreation. Of the 190 retirement counties classified as rural, 99 percent gained population between 1990 and 1994, for a strong overall growth rate of about 4 percent.

Counties with recreational amenities tend to attract retirees. Just over one hundred "recreational" counties also fall into the U.S. Department of Agriculture "retirement" category. As Beale and Johnson discovered in their analysis, "These recreation-retirement counties grew by 12 percent between 1990 and 1994, the fastest pace of any economic group in the USDA categories." Hello, fifth wave.

As might be expected, considering the dynamics of current population shifts and within them the fifth migration, three other types of rural counties are registering widespread inmigration. First, as fifth-migration participants and others settle farther out, 86 percent of rural counties adjacent to metropolitan areas are growing. Of these 73 percent had net inmigration of 2.6 percent per year from 1990 to 1994, double the 1.3 rate enjoyed by metropolitan areas. Second, 84 percent of rural counties whose economy is based on service-sector jobs are growing. Many of these locales show up as entrepreneurial hot spots, and some service-job locales are also classified as recreation or retirement counties. Third, population growth is strong in 75 percent of the 381 rural counties in which the "mailbox economy"—federal transfers of social security checks and corporate transfers of pension proceeds—is important, with 66 percent of them enjoying growth via inmigration.

Migration is not strong, as might be expected, in rural counties that depend primarily on farming and mining nor in very poor and sparsely settled rural places. Of the one-fourth of all rural counties still losing population in the 1990s, most were concentrated in the Great Plains, western Corn Belt, and Mississippi Delta.

Rural businesses of all sorts have been growing, even some commonly associated with dense urban development. Wal-Mart, for instance, became the nation's largest retailer by expanding operations into rural areas, while McDonald's fashioned a smaller prototype restaurant to accommodate life in rural places.

Businesses started by fifth wavers who participate in traditional rural life are also showing signs of activity. Marketing consultants, bankers, lawyers, and other white-collar professionals are working with or on the land. Many are using a portion of their savings or stock-market gains, combined with low-interest loans, to start these businesses, even though many also keep their day jobs, either telecommuting or driving into the office during the workweek. "Hobby farmers," as they are known, are dabbling in minifarms, microranches, and every other imaginable small-scale agricultural endeavor. Fifth-wave inmigrants to rural areas are raising alpacas, blueberries, ginseng, yaks, buffalo, apples, Angora goats, corn, and soybeans. Blake Fohl, marketing vice-president of Tractor Supply Co., a twenty-five–state retail chain, figures that 40 percent of sales are to hobbyists, double the percentage in the late 1980s. Hobby-farm venturers often direct production toward fifth-wave tastes. Demand for gourmet products expands wherever a fifth-wave population takes hold. Organic foods, herbs, dried berries, naturally raised meat, free-range chicken, the freshest vegetables—all find eager customers.

By no means do all fifth-migration settlers in rural areas find work in or near their new homes. Many continue to commute long distances back to their original jobs or to new ones in distant cities and suburbs. As an example, town officials in Prescott, Arizona, estimate that 5 percent of the town's twenty-eight thousand residents commute round trip daily to Phoenix, one hundred miles away. Outside the sprawling northern Virginia suburbs of Washington, D.C., it is not uncommon for professionals who commute into downtown Washington to rise at four to five in the morning to be at work on time.

Eric Pooley, reporting for *Time* magazine, investigated one rural fifth-migration growth town, Wilmington, Ohio, which has a population of thirteen thousand.[10] He wanted to know who some of the newcomers were and what they hoped to achieve by moving. Kathy Wiley, an executive secretary at Warner Brothers in Burbank, and her husband Jim Wiley, a manager at Warner Brothers, came to escape the noise, traffic, crime, smog, and high cost of living in Los Angeles and the cut-throat competition in the film industry. Jim was looking for the close-knit way of life he remembered from his childhood in rural Pennsylvania. Marcy Hawley, a Bostonian who runs a boutique publishing house on Main Street, "wanted the cohesiveness and convenience of a town where you could walk to everything." Ruth Dooley, a pediatrician, and her husband, Mike, a pilot at Airborne Express, whose hub is in Wilmington, abandoned Cincinnati because they saw "a town out of time: lovely Victorian, Italianate and clapboard houses with wrap-around porches and flags fluttering in the

Why People Move to Rural Areas

Although each inmigrant's precise reasons for relocating to a rural area are different, the following excerpts from interviews and printed remarks give an idea of the range.

"Nostalgia plays a significant part of why people want to live in the sticks."

"Life down here isn't as hectic. You go into town, and people stop to say hi."

"Concerns about crime, congestion, and schooling have pushed many people."

"Those who face a long commute say it's worth it, especially when they get to hear hummingbirds in the morning, see starry skies at night, and have peace of mind that the world—or at least their small, green part of it—is still a safe place."

"It reminds people of simpler times when life seemed less confusing and pressured."

"We still have the same old friends. We just drive more to see them. But it's easier to make friends out here. People are not as standoffish."

"You go outside here and there's this wonderful view. You can come home and jump into the pool and just stay there."

"With all of us living longer—including our parents—it is important to choose to live where environmental conditions are right. The cumulative effects of pollution and congestion—plus the newly discovered threat of ultraviolet radiation—can tarnish our 'golden years.'"

"People who come here to vacation fall in love with the natural beaches. A lot of them get ideas for small businesses. They wind up moving here."

"Older visitors end up loving it so much here they buy property."

breeze; a shopping district of three-story brick buildings anchored by a domed courthouse, a gabled hotel and the Murphy Theater, a brick-and-terra-cotta confection with a delightful Art Deco marquee." To Ruth, this was a "protected environment where we could raise our kids in peace."

The Seasonal Resort Becomes
a Year-Round Place

As we have seen, the fifth wave is heading for the best scenery and opportunities for recreation; often they are found in mid-size and smaller resort towns such as Telluride, Santa Barbara, Palm Beach, Aspen, East Hampton, Park City, and Santa Fe. After all, such places offer preexisting amenities, usually an attractive older village or town center, convenient access roads, abundant indoor entertainment such as restaurants, art galleries, theaters, and movies, and all are generally set in a location fine enough to attract seasonal visitors in the first place. In addition, many of the communities are long-established, may possess historic buildings, and can legitimately claim interesting early histories as fishing, farming, logging, mining, or trading communities.

The places I have just listed are well known. But many others are spread all across America. Since the late 1970s resort towns have attracted more visitors than ever before. Many have stayed. Fifth-migration dynamics suggest the inevitability of this trend continuing and accelerating. Nor have resort communities, in general, elected to resist. Instead, one after another has contrived to appeal to visitors over a longer and longer season. Music in the Rocky Mountains has expanded the season from winter skiing to year-round. Theater and opera have been used to similar effect in Santa Fe and in many Florida locations.

In Santa Fe the combination of strong inmigration and growing tourism has created a representative fifth-migration growth town. Not long ago Santa Fe was a quiet resort on hilly terrain with beautiful views of the Sangre de Cristo mountain range, strategically located within sixty miles of Taos, Espanola, Los Alamos, and Albuquerque. Today Santa Fe is populated in large part by relative newcomers. Long inhospitable to major industry because of town policy and water shortages, Santa Fe still attracts individuals who make a conscious effort to move there. "People who move to Santa Fe generally do not transfer to Santa Fe with a company," said Katherine Zacher in 1994, when she was president of the Chamber of Commerce. "Individuals will give up jobs, money, social life, you name it, because this is where they have to be." Any number of them are now doing the "Santa Fe shuffle," a local term to describe how people with Ph.D.'s and others with high qualifications work at three or four jobs, whatever they can get, usually for rather low wages, to be able to live in Santa Fe.

Simultaneously Santa Fe has encouraged the visitor population to expand. Summer fairs devoted to Native American themes and others devoted to colonial ones draw thousands. A vibrant opera season attracts music lovers and countless others who like to be seen where music enthusiasts gather. With a lively art market, numerous resident collectors, small museums, and streets devoted to galleries, restaurants, and upscale boutiques of every kind, downtown Santa Fe is now busy day and night all summer and much of the rest of the year. The convention and visitors bureau, still not satisfied, seeks to attract even more visitors from various unexploited sources. Now they are targeting the "meetings market," particularly during November through May. "We don't promote the summer," said Alan Silow, the bureau's director of sales and marketing, in 1994, "because we feel the summer is packed."

Rocky Mountain Fever

Today, for all their open spaces, the eleven states of the West have the highest concentration of residents in urban settings. Whereas before World War II little more than half of all westerners lived in cities, today 86 percent reside in metropolitan areas. The fifth migration has created a new urban West in which six of the twenty fastest growing metropolitan areas of the country are located (Table 1.9). Trendy, high-tech centers such as Seattle and Portland flourish; desert-defying cities such as Phoenix and Las Vegas have proven a paradise for developers; and Rocky Mountain growth centers such as Denver and Salt Lake City boom with jobs and thrive in close proximity to exceptional, vast natural playgrounds. In 1995, after a trip to the West, Mark Potok reported, "In Phoenix, where developers have been bulldozing the Sonora Desert at a rate of an acre an hour, starving desert termites have been so deprived of their natural foods that they're attacking even chemically treated houses."[11]

The eight states of the Rocky Mountain West—Colorado, Wyoming, Utah, Idaho, Montana, Nevada, Arizona, and New Mexico—whose physical arrangement for the most part had barely changed for two hundred million years, are now in an undeniable boom. New industry, new sources of finance, new people, and with it all new social and physical pressures are pulsing through the bigger cities like Boise, Denver, and Salt Lake City, as well as through resort towns large and small such as Aspen, Telluride, Santa Fe, Taos, and even remote, smaller places such as Bluff, Utah. Nor does the surge stop at settled communities. Many migrants are heading for the back country of the West and commuting to work or just sitting there looking at the view, enjoying their participation in the fifth migration.

As a result, the western economy has been transformed. Utah has been leading the nation in industrial job growth, followed by New Mexico, Nevada, and Idaho. Colorado and Arizona are not far behind. All during the 1990s the area benefited from strong high-technology sectors, active construction markets, and solid tourism growth, which have been added atop a traditional base in certain natural-resource industries. In 1996 the top twenty U.S. towns for manufacturing-job growth included Las Vegas, Phoenix-Mesa, Salt Lake City, Albuquerque, and Denver.

Of the ten states that recorded the fastest rates of international export growth from 1988 to 1996, seven were landlocked western states. While traditional western exports such as farm, ranch, and mine products are being sent to new markets around the globe, technological advances allow new industries such as financial services and computer and telecommunication manufacturing to flourish from bases in the nation's interior. In 1988, the eleven states in the Mountain time zone exported on a per capita basis at half the national average. By 1996 the region's average had risen to two-thirds. By 1996 Japan was the largest trading partner of Utah, Colorado, Nebraska, and Kansas; Britain accounted for a major part of the $400 million invested in Colorado by two hundred companies from twenty-two foreign countries.

For all of the stunning increase in manufacturing and export jobs, the largest private employer and the fastest growing industry in the region is tourism. For example, in 1993, tourism in Utah ran about 12 percent ahead of 1992, a year when a record fifteen million out-of-staters arrived for a visit. Telluride, once a backwater, nearly abandoned silver-mining town perched rather inaccessibly in a high valley, in 1997 alone hosted a jazz festival, a blues festival, a bluegrass festival, a theater festival, a dance festival, and two film festivals. "There are now more summer music festivals in Colorado than in any other state in America," according to Robert Harth, 1997 president of the extremely successful Aspen Music Festival—

the festival that in 1949 pioneered music in the Rocky Mountains. Like other resorts around the country, Rocky Mountain communities seek year-round tourism rather than flourish only during the high season, which for this part of the West is the winter. Efforts to exploit a successful marriage between mountains and the arts are evident throughout the area. Lured by a combination of the arts and attractive scenery, fifth wavers come to town. Each year a number decide to come back—for good.

During the 1990s, western cattle ranching, like skiing, became less profitable. So ranchers began wrangling tourists instead. According to a *Wall Street Journal* reporter, "Guest fever is sweeping the West. Never mind that tending cattle isn't always the best training for tending guests. Tales of city slickers dropping $150 a day at Western cattle ranches are prompting cowpoke after cowpoke to turn innkeeper."[12] Between 1992 and 1997, the number of ranches accommodating paying guests doubled in Wyoming and was up 40 percent in Montana. At the same time, between 1990 and 1997, the number of Montana cattle operations declined by eight hundred.

This region's economic growth has triggered a significant surge in population. Since 1990, the nation's fastest regional population growth, 18 percent, has occurred in the Rocky Mountain states. Colorado has been in the midst of a particularly dramatic fifth-migration boom. As Colorado absorbed four hundred thousand newcomers between 1990 and 1997, the state's population swelled to almost four million. During that time Colorado contained eleven of the thirty-five fastest growing counties in the nation, including Douglas, Elbert, Park, and Custer. As a consequence, in the most sought-out locations, home sale prices and rents have increased by 50 percent or more, while wages have moved up by 30 percent.

In the West, as everywhere else, the fifth migration is selective, centered in particular growth towns or special regions. Most of the West, like most of America, remains sparsely populated. Indeed, during the twentieth century, many western areas have lost population. In Montana, North Dakota, South Dakota, and Wyoming, an area twice the size of France, there are today fewer than three million people. Since 1990, these four large states, with a total residential base of only about one-third that of New York City, have lost population in absolute terms.

In many ways, Utah is a prime example of how the natural beauty of the West has combined with a growing economy to produce a destination avidly sought by fifth wavers. In the early 1980s, Utah was a sparsely populated, often stunning stretch of land, known principally for its clean capital, Salt Lake City, and its deep Mormon heritage. Since then, church-owned Brigham Young University has helped trigger an explosion in high-technology activity, while natural beauty and awesome recreation resources have appealed to alert fifth wavers. Today over fifteen hundred high-tech companies do business in Utah, employing over seventy thousand people, more than 8 percent of the state's work force. The forty-mile strip between Salt Lake City and Provo, where most of the jobs are clustered and 85 percent of Utahans live, has come to be known as Software Valley. Although most people don't think of Utah as a high-tech center, a large and growing number of technology companies are headquartered or have important branches in the state. Among them are Provo-based Novell Inc., a developer of computer software; Thiokol Corporation, a producer of high-propulsion systems; Iomega, which makes storage and safety products for computer systems; Evans & Sutherland, a producer of special-purpose computers; and Packard Bell, a large, privately held producer of personal computers.

The open spaces, clean environment, and strong Mormon work ethic that dominate Salt Lake City have combined to transform the capital and the state into one of the world's largest centers for credit-card processing, airline reservations, and telemarketing. These service jobs can be filled successfully by Utah's unusually well-educated population; the state has the highest literacy rate in the country and ranks high in the percentage of students who earn advanced degrees.

Among the attractions of Utah, and the other principal Mountain states, are relatively low labor costs, affordable real estate, moderate living costs, and as James Wilson, president of the Thiokol operation in Ogden, puts it, "There's a quality of life that makes it easier to attract and hire people from around the country."[13] Although entry-level wages in Utah are 5 to 10 percent below the national average, living costs are also lower. As a result of economic and environmental factors, Utah has been creating thousands of new jobs, more than enough to satisfy the continuing stream of younger, well-educated fifth-migration job seekers.

Looking at the cross-state migration between California and the Rocky Mountain West after the especially severe downturn in the California economy in the first half of the 1990s is another way to obtain a glimpse of the fifth wave. The flight of businesses, job seekers, and retirees from California during much of the 1990s and especially from 1990 to 1996 was a large factor in the growth of the Rocky Mountain area. Beginning early in the 1990s, the six nearby western states—Arizona, Idaho, Nevada, New Mexico, Utah, Washington—began to uncouple from the stagnating California economy and to benefit from it. By 1994, these six states were among the ten fastest growing labor markets in the country. California, by contrast, ranked forty-ninth. In the same year, personal income grew about 8 percent in Arizona and Nevada, but less than half that amount in California.

Data from the Internal Revenue Service (IRS) show that the more affluent and skilled residents left California for Portland, Las Vegas, Phoenix, Salt Lake City, and Boise, while poorer people tended to remain in the state. During the outpouring of 1993 alone, as a result of departed fifth-wave migrants, the IRS estimates that California lost about $4.3 billion in net personal income. In 1994 a quarter of a million people from California found new homes in places like Portland and Las Vegas. Of those leaving, three distinct strands of fifth-migration participants stand out: the self-employed or those able to live largely on savings; young, well-educated households seeking a fresh start in an appealing physical, social, and economic environment; and retirees who elect to move to wherever their fifth-wave options and instincts guide them.

It would surely be a mistake, however, in spite of what occurred during the late 1980s and first half of the 1990s, to assume that California is going to experience continuing erosion of qualified people and top-level jobs. By the middle of 1995 California was turning around and again attracting. Cognetics, Inc., projects that more white-collar jobs will be created in Los Angeles and in the Bay Area by 2004 than in Phoenix, Orlando, Seattle, and Denver combined. Much of the job growth is expected in companies involved in creative services linked to international trade, tourism, multimedia endeavors, and entertainment, the bread and butter of fifth wavers. In spite of its depletion, even in 1995 California remained the undisputed leader in virtually all science-based industries. It had increased its share of the computer industry to 27 percent and was garnering about 30 percent of the nation's biotech sector.

This revival in California has been enhanced by a drop in high real estate prices, which were escalating at a 20 percent annual clip during the 1980s boom; these prices fell during the first half of the 1990s—in some locations by as much as 50 percent. By mid-1997, in southern California, house prices had bottomed out and were rising again in Orange County and in the wealthy neighborhoods of Los Angeles, up about 6 percent in a twelve-month period. At the same time, again as a reflection of the power of the fifth migration, in these same metropolitan areas median-priced houses and modest homes did not increase in value. In fact a decline of about 2 percent was more common. In 1997 it was no more expensive to rent first-class office space in Los Angeles than in Phoenix or Seattle. Huge differentials in housing costs between California and its neighboring states had narrowed. By the third quarter of 1997, the renewal of California was clearly under way.

Back to Town

While rural areas, western states, and the exurbs newly attract in large numbers, there is also a countervailing rotation among fifth wavers back to the most desirable locations in the country's most dynamic cities. Some return to become full-time residents; others rent or purchase a second home, a pied-à-terre. Members of the fifth wave who elect to move back to the cities include many empty nesters who seek places that are well served by medical institutions, cultural centers, and universities with active public programs. Many are former fourth-migration participants who sought a suburban life for a growing family. Some members of the fifth wave who come back to town or who move in for the first time seek the relative ease of apartment living combined with the security afforded by attendants. Older people wish to maintain full personal mobility after automobile driving becomes a burden. Some are also contrarian folks, fifth wavers who never left. Others find long-distance auto travel disagreeable or are drawn by cultural offerings or want the convenient socializing and specialized shopping offered by a city.

Fifth wavers who move into cities are particularly attracted to places that try to manage growth and focus on the quality of life as a part of planning policy. Portland, Oregon, for instance, has become increasingly attractive since 1979, when it became the first city in the United States to introduce an urban growth boundary, as described in Chapter 8. Seattle is a more recent example of a city that appeals to fifth-migration participants because of growth-control and sprawl-control policies. After conventional sprawl consumed thousands of Seattle-area acres in the process of accommodating over three hundred thousand additional people since

1980, an urban growth boundary was established in 1994. This change is preserving open space while stimulating the construction of town houses and apartments, which today account for nearly 60 percent of new residential construction in Seattle. Fifth wavers find the community a more promising place to live than ever before.

The quiet, consistent movement back to older cities by well-off fifth wavers is focused on the most desirable city-center locations, including historic districts, in places such as New York, Chicago, San Francisco, and New Orleans, communities that overall are not gaining population fast. During the 1980s, for instance, about 60,000 suburbanites moved into Chicago, far fewer than the 275,000 to 325,000 people who moved out of the central city. Those fifth wavers who came back headed for high-quality Gold Coast and North Lakeshore neighborhoods and continue to do so. In New York City, the return flow of fifth wavers mixed with a Wall Street boom has kept cooperative apartments full and prices generally rising from 60th Street to 86th Street between Fifth and Park Avenues on Manhattan's East Side, just as fifth wavers have returned to locations within the French Quarter and Warehouse Historic Districts in New Orleans. Historic districts will continue to exert a special appeal. In these areas building design and quality, public-area aesthetics, and growth are all regulated and usually responsibly monitored by an independent public or semipublic authority. As an example of the selectivity of this market, during the much-improved real estate market of 1996–1997 in New York City, for instance, cooperative and condominium prices rose about 12 percent, while the price of the city's most exclusive and desirable residential properties escalated by over 30 percent. But average properties hardly changed in value during the period, and some declined. In Los Angeles the story was much the same, with the prices of the most sought-out fifth-migration locations on the west side up over 6 percent during the twelve-month period.

The number of good jobs is beginning to increase in cities such as San Francisco, New York, and Miami, where mind-based work is flourishing. As these jobs become available, more often than not they are filled by fifth wavers. In New York City, for instance, in the first six months of 1997, over twenty thousand jobs were created. Yet the unemployment rate rose to 10 percent, double the rate for the nation and a level not seen since the depth of the city's recession in 1991. Who has filled these sophisticated jobs? Young graduates, fifth-migration participants who move back into the city, and skilled suburbanite baby boomers who are now thirty to fifty years old, some of whom live in town and others who remain committed to living outside the city.

"Best" Places to Live

In popular magazines and paperback books an emerging industry routinely identifies the so-called best places to live around the country. This proliferating places-rated industry provides contemporary market evidence of the fifth migration because beneath this opportunistic trend is recognition of new priorities, pent-up wishes to relocate, and new abilities to do so. According to a *Money* magazine survey, these were the twenty best places to live as of July 1996 (in order):

Madison, Wisc.
Punta Gorda, Fla.
Rochester, Minn.
Fort Lauderdale, Fla.
Ann Arbor, Mich.
Fort Myers–Cape Coral, Fla.
Gainesville, Fla.
Austin, Tex.
Seattle, Wash.
Lakeland, Fla.
Tampa–St. Petersburg, Fla.
Orlando, Fla.
San Francisco, Calif.
Fargo, N. Dak.
Naples, Fla.
San Diego, Calif.
San Antonio, Tex.
Fort Walton Beach, Fla.
San Jose, Calif.
Jacksonville, Fla.

Many of these places are home to a university, and eight are either small communities (population below 250,000) or medium communities of fewer than 1 million people. Table 3.2 lists *Money*'s survey results as of

TABLE 3.2.
THREE BEST PLACES TO LIVE IN EACH REGION IN BIG, MEDIUM, AND SMALL CITIES, 1998

Region	Big Cities (1,000,000+)	Medium Cities (over 250,000)	Small Cities (over 100,000)
West	Seattle-Bellevue-Everett, Wash. Denver, Colo. Los Angeles–Long Beach, Calif.	Boulder-Longmont, Colo. Tacoma, Wash. Eugene-Springfield, Ore.	Fort Collins–Loveland, Colo. San Luis Obispo–Atascadero–Paso Robles, Calif. Olympia, Wash.
Midwest	Minneapolis–St. Paul, Minn. (Wisc.) Cleveland-Lorain-Elyria, Ohio Chicago, Ill.	Madison, Wisc. Kalamazoo–Battle Creek, Mich. Akron, Ohio	Rochester, Minn. Lafayette, Ind. Sheboygan, Wisc.
South	Norfolk–Virginia Beach–Newport News, Va. (N.C.) Raleigh–Durham–Chapel Hill, N.C. Orlando, Fla.	Richmond-Petersburg, Va. Pensacola, Fla. Tallahassee, Fla.	Charlottesville, Va. Lynchburg, Va. Roanoke, Va.
East	Washington, D.C. Boston, Mass. New York, N.Y.	Trenton (Mercer County), N.J. Duchess County, N.Y. Wilmington-Newark, Del. (Md.)	Manchester, N.H. Portland, Maine Nashua, N.H.

SOURCE: *Money*, July 1998.

mid-1998 for the best big, medium, and small cities to live in in each of four regions. There are predictable overlaps among these selected desirable communities and the entrepreneurial hot spots discussed previously in this chapter.

New computer-sorting programs mixed with inexpensive access to vast amounts of data have enabled the organizations in this new industry to massage published data using their own criteria and weighted priorities, some of which are significantly different. For instance, in 1995 *Places Rated Almanac* ranked Cincinnati at the top of its list; *Money* placed it sixtieth. In the same year *Money* ranked Sioux Falls, South Dakota, and Provo-Orem, Utah, within its top ten; in *Places Rated Almanac* they finished 157th and 172nd, respectively. The same organization may even shift its judgments in sequential years. Between 1993 and 1994, Hagerstown, Maryland, leaped in *Money's* listing from 204th to 34th, while Kenosha, Wisconsin, descended from 25th to 261st. Such radical fluctuations cannot possibly occur in real desirability in the space of a year. Only data massaging or new editorial weightings and priorities can explain the sharp changes.

The criteria used by each publisher vary somewhat, but *Places Rated Almanac* covers the general territory: it examines cost of living, jobs, crime, health care, the environment, transportation, education, the arts, recreation, and climate, along with various subcategories. The result is a subjective statistical mix compounded by the ratings of editors and researchers who impose their own set of subjective factors often not backed up by field visits. Reliance on any of these specific data, rankings, and conclusions without a personal investigation of the sort recommended in Part IV of this book would be a serious mistake. So I present no definitive lists here; no particular collection of data or rating service could possibly be endorsed.

To illustrate the inevitable difference in conclusions based on diverse criteria and individual organizations' and editors' weightings of the importance of various factors, I have included Table 3.3. This cross-section of advice, which ranks different specific places different ways, is a good general guide to places that are currently prospering. Many of these are genuine growth towns being powered by the fifth migration. Some of them are already experiencing the problems that are discussed in Part II. A few will find ways, in the years ahead, to become smart growth towns, as described in Part III.

TABLE 3.3.
THIRTY BEST PLACES TO LIVE AS RANKED BY SELECTED
PUBLICATIONS, 1993–1998

		Publication	
Rank	Places Rated Almanac	Money	Reliastar
1	Orange County, Calif.	Nashua, N.H.	Minneapolis–St. Paul, Minn. (Wisc.)
2	Seattle-Bellevue-Everett, Wash.	Rochester, Minn.	Fort Wayne, Ind.
3	Houston, Tex.	Monmouth and Ocean counties, N.J.	Grand Rapids–Muskegon–Holland, Mich.
4	Washington, D.C. (Md.-Va.-W. Va.)	Punta Gorda, Fla.	Des Moines, Iowa
5	Phoenix-Mesa, Ariz.	Portsmouth, N.H.	Lancaster, Pa.
6	Minneapolis–St. Paul, Minn.	Manchester, N.H.	Sarasota-Bradenton, Fla.
7	Atlanta, Ga.	Madison, Wisc.	Harrisburg-Lebanon-Carlisle, Pa.
8	Tampa–St. Petersburg–Clearwater, Fla.	San Jose, Calif.	Salt Lake City–Ogden, Utah
9	San Diego, Calif.	Jacksonville, Fla.	Madison, Wisc.
10	Philadelphia, Pa. (N.J.)	Fort Walton Beach, Fla.	Detroit–Ann Arbor–Flint, Mich.
11	San Jose, Calif.	Seattle, Wash.	Indianapolis, Ind.
12	Long Island, N.Y.	Gainesville, Fla.	Atlanta, Ga.
13	Riverside–San Bernardino, Calif.	San Francisco, Calif.	Omaha, Nebr. (Iowa)
14	Pittsburgh, Pa.	Lakeland, Fla.	Cincinnati-Hamilton, Ohio (Ky.-Ind.)
15	Toronto, Ontario	Fort Lauderdale, Fla.	Denver-Boulder-Greeley, Colo.
16	Portland-Vancouver, Ore.-Wash.	Raleigh–Durham–Chapel Hill, N.C.	Charlotte–Gastonia–Rock Hill, N.C.-S.C.
			(Continued)

TABLE 3.3 (CONT.)
THIRTY BEST PLACES TO LIVE AS RANKED BY SELECTED
PUBLICATIONS, 1993–1998

		Publication	
Rank	Places Rated Almanac	Money	Reliastar
17	Oakland, Calif.	West Palm Beach, Fla.	Richmond-Petersburg, Va.
18	Denver, Colo.	Orlando, Fla.	Milwaukee-Racine, Wisc.
19	Cincinnati, Ohio (Ky.-Ind.)	Boulder, Colo.	Raleigh–Durham–Chapel Hill, N.C.
20	San Francisco, Calif.	Long Island, N.Y.	Greensboro–Winston-Salem–High Point, N.C.
21	Detroit, Mich.	Sarasota-Bradenton, Fla.	Columbus, Ohio
22	Dallas, Tex.	Los Angeles–Long Beach, Calif.	Columbia, S.C.
23	Chicago, Ill.	Boston, Mass.	Boston, Mass. (N.H.)
24	Miami, Fla.	Oakland, Calif.	Seattle-Tacoma-Bremerton, Wash.
25	Cleveland-Lorain-Elyria, Ohio	Lafayette, Ind.	Cleveland-Akron, Ohio
26	Salt Lake City–Ogden, Utah	Sheboygan, Wisc.	Kalamazoo–Battle Creek, Mich.
27	San Antonio, Tex.	Orange County, Calif.	Portland-Salem, Ore. (Wash.)
28	Milwaukee-Waukesha, Wisc.	San Diego, Calif.	Nashville, Tenn.
29	Orlando, Fla.	Central New Jersey	St. Louis, Mo. (Ill.)
30	Vancouver, B.C.	Naples, Fla.	Hartford, Conn.

Rank	Small Cities	Small Towns
1	Mount Vernon, Wash.	Elko, Nev.
2	Ames, Iowa	Essex, Conn.
3	Morgantown, W. Va.	Page, Ariz.
4	Ithaca, N.Y.	Lebanon, N.H.
5	Traverse City, Mich.	Lander, Wyo.
6	Port Angeles, Wash.	Ukiah, Calif.
7	Sandusky, Ohio	Glenwood Springs, Colo.
8	Columbus, Ind.	Durango, Colo.
9	Concord, N.H.	Lewisburg, Pa.
10	Mason City, Iowa	Culpepper, Va.
11	Wenatchee, Wash.	Littleton, N.H.
12	Rome, Ga.	Pierre, S. Dak.
13	Bozeman, Mont.	Devils Lake, N. Dak.
14	Mankato, Minn.	Kalispell, Mont.
15	Bend, Ore.	Petoskey, Mich.
16	Longview, Wash.	York, Nebr.
17	Frankfort, Ky.	Yreka, Calif.
18	Plattsburgh, N.Y.	Williamstown, Mass.
19	Willmar, Minn.	Shippensburg, Pa.
20	Burlington, Iowa	Anacortes, Wash.
21	Tupelo, Miss.	Plymouth, N.H.
22	Winchester, Va.	Brattleboro, Vt.
23	Albany-Corvallis, Ore.	Beaufort, S.C.
24	Carbondale, Ill.	Monroe, Wisc.
25	Coeur d'Alene, Idaho	Grinnell, Iowa
26	Rutland, Vt.	Easton, Md.
27	Mattoon-Charleston, Ill.	Douglas, Wyo.
28	Harrisonburg, Va.	Grand Rapids, Mich.
29	La Grange, Ga.	Red Wing, Minn.
30	Marion, Ohio	McPherson, Kans.

SOURCES: *Places Rated Almanac* (New York: Macmillan, 1997); "The Best Places to Live in America," *Money*, May 1998, at *http://www.money.com*; *Best Cities to Earn and Save Money* (Minneapolis: Reliastar Financial Corporation, 1998); *The New Rating Guide to Life in America's Small Cities* (Buffalo, N.Y.: Prometheus, 1997); *The 100 Best Small Towns in America* (Upper Saddle River, N.J.: Prentice-Hall, 1993). Table compiled by *American Demographics*, May 1998.

II

Growth Towns
at the Crossroads

CHAPTER FOUR

Causes and Consequences
of Community Decay

TODAY'S GROWTH TOWNS, the receiving sites of the fifth
migration, are at a crossroads. Fast growth induces a reaction.
The kind of reaction depends on the changes that are being
made, the nature of the growth town, and the person or organization that is reacting. If bust follows boom once again in this latest migration, what are the causes and what will be the consequences? What can
we learn from the mistakes made at the destinations of previous migrations? When decay does occur, the damage to residents, the joint-venture
owners of all the assets in each community, is massive.

Causes of Decay

From the beginning and right through to the fifth migration, settlers in
America have been reckless both in how they use the natural environment
and in how they build the communities in which they live. Americans are
also typically suspicious of and resistant to land-use control and land planning. They have long been, as well, often justifiably averse to government
interference and have a deeply ingrained sense of personal powerlessness
over local land-related regulatory initiatives. The causes of decay in the

growth towns of all prior migrations can be found deep in the history and culture of America. They threaten the appeal and the prosperity of some of the most beautiful and currently successful places in the country.

Historic Attitudes

The entire continent was viewed by most early white settlers as a ripe and rich place, one to be tamed and to be exploited. Colonists and subsequent waves of immigrants envisioned North America as a commodity rather than as hallowed ground on which to establish commodious and continuous settlements. Alexis de Tocqueville noted on his 1831–1832 nine-month visit to America, "As one digs deeper into the national character of the Americans, one sees that they have sought the value of everything in this world only in the answer to this single question: how much money will it bring in?"[1] As part of their general refutation of European social and political tenets, new settlers abandoned a primordial love of place while embracing a primordial wish to benefit from the place in which they settled.

This basic attitude characterizes America throughout its continuing settlement history. When a place is no longer able to give up its easily obtained resources, people move on. Gold-mining towns, ranching communities, inland-waterway ports, ocean harbors, industrial cities, close-in suburbs—it is the same story across the continent and across time.

This fundamental part of the American character—to seek, to build, to exploit, and to move on—can be seen at a place like Leadville, in the 1880s the second largest city in Colorado. For its population of thirty thousand, exploitation was paramount. As the easy-to-extract gold, silver, lead, copper, zinc, and molybdenum disappeared, the get-rich-and-get-out ethic left in its wake two legacies: a population shriveled by 90 percent and an environmental disaster so lurid that Leadville has been declared by the Environmental Protection Agency a Superfund site—a site so polluted that it merits federal intervention. In less vivid and less dramatic ways this story was repeated across the continent, as eloquently recognized in 1892 by Frederick Jackson Turner, who remarked so aptly, "The existence of an area of free land, its continuous recession, and the advance of American settlement westward explain American development."[2]

From the beginning, the way architecture and planning in America have been carried out has also been problematic. Design and planning professionals, often joined by engineers, have been with few exceptions preoccupied with growth, development, expansion. Architects, for their part, wish to put up buildings that accommodate required activities but that will also redound to their personal credit as designers. This legacy may be coming to an end. Vincent Scully, the most admired living architectural historian in the United States, accurately relates this tradition to American designers' awe since the 1920s with modern architecture's iconic figures such as Frank Lloyd Wright, Le Corbusier, Ludwig Mies van der Rohe, and Walter Gropius:

> It now seems obvious to almost everybody…that community is what America has most conspicuously lost, and community is precisely what the canonical Modern architecture and planning of the middle years of this century were totally unable to provide. This was so for many reasons; foremost among them was the fact that the Modern architects of the heroic period (Wright, Le Corbusier, Mies van der Rohe, Gropius and their followers) all despised the traditional city—the finest achievement of Western architecture, put together piece by piece over the centuries—and were determined to replace it with their own personal, utopian, idiosyncratic schemes.[3]

Traditional planners and engineers, for their part, have typically promoted development and new extensions to cities at the cost of both older city areas and the natural environment: they have willingly cleared already settled areas as well as fields and forests, fouling rivers and the air, leveling mesa and mountain. To most of the engineering community, especially those associated with road and highway construction, more is desirable and bigger is better. As is evident in the new-urbanism movement, a new breed of architects and planners increasingly espouses a more promising direction, but most architects and engineers still tend to focus on building rather than preserving, on changing rather than improving, on making a reputation rather than making a substantial if less visible contribution.

HALLOWED PRIVATE RIGHTS

Displaced, disadvantaged, dissatisfied immigrant settlers brought across the sea a mistrust of government coupled with fierce independence and a profound belief in the private rights of individuals. This viewpoint was written into the laws of the country, which accorded individuals or companies who owned land the right to use it primarily for their own benefit. The Constitution of the United States guarantees that private property cannot be taken by any level of government without due process of law. And if the property is needed for proven public purpose, the owner must be fully compensated. In addition, the Constitution places the regulation of land use at the lowest level of decision making, local government. When one remembers that many framers of the Constitution were locally influential large-property owners, it is no wonder that in American law the landowner exerts great influence.

From the outset the federal government was eager to sell at nominal rates or to give the land of America to the private sector, even though, considering Native American prior rights, title to this property was technically questionable. Through various laws, culminating in the Homestead Act of 1862, the federal government used migrating settlers and opportunistic commercial enterprises as instruments in the occupation and control of a vast continent. In return, private interests were accorded near absolute rights of use, exploitation, and transfer. Homesteaders are but one well-known example. An individual who simply settled on and "improved" a parcel of land during a five-year period was deeded 160 acres.

Through different federal laws, beginning in the 1840s, railroad companies were awarded long and wide swaths of property, eventually totaling one hundred million acres across the country. Their sole obligation was to build rail lines for the transport of goods and people; they thereby created access, which in turn automatically added value to the lands made newly accessible. Thus, at nominal cost, railroad companies were given enough territory to found towns wherever they elected to create station stops. The towns themselves became centers of commerce and land speculation.

Zoning is the most pervasive form of government restriction on the use of privately owned land. Yet, although reasonably simple and operative since 1909, and confirmed by the Supreme Court in *City of Euclid v. Ambler* in 1926, zoning is still not extremely common or dearly loved. In many sections of the country, municipalities have not enacted local zoning ordinances. However, public and private awareness is increasing. In the whole 2.3 billion–acre land mass of the contiguous United States, of which approximately 58 percent is privately owned, none of the 86,692 land-use jurisdictions is now without some form of municipal, county, state, federal, or special-district regulation.

Indifference to Natural Resources

While the land was being distributed, few were concerned about its protection. The vision of property as a commodity was unchallenged until the last quarter of the nineteenth century: Yellowstone was established as the first national park in 1872, and the National Park Service was inaugurated in the 1890s. Once President Theodore Roosevelt pushed through the 1902 Reclamation Act, Congress began to give land serious consideration as a national resource to be protected. But not until the environmental movement began in the mid-1960s did public concern about deterioration of the natural environment in and around inhabited communities become widespread. The 1966 National Historic Preservation Act and the 1969 National Environmental Policy Act eventually led to a focus on environmental sustainability and its relationship to land conservation, as discussed in detail later.

When a place is in the midst of growth, its environmental amenities are under siege. The once taken-for-granted high meadow, long used for grazing, is identified by an outsider as an ideal site for a housing development. The nearby lake attracts a resort builder. All of a sudden, traditional access to a stream is cut off; a fence is thrown up; trees and trails are removed; and the once-serene natural landscape becomes hardly recognizable, certainly no longer freely frequented by town residents.

In fast-developing places environmental issues are many. They include loss of farmland and woodland, the degradation of wetlands, the crowding out of animals and overcrowding by people, the noise of construction, and the incessant hum of the highway. Growth seems traditionally to demand environmental sacrifice. For example, at a fundamental level, water resources become an issue. Is there enough water? Who is entitled to how much? And who will pay for the extension of public water lines, filtration plants, and sewage disposal systems? Fear becomes an emotion associated with water: fear that it will become insufficient or no longer pure and safe to drink or expensive to obtain. For a discussion of the many natural-resource issues with which growth towns must grapple, of which water is just one, see Chapter 8.

The Property-Tax Syndrome

In America, real estate tax revenue constitutes the lion's share of funds available for local community expenses such as schools, the police, maintenance of public space, and fire service. On average, 75 to 90 per-cent of locally available revenue is derived from a tax on real property within the community. The largest single expenditure from these rev-enues is for the school system, which tends to absorb from 40 to 60 per-cent of property taxes.

In most cases, the public cost of educating children exceeds whatever their family may contribute through real estate and other taxes. There-fore, each new family with school-age children creates a financial burden shared by each property owner. Dynamic population growth, as opposed to the occasional new family in town, inevitably triggers school expansion, hiring of new teachers and administrators, enlarged athletic teams and athletic facilities, new extracurricular offerings, and new staff experts put on payroll. Often a school district's expansion is so costly that capital funds must be raised through a local bond issue. A long-term community indebtedness is thereby incurred, one that assures higher taxes for years to cover interest and amortization payments. For this reason, school bond referenda often become hotly contested, especially in towns with large numbers of people with no school-age children.

Along with expanding school facilities, other municipal amenities are costly in growth towns. There is likely to be pressure to enlarge the town hall, to build a new police station, or to provide a firehouse with the latest interactive communications equipment. To pay for these services and to cover the swelling municipal payroll, many communities, as they begin to experience growth, opt to continue to expand at a rapid rate, adding new private commercial and residential buildings to raise needed property-tax revenue.

A vicious cycle begins, and eventually the tax burden becomes oner-ous—an unacceptably high and accelerating expense, even for middle-income residents. Questions then arise among property owners about the wisdom of growth and its impact on those already in town. Even before this stage, childless people, older residents who no longer have children in school, and emigrant retirees who never did have been troubled by the trends and may well have been leading the resistance to new capital ex-penditures, particularly for school expansion. As growth towns expand, elderly voters, and sometimes even young people, often vote against in-creased school budgets.

What most fast-growing communities fail to understand is that most new houses require greater public expenditure on infrastructure and services than real estate and sales taxes bring in. Put bluntly, new houses cost taxpayers extra money annually. A typical study undertaken by the Pittsford, New York, planning department, for instance, concluded that conventional development of a proposed 1,200–acre subdivision would cost each taxpayer $200 a year indefinitely for services and additional school expenses. By contrast, a twenty-year bond issue floated to purchase the property would cost each person $67 per year. Officials in Loudoun County, Virginia, estimated in a 1994 study that a new home had to sell for at least $400,000 to provide enough property taxes to cover the cost of county services. The average selling price in the area, however, was less than $200,000. Similarly, the Piedmont Environmental Council authored a 1994 report called "Fiscal Impact of Major Land Uses in Culpepper County, Virginia," which concluded, "For every dollar of revenue collected from residential land, $1.25 is spent on county services; for every dollar collected from farm/forest/open space, 19 cents is spent on services." This kind of analysis has been validated in study after study over the years. When such analyses are ignored as rapid development begins, the increasingly needy municipality, now beset with more people and all their demands, sees open space as a commodity for conversion to taxable houses, offices, and shopping centers. The result is segmented sprawl— pasture after pasture, farm after farm, one wooded tract after another.

Myopia of Local Governments Regarding Land Use

Ironically, local regulation of land use often hastens the destruction of fast-growing places. For instance, once development begins, farmland and forests are often zoned for residential use. With the new zoning comes an increase in real estate taxes, so owners are not inclined to leave property idle; they become increasingly eager to sell or develop.

As a dramatic example of the role of increased property taxes consider a single undeveloped 240–acre parcel in East Rutherford, New Jersey. Although situated amid wetlands, the parcel was zoned by the local community to accommodate a sports complex, office buildings, luxury high-rise apartments, and an outlet shopping mecca, and it was assessed at $20 million, its full development value. In a challenge by heirs, based on state and federal wetlands restrictions, Judge David E. Crabtree ruled that the property's proper value was not $20 million but $1 million, causing local property taxes to be reduced from $300,000 to $17,000 a year. The lawyer for East Rutherford, Kenneth A. Porro, abashed at the outcome and try-ing to preserve East Rutherford's potential income stream, argued, "This decision is a travesty. The problem with it is that even though a property is considered a wetlands doesn't mean that the property is undevel-opable."[4] And, of course, this is precisely the problem. If the owners re-mained obligated to pay a $300,000 annual tax bill, they would indeed develop or sell to someone who would figure out a way around the wet-lands regulations in order to exploit the land's location within the core of the New Jersey meadowlands.

When towns are growing rapidly, planning for the unbuilt terrain is generally ignored. Most often towns have no plan for areas that should re-main open for public recreation or to conserve important natural envi-ronments; such a plan, sometimes referred to as a communitywide "site analysis map," would identify unbuildable areas and designate buildable lands that merit conservation. Without such a plan, open areas are pushed farther and farther away from the residential centers. At some point, the deficit is noticed; only it is too late. In many other instances, as growth gathers steam, near-in public recreation space is sacrificed to parking ar-eas, municipal buildings, and school facilities.

Countless other examples of local land-use regulatory myopia are en-countered in growing communities. One of the most destructive is the lack of appropriate planning for the automobile and other forms of trans-portation. Routinely, the car is given priority and too much land. Need-lessly wide subdivision streets consume vast acreage. On-grade parking paves much of the town center. Traffic and parking congestion then occur, and residents become dissatisfied and aggravated. Growing towns also fail to designate zoned, design-controlled retail areas near the locations where new residential development is taking place so as to relieve conges-tion in the original town center. In many larger towns myopia regarding land use has led to the near absence of public transport.

Local governments have also been slow to offer businesses market in-centives for long-term planning. Business planning in America is notori-ously short term. And the term is getting shorter. Businesses in many parts of the world measure achievement in decades; businesses in the United States do so monthly, quarterly, and yearly. In private enterprise, a five-year plan is generally viewed as purely hypothetical. The short time frame for private-enterprise planning collides with the reality of town growth and community development, endeavors that proceed at a slow pace and require long-range solutions. Some jurisdictions now offer tax breaks and other incentives to businesses that meet community-development objectives (see Chapter 9); more need to.

ABSENCE OF RESIDENT INVOLVEMENT AND COMMITMENT

Places where private individuals refuse to participate in community affairs and thus leave all decisions to elected officials are likely to have troubled economies, so-so schools, insufficient planning, disturbing social relations among groups, inadequate security, a clash of official values, and decision gridlock. Because there are too many options for local government to handle alone, there is a correlation between the involvement of private citizens and wise community growth. Government oversight and management alone do not suffice.

Take, for instance, the schools. If citizen oversight and participation are inadequate, quality often languishes. The eventual result is a less desirable town. This is just one case in which the involvement and commitment of private individuals or nonprofit groups make all the difference. Historical societies advocate while serving as guardians of a community's historical resources. Environmental advocacy groups work to maintain land, water, and air quality. Volunteer auxiliaries, lay boards, and professional staff of hospitals, colleges, and cultural institutions can be catalysts for sensible town development policies. When private commitment to the public and semipublic physical, social, and institutional endeavors of a community are weak or absent over the long term, it is likely that a growth town will fail to thrive. This kind of help evaporates when fifth-wave residents move away from older urban and suburban centers.

FOURTH-MIGRATION SPRAWL AND MELTDOWN IN THE SUBURBS

The fourth migration, now over fifty years old, illustrates the contemporary continuation of self-destructive tendencies in community building. Fifth wavers are moving into a few special suburban places. But, more frequently, because of self-induced problems, the reservoir of the older, near-in suburbs is being drained by the fifth migration. The situation merits a close look and a bit of review.

One combined federal, state, and local policy alone—the proliferation of highway building without associated community planning—is the single most direct cause of community decay. With the spread of roads, sprawl is fed; its companions, congestion and pollution, follow. In the suburbs, all are twined around once placid, pristine places that are now metastasizing out of control.

Before the 1920s, most suburbs evolved as closely linked, integrated extensions of the nearby city. They were most often attached by streetcar and rail line to central-city job locations and commercial outlets. Most were platted on rather dense grids that made subdivided land as valuable as possible, easy to describe in public records and easy to sell. These early development clusters tended to radiate only as far from a transit stop as a person might comfortably walk.

After World War I, when cars became affordable for middle-class families, participants in the fourth migration rushed in unprecedented numbers to escape into the newer auto-accessed suburbs, into this open land in which lax building codes and popular zoning ordinances ensured the segregation of coveted residential enclaves from town-related commercial and manufacturing activities and ensured as well the absence of social and economic mingling with those who could not afford cars.

A typical modern suburb is composed of one to four dwelling units per acre; in most cases these are single-family houses positioned in the middle of a lot. This layout privileges the car, with driveway and garage readily accessible from an ample street. Most suburbs contain almost no civic space except for the streets and no semipublic space other than shopping malls. Of the land not consumed by streets, more than two-thirds is devoted to private yards. Typically kids have no close-by public place to meet and play in; they do both in the streets. Adults, disadvantaged in much the same way, encounter isolation. The health club located in a shopping mall is the closest replacement for the market square, church, and concert hall.

Bereft of many of the conveniences and amenities of a genuine community, the typical suburb dictates a lifestyle that is socially isolating, inconvenient, and time-consuming. A one-hour door-to-door commute, not uncommon for suburban working people, consumes ten hours a week, the equivalent of more than one additional working day. Reliance on a car chains parents to the children's school schedule and sometimes chains the elderly to their homes.

The standard suburban zoning code forbids the intermingling of stores, recreation places, and houses. Based on outmoded fears about the contamination of residential areas by the workplace, which hark back to unsavory conditions in third-migration industrial cities, suburban zoning usually disallows a mixture of uses that might enliven any place for much of the day and part of the evening. Even small apartments for elderly relatives and home offices for property owners are commonly forbidden in suburban residential zones.

Nor do suburbs generally contain any obvious physical boundary, no planned edge that preserves natural features or protects needed water or land resources. Clear definition on and in the land is rare. Typically there is no bounding forest, open fields, or natural park. The sprawl, its roads, its parking lots, its highways, and its continuous housing and commercial strip go on and on. The sameness and nondescriptiveness lead to a feeling that, as Gertrude Stein said about Oakland, California, in her day, "there is no there there."[5]

A few statistics explain the ascendance of sprawl. For example, as California's population grew by 50 percent between 1970 and 1990, the number of miles people had to travel by car increased 100 percent. In the decade 1980–1990, the population around Seattle rose 22 percent while the number of miles driven in cars in the region quadrupled. In Denver traffic has increased at twice the rate of the population. Today vehicle miles traveled are still growing three times faster than the population, as they have since the late 1950s.

During the fourth migration jobs followed the roads out of town. From 1973 to 1985, nationwide, as five million blue-collar jobs were lost, about one hundred million service and office-based jobs were created, and many of these jobs were housed in the 1.1 billion square feet of new office space in suburban office complexes. By the mid-1980s, over half the office space in America was outside of central cities, a 100 percent increase in fifteen years. So the suburbs spread as an inevitable consequence of being the new location of so much work. As commute time in all directions lengthened, peak-time traffic patterns shifted from predominantly suburban-to-urban to a mixture, including intersuburban. Between 40 and 50 percent of all commute trips are now exclusively in cars from suburb to suburb.

Years of federal stimulants were required to trigger the fourth migration—support for highway building, guaranteed home mortgages, interest deductions for mortgage payments, the placement of defense contracts worth billions of dollars in suburban and exurban locations. Grateful communities matched these federal incentives with zoning practices that for the most part ignored natural-resource conservation and also with permissive building codes that guaranteed obsolescence. Both were calculated to attract and induce rapid development. Both ignored long-term consequences and many fundamental precepts of community building. These coordinated federal, state, and local policies, which reveal the commercial interests of powerful automobile companies, banks, road contractors, and utility monopolies, have scattered the debris of suburban sprawl across the landscape.

As a direct result of these policies, more and more land outside original town confines was transformed into a sprawling arrangement of destinations linked to town and to one another by an ever-widening and proliferating network of concrete connectors; consequently, much of the built-up part of America now consists of a visual wasteland and dysfunctional terrain. In addition, cars now generate traffic jams, pollution, and accidents within suburbs at rates once found only in the densest third-migration cities.

Suburban sprawl has engendered a significant backlash. After studying land-use patterns in more than three hundred urban areas, David Rusk, the former mayor of Albuquerque, concluded, "My rule of thumb is that the faster the rate of sprawl, the faster the rate of abandonment."[6] In 1995 the Brookings Institution sponsored an "Alternatives to Sprawl" conference. Participants were stunned to receive a negative report from California's Bank of America, which in prior decades, through its mortgage programs, had been one of the great stimulants to and beneficiaries of sprawl. The bank's new view is that sprawl in California has created "enormous social, environmental and economic costs, which until now have been hidden, ignored, or quietly borne by society. . . . Businesses suffer from higher costs, a loss of worker productivity, and underutilized investments in older communities."[7] A less-elevated summary of the backlash was offered by Bill Wolfe, acting director of the Sierra Club's New Jersey chapter: "I think the public has reached the point where they are fed up. They don't like being stuck in traffic. They don't like a two-hour commute to work. They don't like overcrowded schools and rising property taxes. All those things can be traced back to poor land-use decisions."[8]

Indeed for the first time major environmental organizations have declared war on sprawl. The Sierra Club finds it to be their members' top concern. "There is a rising crescendo of concern about the impact of sprawl development on communities and the environment," says Larry

Bohlen, cochair of the Sierra Club's "challenge to sprawl" campaign. Bohlen also notes that sprawl is becoming an increasingly contentious political issue.[9]

The absence of wise planning during the growth boom has left suburbs unable to accommodate many current demographic and socioeconomic realities. The stereotypical American household is vanishing. The size of a typical U.S. household has shrunk since the 1970s from three people to around two and a half. The percentage of singles and single-parent families has increased 10 percent, to about 38 percent of the total. Households with children now typically have two workers. Married couples with children represent 25 percent of households, down dramatically from 40 percent a generation ago. So the two ingredients essential for middle-class suburban life—children and a mother who is available all day to drive the car and take care of the home—are becoming scarce commodities. All these trends added together challenge the dominance of the suburb as the place to live.

The absence of wise long-term planning, the destruction of an agreeable natural environment, social isolation, all are catching up with these communities. But there is another important factor. Suburban residents once thought of themselves as isolated from the problems of the central city. Time and reality are proving that they are not. Not by a long shot. And residents of the suburbs are afraid. This fear surfaces quickly in suburban communities that permit especially dense housing developments such as attached town houses, particularly when the new houses become rental units. Opposition to proposals for new town-house development throughout the suburbs has increased. As a typical example, in a meeting in suburban Sloatsburg, New York, Rebecca Kern, a leader of the Little Town Forum for the Historic Preservation of Sloatsburg, speaking in opposition to a development proposed by K. Hovnanian Enterprises, the biggest suburban town-house developer in the country, expressed the fear that has crept into the suburbs about the kind of people who might come into town: "I want growth—I want development. But not condos." And one meeting participant went further. He asked "whether or not social service agencies would be allowed to rent any of the new row houses for clients.[10]

These remarks and countless others like them point to a changed mood within suburbs that is evident in physical design. Newer, farther-out suburbs today are dotted with gated enclaves. Fear has become an ever-present neighbor. People who can afford private guards and elaborate physical barriers seek to live safely and quietly in the midst of perceived turbulence and social danger. To most residents of gated enclaves, the older near-in suburbs and the not very distant city are now places to avoid at night, to dread all the time, and to try to protect against. Michael Casale, an entrepreneurial former New York City homicide detective, supplies round-the-clock guards to two thousand suburban homes in fifteen different gated developments. "Years ago people who were wealthy just wanted to be on two acre estates," he commented. "With crime what it is, now they want to be in a gated community with a guard and a patrol." Marcia Greene, a recent move-in with her husband to gated Gracewood development, confirms Casale's observation: "There's nothing that's 100 percent foolproof. But Gracewood to me is that much more secure because of the total perimeter fencing. I am very, very comfortable. I did not want to be on a couple of acres by myself on Long Island."[11]

Suburban residents, never a group intimately involved in community governance and management, increasingly despair of solving the physical and especially the societal problems that threaten. The acronym PLU (People Like Us) sums up their attitude. It denotes distinction and exclusion and, lately, as Whit Stillman, producer and director of the 1990 movie *Metropolitan*, has said, "defensiveness and escapism."[12] In talking to Ron Suskind of the *Wall Street Journal*, Nancy Corkery, a thirty-three-year-old housewife living in the Boston suburb of Needham, Massachusetts, who describes herself as a PLU, explained, "It's not that PLUs don't care about other people, it's just that they are focused more on people who are like them. By and large, they give their time, effort and money to things that return a benefit to them. Is that wrong? I mean, where do you begin with some of these awful problems out there?"[13]

The perception of PLUs that diversity is increasing in the suburbs is accurate. During the 1980s and into the 1990s the migration into the suburbs of middle- and working-class blacks, Hispanics, and Asians increased dramatically. Between 1980 and 1990 the minority population within the suburbs increased at a higher rate than it did in the nation's central cities. The black population grew by 34 percent; the Hispanic population increased by 69 percent; and the Asian population skyrocketed by 125 percent, while the white suburban population increased by only 9.2 percent. In spite of strong black, Asian, and Hispanic migration, which continued even more dramatically during the 1990s, the suburbs remain predominantly white. As of the 1990 census, minorities constituted less than 18 percent of the suburban population, while accounting for over 40 percent of the nation's central-city residents. In contrast to the total minority suburban population of about twenty million, about ninety-five million whites lived in the suburbs in 1990. It is my guess that most black, Hispanic, and Asian fifth-migration participants are now finding their way into suburbs. But unless they choose carefully, new migrants to the older suburbs are likely to find disappointment lurking in the years ahead. They may be a generation late, as the fifth migration gathers speed.

In 1995 Richard Voith, senior urban and regional economist for the Federal Reserve Bank of Philadelphia, completed a telling study. After reviewing twenty-eight major metropolitan areas in the Northeast, North Central region, West, and Washington, D.C., Voith felt ready to ask and to answer this question: Do suburbs substitute for cities, or do they complement each other? His conclusion:

> Decline in the central cities is likely to be associated with slow-growing suburbs. Even if the most acute problems associated with urban decline do not arise in the suburbs, central city decline is likely to be a long-run, slow drain on the economic and social vitality of the region. Suburban residents may not notice the damage at first, but eventually even those satellite areas that are relatively unscathed by regional urban decline will not be as healthy as suburbs near healthy . . . cities. . . . The symptoms show up in: falling suburban property values, . . . rising taxes and crime, . . . slower growth . . . [and] lower incomes.[14]

The Decline of Edge Cities

Edge cities are no exception to the rule that places which grow fast but not wisely are likely to languish. A fully developed edge city usually consists of a shopping mall connected to an array of linked offices, stores, and services such as movies and hotels. Today nearly 190 identifiable edge cities are spread around the major metropolises of the country. Each of these has at least the working population of Orlando, whereas fewer than forty inner-city downtowns match Orlando's size. These edge cities are not suburbs; they are not sub-anything. They are burgeoning service-job sites and magnets of regional commerce. Arising along the edges and interchanges of highway systems, they are relatively new centers like Houston's Galleria area or Las Vegas's Summerlin; sometimes they evolve around airports, as in Miami and Los Angeles.

Although edge cities are a relatively recent development, many are already facing problems of various kinds. It is not unusual for two or even three distinct public jurisdictions to exercise authority within a single edge city, so governance is difficult. The sterility and place-less-ness of most edge cities and the absence of public gathering places such as churches and parks make them unattractive domains in which to live and work. An edge city can be characterized as a suburban downtown, and, like older city-center downtowns, it experiences a shock wave when there is a tremor in surrounding feeder residential areas. At risk are edge-city complexes dependent on once-thriving near-in suburbs that may now be deteriorating. In many metropolitan areas, the traffic congestion, high costs, and crime that corporations and individuals thought they had left behind in the center cities are undermining edge cities. Gangs have invaded shopping malls in suburban Detroit, Houston, and Los Angeles. In any number of places, as Charles Lockwood, a leading writer about American cities, has observed, "shopping malls near troubled suburbs are losing their best retailers and suffering economically depleting vacancies, ironically, just like the downtown shopping districts they largely replaced after World War II."[15]

Most edge cities develop at a considerable distance from the city center, past the first and often the second circle of ring highways. Because of this pattern of settlement, there is a lot of sparsely settled land between edge cities. To expansion-minded industry, retailers, and residents, this in-between terrain provides a logical "infill" opportunity. Within these infill zones much conventional metropolitan growth is likely to occur during the coming decades. But these zones and the edge cities that define them are not the sort of places in which most fifth-migration participants prefer to live. For people with a fifth-wave mind-set, a potential destination must have more to offer.

Unless fundamental precepts of community planning are applied, some edge cities are not going to survive with vigor and health deep into the next century. Joel Garreau, the journalist-author who first coined the term *edge city* and the nation's most attentive observer of edge-city evolution, recognizes the whiff of self-destruction as he observes these dynamic and diverse places. "As we approach the third millennium," he says, "some edge cities will boom, and some will probably die. Who will the winners and losers be? The top edge cities are all strikingly efficient at delivering anything you can measure with dollars—proximity to airports, executive housing, worker housing, shopping, whatever. The real competition will be over intangible features like civilization, soul, and community—the things that define quality of life."[16]

Consequences of Decay

In all the movement, development, growth, struggle, and excitement of building communities there has been great flux, but one constant: boom and bust, at the scale of the town itself. Traditionally, a small place grows as a result of valuable resources, newly acquired accessibility, leadership, luck. The growth soon takes on a life of its own, a feeding frenzy of new-comers and new construction. Then one day it is over. The resources give out. The energy wilts. The boom slides into bust.

There are not enough ways to measure the disastrous consequences of community decay. To suggest how varied and dire they are, I will enumerate a few of the most obvious losses. When it is all over, great portions of long-in-the-making reservoirs of social well-being, public and private wealth and investment, and institutional achievement evaporate, leaving only problematic remains.

The Cautionary Tale of the Suburbs

By now, the distinct whiff of self-destruction within near-in suburbs is causing residents with a choice to move on and jobs to disappear. The major beneficiary, in most cases, is the surrounding counties, as well as attractive communities elsewhere, newer fifth-migration destinations. The secondary beneficiary is the best locations in the nearby city, as a select group of fifth wavers move back into town. In a 1998 editorial, the *Observer*, a New York City weekly geared to fifth-migration urban preoccupations, sketched an accurate picture when it gleefully declared:

> In the past few years we have seen the suburbs' image curl and wither a bit, like a postcard left out in the rain. In fact, as cities like New York have become more livable, many suburbs, especially those just past the

city limits, the so-called "inner ring" suburbs, have seen their standard of living drop. Many of those who live in the suburbs are finding they have the worst of both worlds. Urban problems like crime—with the grim, added twist of carjackings—and there's still nothing to do after 6:00 P.M. or on a weekend. No theatre, no museums, precious few restaurants. . . . The moral of this tale? Go ahead and buy that co-op and watch the grass grow in your window box.[17]

The 1990 census reveals the trend. Between 1980 and 1990, 35 percent of suburban towns experienced significant declines in median household income. The loss of income reflects the catastrophic loss of several million jobs in these areas and the relocation of many well-off people, which began in the 1970s as jobs and residents participated in the fifth migration. As a result, suburban towns that were once family-oriented, such as Parma (outside Cleveland), Brockton, Lowell, and Somerville (outside Boston), University City (outside St. Louis), Cicero and Harvey (outside Chicago), Upper Darby (outside Philadelphia), and many others all along the social and economic spectrums, are experiencing social destabilization together with the erosion of jobs, taxable resources, and private capital.

By the mid-1990s it had become abundantly clear to competent researchers and observers that it was a mistake to take continuing suburban prosperity for granted. As William Lucy, a well-known professor of urban and environmental planning at the University of Virginia, advised the professional planning community in 1995, "Many of our metropolitan areas have entered a 'postsuburban era' in which we are seeing two things— continued exurban expansion and increasing decline of older suburbs."[18] Increasingly, corporations and professional firms are deserting existing cities, edge cities, and suburban downtowns for entirely new locations, leapfrogging to the outermost fringes of metropolitan areas or to distant small towns geographically remote but technologically connected to the rest of the country. A *Wall Street Journal* article concludes, "If it comes to a choice between redeveloping a congested, worn-out suburban downtown or moving on to a newer and cheaper outlying site, guess which option most corporations and Americans will choose? The nation that invented the throwaway central city after World War II may now be perfecting the disposable suburban downtown."[19]

Economic Waste and Ruin

The development philosophy and financial blueprint followed by most growing towns today are out of date. To accelerate growth to pay the bills, land-use regulation is relaxed. Development accelerates. And, as previously discussed, the deadly cycle sets in. Slowly, at first imperceptibly, the quality of physical life in the town begins to deteriorate. Maybe it's congestion, maybe poor road maintenance, maybe problems in the schools, maybe noticeable increases in crime. Public expenditures rise again. More police are hired. The highway department requires additional people and equipment. Taxes increase.

Once decline begins, the enormous fixed investment in houses, stores, streets, landscaping, and all the other trappings of community life owned by the private sector but regulated or operated by public agencies is at risk. A town is a joint public-private investment venture. Each contributes, in its own way, although all the cash comes from private citizens and companies. At the end of the day, the residents are at risk for the investment in a place. When values are depleted, and in some cases entirely wiped out, an awesome loss is sustained by the private sector.

In the midst of community decline commentators characteristically describe the loss of private-property values. Rarely do they consider the sometimes even more appalling loss of value in infrastructure, such as roads, sidewalks, lights, which have been purchased with taxpayers' money. Add in the lost value of public and quasi-public organizations and institutions such as museums, schools, hospitals. When the music stops, and the growth community is no longer so appealing, it is the private stakeholders who are damaged.

In the beginning of a community's decline, the incremental loss of value creates a domino effect. There is less real property value to tax, so the government has two choices: raise the tax rate on what remains to obtain the same revenue or diminish services. Usually both happen. Eventually, when the diminishing value of tax ratables can no longer provide adequate revenue, either expenditures for community needs are rationed or increased debt is incurred, raising interest and amortization costs. Political argument ensues. Discontent is rampant among all who must pay property taxes and once received services at an acceptable level in return. Those with an option move on.

Once a decline is firmly under way, loss is experienced by all social and economic groups. Property owners find their assets devalued. Tenants encounter landlords unwilling to maintain properties at previous standards or, in extreme cases, at all. Educational standards decline, and school-building maintenance is deferred. In time the impact is felt throughout the region surrounding the declining community. More is demanded of county health, social-welfare, and educational programs and resources. And so on up the chain to the state government. Eventually, in a variety of ways, the impact registers at the federal level. The boom town, once a thriving generator of jobs, of social networks, of institutional achievement and growth, of wealth itself, becomes the reverse. The loss to all concerned is nearly immeasurable.

The difficulties encountered in providing public education exemplify the dilemmas and pitfalls growth towns face as they attempt to avoid decline. Nationwide, the crop of school-age children is turning out to be much larger than predicted in the late 1980s. The 1990 census predicted that school enrollment would drop by the year 2025 nationwide by about 1 percent. That prediction was way off the mark. Between 1990 and 1993, kindergarten enrollment shot up by 22 percent. Late-blooming boomers are producing far more children later in life than experts predicted; immigration is stronger than foreseen; and Generation X women are having babies later, but before it becomes physically risky. All these developments have sent demographers back to their crystal balls. The Educational Research Service, an independent firm, now anticipates that by 2025 the school population will increase by ten million to around fifty-eight million children, an 18 percent increase from current levels.

Many growth towns have been caught off guard by the increase and by resistance from those who oppose costly school expansion, including many retirees and second-home owners. School-construction bond issues have been rejected; in a few places property-tax ceilings have been imposed, crippling local government's ability to finance school expansion. In many growth towns these days, school officials construct complex schedules for using existing buildings to capacity rather than constructing new edifices. Low-cost temporary buildings have a way of becoming a permanent part of the school plant. Pupil-teacher ratios, normally the lower the better, creep up, while the mood of increasingly overworked staff and faculty deteriorates. In many fifth-migration growth towns one of the foundations of their appeal—an affordable, civil, and quality public school system—is increasingly at risk.

Growth towns all across the nation are debating how to pay for education without compromising their future. What happens if all those kids move away because the town falls into decline? The cruel irony is that the overwhelming debt from school expansion would then have to be paid by those left sitting on the front porch, the least mobile and least flexible residents. Yet by holding taxes down in a continuing effort to appeal to ever more migrants, these same growth communities cripple schools.

SOCIAL INSTABILITY

Social instability tends to accompany a reversal of fortune. This experience is as evident in the life cycle of places as it is in families. Community-wide job losses, diminished public revenue, compromised educational standards, and the curtailment of private, semiprivate, and public institutional activity generate destabilization. Relationships of long standing are shattered—whether it be loss of a job, of a particular social service, or of a circle of important friends. The wish and the need to leave are increasingly manifest as social shattering becomes normative. Out of personal necessity in some cases and opportunism in others, crime rises just at a time when budgets are reduced and law enforcement is diminishing. Charities, medical facilities, and social services cannot meet the demand.

In community decline, the social fabric binding groups of people together frays and eventually tears. Key officers of institutions begin to leave town; key members of community boards no longer live nearby. Replacements are sought and found; but the fabric they have to work with is so fragile it may not even hold together. Familiar faces are no longer at their traditional posts behind the store counter, at the post office, in the town hall, at the bank, in the classroom. A place once inhabited by an extended family of the recognized, the comfortable, and the known becomes a collection of strangers. Many feel isolated who once felt integral. With this feeling comes an accompanying yearning to recapture what was lost, to find it somewhere else.

If and when the bust sets in, it is the remaining residents who suffer most. A substitute for the depleted institutions will spring up somewhere else. But the social fabric cannot be replaced. The vast public and private investment loss sustained by the residents is not easily recovered. Individuals are the angels who finance the show—this chancy, dynamic drama of community growth and change. Only, very often, they are not aware of what is happening on stage.

CHAPTER FIVE

The Whiff of Self-Destruction in Particular Growth Areas

A S FIFTH-MIGRATION GROWTH TOWNS display strong appeal and attract jobs and residents at over twice the national norm, problems are emerging; a storm is gathering on the horizon. Many growth towns are finding it increasingly difficult to maintain their appeal. The original promise that attracted fifth-migration participants—a pristine environment and abundant natural resources, accessible outdoor recreation, uncongested roads, quality schools, pleasant commercial centers, moderate living costs, the absence of crime—is fading fast.

A million fifth wavers a year are moving into fifth-migration growth towns. This adds up to ten million during the next decade, fifty million in the next half century—a short time in the history of communities. What is the impact likely to be? Given the problems already emerging, are we in for another boom-and-bust cycle? What has the effect been in the areas already hardest hit—the West, rural America, and resort and tourist towns?

The West

There is ample evidence that most current growth towns are moving, without recognizing it, in the traces of their predecessors. After traveling around the booming West late in 1996, *New York Times* correspondent

Timothy Egan observed, "Some of the shiny Western cities are becoming their worst nightmare. Los Angeles symptoms—bad-air alerts, traffic gridlock, loss of open space, huge gulfs between the rich and poor—are becoming impossible to ignore."[1] The headlong growth of the major western metropolitan areas is being stimulated by some of the same policies that encouraged earlier migrations: rapid road building, cheap land, low taxes, and minimal government interference.

New subdivisions have sprawled across pasture and farmland. In Denver, Phoenix, and Salt Lake City highway traffic has slowed to a crawl during rush hour. In many places school districts are choked, and the loss of a cherished and familiar landscape is provoking a backlash. Looking over the results in places like Phoenix, Denver, Las Vegas, and Salt Lake City after ten years of dramatic growth in the region, Robert Liberty, the director of 1,000 Friends of Oregon, a group that monitors urban-growth issues, warned, "These cities all think they're special because they're set in special places. But they are delusional." Terry Goddard, a former Phoenix mayor, summed up much of the frustration and concern in an opinion piece published in the *Phoenix Gazette* in May 1995: "If you are a recreational bulldozer driver or enjoy the tangy smell of exhaust fumes in the morning, times are great in Phoenix. For the rest of us, Paul Revere has left the stables. The qualities that brought us or kept us here are vanishing. No tea party sentiment is going to bring them back—it will take a full-blown revolution."[2]

Limits on property taxes are often imposed in the West, and problems follow. Officials in the fast-growing Salt Lake City metropolitan area, which attracted over two hundred thousand people in just five years during the 1990s, lament that each new subdivision puts Salt Lake City further into debt. The problem began when Utah residents understandably passed legislation that caps property taxes. In Colorado, where various tax caps and restrictions have also been legislated, local governments in growth towns are forced to obtain funds by promoting large regional shopping malls and other commercial development; such growth depletes existing town centers and consumes vast tracts of land. In Douglas County, near Denver, one of the fastest growing in the United States, the ten thousand–home Highlands Ranch development is not bringing in enough income to cover the cost of new schools and services. As a result, its school district, among the fastest growing in the state in the mid-1990s, spends nearly the least per student.

Even San Diego, generally considered one of the most thoughtfully conceived and managed communities in the country, has had great difficulty with its strong growth. To contain sprawl and to preserve open space, a "tier" approach was agreed on in the 1970s. The city demanded that the farther development sites were from the city center, the less densely built up they could be. However, as usual, pressure from developers and political temerity eroded this sensible growth-management plan. In San Diego today residents have the same worries and concerns as residents in most fifth-migration growth towns, and they have most of the same internal conflicts as well. Warnings were issued as long ago as 1974. That year, two experienced urbanists, Donald Appleyard and Kevin Lynch, undertook a "regional reconnaissance" of the San Diego area, commissioned by Hamilton Marston, whose father, George, had commissioned John Nolen's original 1908 plan of San Diego. Appleyard and Lynch implored the community to preserve its "green fingers," the canyons that snake through the broad coastal mesas, and to protect view corridors between neighborhoods. They also noted that in the vast northern section of the city, development was "too rapid, too poorly coordinated with public services, too extensive and homogenous, too destructive of the land, inappropriate in form, and in the wrong place."[3]

Since then, continuous efforts in San Diego to attack urban-core decay, waterfront deterioration, and traffic congestion have not been particularly successful. The San Diego Association of Governments warns that by 2020 traffic congestion will overwhelm the area's freeways. Public transit, a possible solution even at this late date, would cost almost $25 billion. San Diego has other growth-related problems as well: as a result of long-deferred maintenance water pipes are breaking; storm-drain runoff regularly closes area beaches; areas along the docks are blighted; affordable and rental housing is in short supply; and precious open space in canyons as well as farmland continue to disappear.

In San Diego, as in so many other fifth-migration growth towns, poor planning for population growth causes the problems. When Nolen wrote his plan in 1908, San Diego was a quiet town of thirty-five thousand, isolated from the major rail network along the West Coast. But the town's fine year-round weather and attractive setting were eventually enough to appeal to aerospace companies, which recognized and appreciated the marine-influenced absence of temperature extremes. During World War II San Diego became a major military base; thousands of Americans were exposed to the city's balmy climate. In spite of the reduction in aerospace and military employment, the city and its suburbs are growing at an even faster pace than before, a consequence of the fifth migration. In 1980, San Diego's population was 1.8 million; ten years later, 2.5 million. By 2015, the region's population is expected to top 3.6 million. These figures do not include the 4 million residents projected for the Mexican city of Tijuana, just across the border from the San Diego suburb of San Ysidro.

Growth is now a dominant issue throughout the fastest growing regions of the Rocky Mountain West. In 1995 a statewide poll found that excess growth was the top concern of a third of Colorado residents, more than any other issue. And 22 percent said that they had been negatively affected by the expansion of the past few years. In the same year the May 10 *Idaho Statesman*, Boise's newspaper, found that 78 percent of Idaho residents had serious reservations about growth. Almost one-third said that the state's recent population boom had hurt their quality of life. In many areas in the West, as subdivisions and "ranchettes" replace grazing spreads, alarmed ranchers are now joining with environmentalists who once objected to cattle as harmful to streambeds and grasslands. The threat of an entirely new way of life has forged an alliance between these two groups, who now jointly advocate "cows not condos" and "Herefords not highways."

Time magazine devoted its September 6, 1993, cover story to "Boom Time in the Rockies," noting that "more jobs and fewer hassles have Americans heading for the hills." The story ended with a representative if wistful observation from William Kittredge, a short-story writer in Missoula, Montana: "Is this the old dream—America the beautiful, and I want my share?" he asks. "Yeah, except it may be more accurate to say that this is all that's left of the dream—a hideout in the Rockies, the last safe place. And afterward, in a couple of more generations, where will we go then?"

Rural Communities

As detailed in Chapter 3, for the first time in decades, during the 1990s rural America gained population. However, settlement in rural communities was highly selective. Most are not growing and wonder how long into the twenty-first century they will survive. And people living in rural towns that are growing have mixed feelings. In fast-growing St. George, Utah, for instance, where residents used to leave doors unlocked before the heavy southern California inmigration, the crime rate has doubled and congestion is rising. Although most newcomers are retirees or self-employed fifth wavers, others are struggling young families who are seeking a fresh start. Many of them bring children attuned to contemporary social and political trends long shunned by predominantly Mormon and conservative St. George residents. Rancher Farrell Hall expresses a common sentiment when he says, "People don't like it where they are, so they come here and try to make it just like the place they left."[4] Some especially offended residents have started home schooling their children. Locals also complain that the newcomers—usually called "move-ins" or "imports"—are driving up rents and home prices beyond the means of home-grown young families.

Unanticipated problems and negative incidents are commonplace in growing rural communities. Many newcomers to Wilmington, the fifth-migration Ohio town described in Chapter 3, have discovered that the poster-perfect place they expected to find is in reality quite different, with crime, drugs, outsider-insider prejudice, unplanned sprawl, increasing traffic, youth gangs, and indifference to the historic downtown. Newcomers are not told that Wilmington's felony rate is on the rise, racial tension in the high school has led to fights, the Ku Klux Klan has twice staged rallies at the courthouse, the Aryan Nation has set up headquarters in New Vienna, ten miles from town, and a black gang that claims affiliation with the Los Angeles–based Crips has been committing armed robberies and assaults on whites. As the ladies of the sixty-year-old Wilmington Wednesday Book Club know, "Wilmington isn't a community anymore—it is dozens of overlapping ones."[5]

As sprawl sets in, the comforts of previous ways disappear, as does the physical organization of the town and the beauty of the long-familiar landscape. Dayton, population 1,580, a case in point, is the fastest growing town in York or Cumberland County, Maine. Once skipped over by developers, this farming community faces nearly complete transformation as fast growth reaches into scenic rural corners of southern Maine. Since the late 1980s, the number of houses in town has increased by a third, and subdivisions now outnumber working farms by about five to one. "I've always said Dayton is a piece of heaven that no one had found," said Constance Lambert, principal of the Dayton Consolidated School. "We're hoping to keep it that way. But we've been found." Extensive new services are needed, and costs are mounting for everything from road salt to education. Dayton spent nearly $1.5 million on schools in 1996, including nearly $500,000 to send 115 students to middle school and high school in neighboring Saco, up

36 percent in five years. Isolde Cole, chairperson of the town planning board, reports, "Dayton residents are increasingly concerned about the cost of new development and the deterioration of rural character; we haven't lost it yet, but the time is approaching when we might lose it."[6]

Resort and Tourist Towns

Special problems arise as change occurs in fifth-migration seasonal resorts such as Jackson Hole, Telluride, East Hampton, Bozeman, Aspen, Sedona, and Naples. Slowly but surely, resisting or not, these towns will have to adjust to a new status as fast-growing year-round communities. What is the downside as a highly desirable resort becomes a fifth-migration year-round growth town?

Vibrant tourism, although promoted by local officials as an economic revitalization tool and by large landowners with well-positioned property as an economic necessity, is not always beneficial for most of the residents. Wages paid in the tourism industry are rarely high enough to support a family, and jobs are only seasonal. Thus high rates of off-season unemployment plague towns dominated by tourism. Paying for the seasonally overburdened roads, police, medical facilities, and sewage-treatment infrastructure raises property taxes for local residents all year round. And when tourism becomes so successful that more people are attracted as second-home and year-round residents, property values escalate beyond the means of most longtime residents. In the now chic small former mining town of Telluride, Colorado, for example, which is perched in a stunning valley near awesome physical recreation, good fishing, fine skiing, and which offers an extensive schedule of cultural entertainment, nearly 70 percent of the town's housing units are second homes. The surrounding working ranches, now owned predominantly by well-off newcomers, trade for a price above their intrinsic economic value. As a consequence, most former residents have left—some with regret, others with a teeming bank account and pleased to escape the momentum of the new Telluride.

Many resort growth towns have the complex task of not just managing growth but of simultaneously managing change in character. A transition occurs from being a quiet small town busy during one season and inhabited by a relatively few year-round residents to being a year-round place hosting many more visitors over a much longer season and inhabited by increasing numbers of new full-time and second-home fifth-migration newcomers. Resorts often cannot manage this transition skillfully. Decisions become ad hoc and often adverse. Scarcely noticed, application after application for land development is approved, until one day residents wake up to find the place they once loved all but gone. Inexperienced town management and inadequate planning permit changes that make it impossible to retrieve qualities now lost.

Many resort and tourist towns find it understandably difficult to resist a new cash crop, the second-home owner. Part-time town residents build expensive new houses and renovate others, stimulating construction jobs that pump money throughout the local economy. They pay property taxes just as if they lived in town all the time. They often contribute to local charities and to nonprofit groups, shop and hire professional services locally, and best of all do not use the schools or most government services. Well-off, full-time-resident retirees are welcomed in many resort growth towns too. They offer most of the same advantages, although this group is more likely to use some of the local social, medical, and governmental services.

Resort- and tourist-town growth is accompanied by familiar problems and questions. Consider Aspen, Colorado. An affordable-housing program there requires large-project residential builders to make 60 percent of their units affordable and requires commercial lodge developers to provide housing for 60 percent of potential employees. Yet Aspen's growing year-round popularity as a tourist and recreation center has gradually forced even middle-class residents, such as doctors, dentists, and lawyers, to move farther and farther away as prices of land and buildings escalate. Some move "down valley" so far they abandon Aspen and find jobs elsewhere. The affordable-housing program has failed to meet demand. It is sometimes necessary for seasonal workers and full-time tourist-industry employees with lower-paying jobs, such as hotel clerks, housekeepers, and waiters, to live as far as thirty miles outside town. Commenting on the long columns of help-wanted ads placed by stores, hotels, and restaurants, the *Aspen Times* editor-in-chief Andy Stone remarked in the winter of 1997, "This is one of the worst years ever."[7]

Small resort and tourist towns at the edge of scenic attractions such as national parks are among those being inundated. Residents in towns as far apart as Durango, Colorado; Maryville, Tennessee; and Tremont, Maine, are feeling the impact as many of these towns grow out of control. These communities, some gateways to the parks, are sometimes unincorporated rural towns with no elected officials and no organized planning effort. Yet they must deal with hordes of tourists, pressure to expand roads, demands for expanded overnight accommodations, and the need to house workers. Many residents, such as those surveyed in towns near Acadia National Park in Maine, complain about the high cost of land and housing in their communities and the noise, litter, and traffic generated by visitors. They also perceive increased rates of alcoholism, crime, vandalism, and drug abuse. In 1989, the most recent year the National Parks and Conservation Association assessed such issues, it identified land-use problems near 175 of the 375 national parks in the country, which attract in excess of sixty million visitors a year. The pressure has increased since then.

More recently, a group of experienced environmental consultants interviewed a variety of people in communities that are gateways to parks from Maine to California. They also surveyed the land-use patterns and economic forces shaping these gateway communities. They published their findings in 1997 and concluded: "(1) Many gateway communities are overwhelmed

"Our state and town taxpayers have been paying for growth, by themselves, for much too long. New residents and businesses that benefit directly from growth should pay for it."

"We need to decide how to manage tourism before the visitor who is returning for the fourth or fifth time goes home and tells his friends, 'It isn't the same anymore.'"

"Don't build an airport. What would we do with all those new people, and the noise?"

"We just grew too fast. Originally this was not a business center; people came to get away from the heat or those who needed the dry, clear climate. It was a summer getaway, and summers were ideal. Now it goes year round."

"We need the jobs, and we need them year round. I only hope they make it easier to apply for a building permit than to go on welfare."

"By 2020 traffic congestion will overwhelm the area. Pipes are another issue; breaks and leaks are now a frequent occurrence. Beach pollution is a related problem. It's growth, of course, that's causing these problems."

"This boom is giving our region its worst nightmare, symptoms like bad-air alerts, traffic gridlock, loss of open space, huge gulfs between the rich and the poor—these are becoming impossible to ignore."

by rapid growth that fails to meet local needs and aspirations. (2) The vast majority of residents in gateway communities, both longtime residents and newcomers, feel a strong attachment to the landscape and character of their town. They want a healthy economy, but not at the expense of their natural surroundings or community character."[8]

Tension and Fear in Growing Communities

Places have a spirit. It is felt in the way people walk at night along Main Street. And it is a sign if they do not walk at night. It is obvious in the aisles of the supermarket. Almost as in a personal relationship, it is noticeable in the faces of residents on the streets of town. In the most successful places, on most days, there is a relaxed expression, even a smile—maybe just in the eyes or in the gait. In less successful places, tension and fear become dominant, encouraging those with a choice to move on.

Residents of growth towns at the crossroads are tense. Recently established newcomers, whether full-fledged new residents or second-home owners, are preoccupied. Natives are divided. Unconventional alliances are forged based on social status, residential status, wealth, landowning status, level of activism, and interest in making a profit.

Whatever the viewpoint, in the growth towns of America, the conversation is hot—and continuous. It goes on at every level, sides opposed, overlapping, revealing chaos and contention at the crossroads. You can hear the babble of the battle in places as different and diverse as southwest Utah, the Eastern Shore of Maryland, north-central New Mexico, and the southeastern shore of Long Island.

Fifth-migration growth towns are where fourth-migration suburbs were in the early 1990s, when disintegration began. Most of the fastest growing places in prior migrations, such as New York, Los Angeles, Chicago, Philadelphia, Brooklyn, Detroit, Boston, are recognized as being far beyond and below their prime, although rejuvenation is in the air in certain privileged parts of each of these. If fifth-migration growth towns do not modify their traditional ways, another round of destructive loss will be sustained.

III

Wise Future Growth

CHAPTER SIX

What Is Wise Growth?

WILL TODAY'S GROWTH TOWNS, vibrant centers of new jobs and prosperity, be destroyed eventually by their own success? Will they go through the same boom-and-bust cycle that diminished so many other towns in previous migrations? Or will some of them be wise enough to remain highly desirable for an extended period of time, perhaps permanently?

Fifth migration growth towns have a choice, a luxury many places do not possess. They can decide to become attractive, high-quality communities by becoming wise now. Becoming wise requires deciding on new priorities based on a set of simple, proven principles, which I discuss in the remainder of this book. Any community—growing, static, or shrinking—that understands and embraces these principles will be on the way to a healthier future. Implementation of the principles in a planned, prolonged, purposeful way by town managers, policymakers, and insistent residents will assure longevity for a community.

But one idea must precede all the others. In the past, growth towns have targeted their efforts toward sustaining growth itself. No sacrifice was too great, no scheme too expensive, no promotion too short term. However, a smart growth town will realize that what must be preserved is not the growth but the qualities that attract people in the first place. Desirable consequences will follow. Wise policies will permit growth and change on a manageable scale and at a desired rate. The depletion of natural, social, and historic resources and attributes is not inevitable.

Informed residents, savvy managers, and astute investors are beginning to recognize that a mixture of modern capitalism and restrained regulation creates wise growth. They believe in growth and change. But with equal vigor they insist on finding ways to enhance the quality of residents' lives, to introduce aesthetics and good design into construction, to protect what is precious in nature, and to preserve the best that has already been built. Wise growth reconciles the consumption and depletion that result from physical and economic development with those seemingly competing principles of conservation and enhancement that promote quality of life and environmental protection. This goal is obviously laudable. But to achieve it is far from easy. To do so requires new awareness and new attitudes. Wise growth will not magically dissolve conflicts among economic, environmental, and social interests. Rather, by using some of the principles and objectives discussed here, towns can begin to test resolution recipes. A utopian proposal? I think not. Practical and possible? I think so.

Clues in the History of Natural-Resource Management

When Rachel Carson published vivid and alarming warnings about the environment in *The Silent Spring* in 1962, few would have predicted the advances made since then in the protection of the natural environment. At lower cost than originally estimated by antagonistic and skeptical conservatives and to greater positive effect than even environmental liberals could imagine at the time, much has been achieved. The country's air and water are becoming purer, forest coverage is expanding, and acid-rain destruction is diminishing. Harbors are cleaner; toxic dumps are being purged and their spread stopped; 20 percent of household trash is now recycled.

Changes in federal policy and new attitudes evident among key managers of federally owned land point in a promising new direction. We can clearly see the first glimmers of public leadership in the protection and replenishment of the natural environment. The Bureau of Land Management, the Forest Service, and the National Park Service manage more than seven hundred million acres, nearly one-third of the United States, technically on behalf of the American people. But for most of this century, as in the past, a narrow set of commercial interests, particularly ranchers, loggers, and mining companies, have received most of the benefit. Now these agencies are listening to rising complaints in the New West, site of most of the nation's public land. As a result, Patrick Shea, director of the Bureau of Land management, which governs 264 million acres, has proclaimed, "In an ever-crowded West, public lands provide us with perhaps the greatest of all assets: open space." His counterpart at the Forest Service, Michael P. Dombeck, supported a proposal to halt road building into large sections of forest land. He believes the agency should return to its roots as a restorer and protector of public land. The Forest Service has recognized that about 75 percent of the jobs linked to the 190 million acres of national forest are in the recreation industry, compared with just 3 percent in logging. And so, as the finite scale of the forests becomes obvious, in national forests (and increasingly on private lands) the accepted practice is to cut selectively and to replant rather than to clear-cut.

Other parts of the environment are also benefiting from government regulation. The 1997 Surface Mining Control and Reclamation Act at long last required rehabilitation of areas mined by private companies on public lands. The cleanup of rivers, lakes, and near-in ocean areas is just getting under way, with new controls on sewage discharge and industrial exhaust. Air quality, too, is newly susceptible to government regulation. Controls affect exhaust and discharge of every kind—leaf burning in yards, boat discharge and sewage dumping in the water, emission from vehicles on the road, the exhaust from factories and utility installations.

Most traditional, conservative western business interests continue to resist these new conservation initiatives. Loggers call the moratorium on forest roads a theft of their rights and a compromise of their livelihood. The mining industry complains about job loss, although the New West is growing jobs at a rapid clip. Ranchers long accustomed to bargain-basement terms for access to public grazing lands still resist policies to preserve grasslands.

Nevertheless, less than three decades after the landmark environmental-protection legislation of the early 1970s, environmentalism has become a core American political value, one of the few regulatory areas in which a voting majority is willing to approve more government expense and control. In his excellent report "Here Comes the Sun," written to summarize experience twenty-five years after the first Earth Day, Gregg Easterbrook accurately observes, "In the main, ... conservation has been an excellent investment for society. Environmental initiatives worked well even in the early years, when they were driven by top-heavy federal edicts. They work even better as new regulations have centered on market mechanisms and voluntary choice. ... Western market economies excel at producing what they are asked to produce, and, increasingly, the market is being asked to produce conservation."[1]

I believe that wise community development will achieve similar support when communities are accurately recognized as the human environment, one even more fragile and more helpless than the natural environment. Direct and useful analogies are already being made between the advances in natural-resource management and the potential for smart community growth. William D. Ruckelshaus, former administrator of the Environmental Protection Agency, outlined in 1989 a hopeful vision of wise growth as applied to land use: "The emerging doctrine is that economic growth and development must take place, and be maintained over time, within the limits set by ecology. ... It follows that environmental protection and economic development are complementary rather than antagonistic processes."[2]

Attempts to ensure a clean, productive, protected, renewable environment are thus now converging with issues related to community development and community conservation. In the years to come, the long-term survival of places will out of necessity gain a broader set of advocates, as was the case with the natural environment. It is quite likely that in the future conservation and environmental advocates will find in the trenches with them private entrepreneurs who depend on the nation's natural resources such as clean air, healthy forests, abundant grazing lands, productive soils, and ample water. The lessons learned from the growing scarcity of natural resources are spreading to communities. In the most enlightened locales, we can expect broad initiatives supported by new coalitions dedicated to making settlements evolve wisely.

A national consciousness raising was sparked in 1993 when President Bill Clinton formed the President's Council on Sustainable Development. This twenty-five member council includes five Cabinet members plus leaders from industry, government, and environmental, labor, and civil rights organizations. It recommends strategies to help the United States meet future economic needs without unnecessarily depleting available resources and without compromising the environment. During his speech inaugurating the Council, President Clinton asked that the Council be guided by three principles. The first of these applies to community growth as much as it does to environmental care: "We believe a healthy economy and a healthy environment go hand in hand. Environmental problems result not from robust growth, but from reckless growth. And we can grow the economy by making our people healthier, our communities more attractive and our products and services more environmentally conscious."[3] It is necessary to reword this statement only slightly to have it apply in full measure and with equal validity to the evolution and future of towns in this country. The rewording I propose: "We believe a healthy community and a healthy environment go hand in hand. Community problems result not from robust growth, but from reckless growth. And we can grow our communities by making our people more aware, our public and private spaces more attractive, and our development more aligned with smart principles of growth."

I am hopeful about the potential for smart community growth because, like the environmental movement, it is ultimately related to broad-based self-interest. Unlike the environmental outcome, the outcome for a community is entirely within the control of local private and public entities. My hopefulness grows out of a conviction that free-market forces and competitive necessity will guide citizens and town managers, and everyone with a vested interest, to tilt toward smart growth.

Awareness

Before the dominance of the automobile, before the luster of post–World War II heroic architectural figures who dominated not only practice but also professional architectural teaching, before the ascendance of engineers who have come to set community-development standards and priorities, planning was based on older traditions and was more incremental and people-oriented. In the wisest places these are once again becoming important considerations. The revival of these ideas may be justly credited to a few architectural historians, the most notable being Vincent Scully; to a number of architects and planners first inspired by the seminal designs and writings of Robert Venturi and Denise Scott Brown; to the influential architect-writer-historian Robert A. M. Stern;

and to increasingly well-known, younger new-urbanist architect-planners such as Peter Calthorpe, Andres Duany, and Elizabeth Plater-Zyberk.

But professional architects and planners can do little that is effective without the informed cooperation of other interests throughout a community. When the mechanisms of political activism and the entrepreneurially driven marketplace are involved in the service of an idea, it is likely to be realized. Individual citizens are also crucial. In a wise growth community private citizens are willing to help; awareness and work and commitment by the town's public officials are supplemented by the work of residents who function through many kinds of private and not-for-profit entities. The responsibility for community must shift from "those guys," the elected officials, to "us guys," all who are stakeholders in a place. As is true in most suburbs and in many other places, when individuals do not get involved, when they think it impossible to make a difference, when they feel incapable of making a contribution, or when laziness prevails over goodwill, a vacuum is created by so much talent being withdrawn into its private vortex, a lamentable loss of one of a community's most valuable nondepleting resources.

Awareness is also heightened when a town looks beyond its own borders at examples of success elsewhere. For instance, if a community wants to tackle its pollution crisis, it could look to Chattanooga, Tennessee. Named the most air-polluted city in the country in the late 1960s, Chattanooga decided in 1984 to literally clean up its act when it launched Visions 2000, which brought together thousands of local residents for twenty weeks of "visioning" sessions that resulted in 223 projects all directed toward a single objective. Much was achieved. Diesel buses were replaced by locally manufactured electric mass-transit vehicles. A new nationally recognized "greenways" program created a river-front park where abandoned factories once stood. A large land-trust program was begun. A zero-emissions industrial park was inaugurated, and a hazardous waste site was replaced by the world's largest freshwater aquarium. Revealing the importance of awareness, and reflecting on the dramatic changes in Chattanooga, city-council member Dave Crockett remarked, "We were shocked into getting into healthy habits the way a thirty-five year old gets a second-chance after a heart attack."[4]

Although most fifth-migration participants are complacent, believing they have made a brilliant move, increasing numbers of residents, industry leaders, and policy experts are alert to danger. In Boise, for instance, there is "fear that beneath this gloss is another story, one that raises the question of whether cities like Boise are a model for the twenty-first century, with a sustainable base of good jobs, or just low-wage exurbs of Southern California that will soon be overrun and suffer problems familiar to both coasts. The sharp growth is creating its own problems. Housing prices are soaring, repeating the pattern in California and later Seattle. And every new company and every new worker coming here may detract, in some small way, from the vaunted quality of life that brought them to begin with."[5]

Utah is a prime example of a place where awareness is increasing. Since 1990 Utah has added about three hundred thousand people, the equivalent of another Salt Lake City, and the numbers are expected to swell even more. For ten years starting in the late 1980s Utah's economy grew at about 5 percent a year, creating jobs at a rate second only to Nevada's. Tourism revenue is now greater than revenue from mining, ranching, and farming combined. Park City, Utah's largest skiing center, was listed half a century ago in the specialized guidebook *Ghost Towns of the West*. Rather than survival, the top concern years ago, now development, population expansion, affordable housing, and loss of historical character concern residents. Sensing the mood in Utah, Governor Michael O. Leavitt called a "growth summit" in 1996. Enlightened community leaders demanded construction of fewer houses and more apartments and a light-rail line along the Salt Lake corridor. In an interview at the time, referring to new subdivisions that now blanket former ranch land, the governor remarked, "Local governments must realize that they can't keep on zoning for quarter-acre lots."

Austin, Texas, one of the most dynamic fifth-migration growth towns in the country, with its region growing faster than any other metropolitan area outside of Las Vegas, also is becoming cautious and thoughtful. Set amid hills and watercourses, the Austin area is now home to more than nine hundred software companies, the world headquarters of Dell Computer, the state capitol, and the University of Texas. Population in the region has soared to over one million, more than doubling since the late 1970s. The city of Austin, at 540,000 people, will soon be larger than Boston and Washington, D.C. With growth in and around Austin has come predictable traffic congestion along Interstate 35. By 2010 traffic is slated to increase in that corridor by 75 percent. Air quality is a concern. The loss of the once-steep hills on the edge of town, now flattened platforms for shopping malls and subdivisions, troubles long-time residents.

Ambivalence about rapid growth is spreading in Austin. The mayor, Kirk Watson, ran in his last election with the support of both environmentalists and business groups. When asked whether growth had been properly managed, Mayor Watson gave a candid if somewhat diplomatic answer: "It has not been managed so poorly that we are now in a position where we can't get a handle on the next ten, fifteen, twenty years, but if we don't do it right, we're in big trouble." Brigid Shea, a former Austin city-council member and now executive director of the Save Our Springs Alliance, a local environmental group, has a more comprehensive vision of how to proceed. She feels the special character of Austin can be maintained in the face of rampant growth: "What's happening right now is, we're trying to see if we can't marshal the intellectual resources of the high-tech community, the economic self-interest of the business community and the preservation instincts and the passion of the environmental community to grow smarter so that we don't foul our nest."[6]

Attitude and Vision

ALICE: "Would you tell me, please, which way I ought to go from here?"
CHESHIRE CAT: "That depends a good deal on where you want to get to."
ALICE: "I don't much care where."
CHESHIRE CAT: "Then it doesn't matter which way you go."[7]

Each community does have a different spirit, a different attitude. What do most residents want? A place in which merely to sleep and work? A place in which to raise children? A place to invest in? A place to exploit materially or socially? A place where the generations to follow will want to reside? Answers to these and many other questions constitute the attitude of a place. In America, most communities, like Alice, have no idea where they are going in the long term. When change is occurring rapidly, communities need to clarify their goals and priorities, where they want to go. Only then can they decide how to get there. Achieving what might be called a community vision is a difficult but essential step toward wise planning and development. And it requires a not especially common American trait—a commitment to place.

Boulder, Colorado, has employed new awareness and attitude to facilitate smart growth. Alarmed by rapid inmigration beginning in the early

1990s and then by national polls proclaiming Boulder to be "the American entrepreneurial hot spot" in the mid-1990s, Boulder residents and community leaders recognized they had serious problems: fast population growth, chronic traffic jams, escalating housing prices, the rapid loss of precious open spaces and vistas.

Rather than get mired down in the shallow growth–no growth debate, in which quality-of-life viewpoints directly clash with economic-development interests, Boulder devised a new strategy to reframe the issues. In January 1995, thirty-two Boulder County high-profile business, government, educational, and cultural leaders began to meet together to figure out how Boulder could create a smarter community, a place that in the broad sense might resemble a living system in which all resources—human, natural, and economic—would be interdependent and would draw strength from one another. The overall goal was to sustain the quality of life from the plains to the mountains of Boulder County and to do so without suggesting a controversial, perhaps publicly unacceptable, no-growth agenda.

Once new attitudes were in place, Boulder leaders decided to restrict population and commercial proliferation while vigorously protecting and acquiring open space. In an effort to impose a still healthy 2 percent per year population growth rate, new residential construction permits in the city of Boulder were restricted to four hundred annually, down from eight hundred. Boulder proceeded to restrain commercial growth as well by deciding that annual rates of new commercial development in the city should decline by 5 percent annually. These two policies produced one of the most powerful growth-management programs in the country, although scarcity induced higher housing prices in Boulder, and a great deal of sometimes unappealing spillover growth did occur in nearby communities. But Boulder demonstrates that once a vision is sufficiently set and agreed on so that political action is possible, a growth town can regain control of its own destiny, can assert its own residents' values. As a result, in broad-based national polls Boulder is routinely declared one of the best places to live in America (see Tables 3.2 and 3.3).

Involving the Entrepreneurs

New attitudes are also needed to understand and ultimately to capture the energy and contributions of entrepreneurs. It is commonplace to blame real estate developers for short-term thinking and exploitive behavior—and in fast-growth towns for the eventual degradation of the built community. Few critics recognize, or perhaps admit, that most developers follow the rules promulgated by public officials. Variances are obtained through a process that public officials control. Due process determinations exercised through court appeals are the rare exception. Most of the physical development of a community is worked out in the town hall with the compliance and approval of local government officials. Complaining about the venality of real estate developers misses the point. The weak link is usually the public policies and regulations by which entrepreneurs are guided. In most cases people who routinely transform land use or re-develop existing properties want as little trouble as possible in the planning and approval process.

Growth towns always have a vibrant real estate community, one stimulated by change, demand, and opportunity for profit. The entrepreneurially driven market—in real estate or anything else—is the most powerful and most economical way to create change. Offering that market financially sound incentives when profit is possible will get results. If planners, town managers, and civic leaders have a clear vision of the long-term results they wish to obtain, operations of the marketplace will supply the capital and the implementation. But to obtain quality results the basic mechanisms of entrepreneurial real estate investment must be well understood by public-sector negotiators. A town must first have objectives that are achievable, and these need to be clearly articulated in public-policy documents available for review by property developers before they submit proposals. The town must then require the private sector to incorporate these objectives into its physical and financial plans. If town management takes this step, entrepreneurs will comply; if they do not, the time is not right, the economics are not right, or the right builders have not come along.

But it is important to start early and to make requirements plainly known. By the time new development projects are publicly disclosed in applications and meetings, developers have already incurred costs, raised their own expectations, and hardened their negotiating positions. They have invested in land acquisition or in securing options; they have likely paid substantial consultant fees; and they may have formed a prodevelopment constituency composed of brokers, lenders, utility companies, engineers, road contractors, and perhaps some local political officeholders who welcome the prospect of increased real estate tax revenue.

Most towns miss a great opportunity by creating an adversarial relationship with real estate entrepreneurs rather than figuring out ways to encourage them to participate in creating a smart, well-planned community. Encouragement to enhance quality, reduce density, mitigate off-site impacts, or ensure reduced communitywide environmental or fiscal impacts can take any number of forms. It can be as simple as rapid, priority review for projects that conform absolutely to guidelines. It can entail valuable rewards for supplying specified public facilities. The rewards might take the form of reduced real estate taxes for a period of time or permission to build a larger structure or denser housing development than would otherwise be approved. More innovative rewards are also possible, such as assistance with space rental.

Frank Jossi, a writer in St. Paul, studied small-town survival strategies all over the country for an article published during 1997 in *Planning*, the journal of the American Planning Association. After examining small towns that thrive and the majority that do not, he came to this conclusion:

> In the long run, the towns that make it are those that manage to encourage entrepreneurism and to retain local businesses. They start with good planning that shows them how to pay for infrastructure improvements and special projects like downtown revitalization. Most important, these towns are blessed with strong leaders: bankers who are willing to take risks, government officials who understand how to write grant applications, and businesses that are eager both to expand and to help attract other companies to the area.[8]

Where to Start

The starting place for wise growth is inside each community. In America the most important land-use decisions are hammered out at the local level. The founders of the country were landed gentry strongly committed to local control. Besides, for the microcontrol of land in such a large country, federal or state planning schemes and legislation don't generally work well. Their command-and-control approach is centralized, inflexible, necessarily bureaucratic, and therefore not responsive to local needs.

For these reasons, land-use decisions are usually left to local communities. Even in areas with state land-use planning, such as Oregon, Florida,

New Jersey, and California, once consistency with overall state goals is demonstrated, the local community has most of the decision-making power. During the mid-1980s, after more than a decade of conflict in coastal areas under the California Coastal Act, even the state of California found it practical to return land-use decisions to local communities. The special nature of each place is revealed in its land-use policies as worked out over the years. As Greg Low, vice president for major program development at the Nature Conservancy, wrote in early 1995, "Ultimately the solutions for sustainability must come place-by-place, at the local ecosystem and community level. Experience shows that the keys to success are local leadership and institutions working together over time towards a common vision."[9] This is the approach architect-designer William McDonough has called "a new declaration, not of independence but of interdependence."

Why would anyone think it remotely possible that an idealistic vision of increased collaboration at the local level might be embraced in growth towns? Because of this truth: the old way is not working. Wise growth is in step with the realities of our time. It is economically sound. It is mindful of the need to conserve resources and capital and to preserve rather than use up and discard. Smart growth becomes increasingly imperative because millions of fifth-migration participants are voting with their feet. They have the option of moving to a new place that will provide greater benefits, exhibit greater long-term promise—a place that is acting like a smart growth town. Observed *Time* magazine in 1997, "Whether young or old, the new *émigrés* share a sense that they're reinventing their lives in places that seem purer."[10] By making a radical move to improve their quality of life—arguably the signature preoccupation of the 1990s—these new *émigrés* are acting out a fantasy shared by tens of millions of Americans.

Although I would describe no growth town in America at this time as "wise," signposts help identify those that are on the way. Chapters 7 to 10 contain my selection of the most important initiatives that, if utilized simultaneously, will add up to wise community growth.

CHAPTER SEVEN

Planning, Zoning, and Land Use

SINCE MID-CENTURY many of the most important local planning, zoning, and land-use policies necessary for wise growth have been working in one place or another. In this chapter I present the most important ingredients smart growth towns must incorporate, along with examples of successful initiatives. Wise local land-use regulation will be consistent with smart growth policy. Once a direction is set, review and revision of any initiative at specific intervals are required so that fine tuning is ongoing. As time goes by, changing market conditions must be monitored and changing community priorities must be incorporated into planning, zoning, and land-use rules.

Using Common Sense Planning Concepts

Too much of anything in too small an area is a mistake. A disorganized closet overstuffed with garments doesn't work well. Neither does a block or a neighborhood or indeed a whole community too stuffed with people or cars. Density is a relative matter. In older, high-rise cities, hundreds of units of housing to the acre are commonplace, and that arrangement works. In contrast, in many parts of the West, one unit of housing on thirty-five acres is considered a bit crowded. Just as how much a closet holds efficiently depends on the interior organization of its space, the convenience and efficiency of a town depend on its organization. Allowable density buildup must be calibrated by paying attention to how the blocks and the streets and the infrastructure and the open space and all the other aspects of place are organized, including the location of natural resources and the availability of water. Otherwise town dysfunction and resident dissatisfaction are assured.

Revitalizing Core Areas

A sure way to wipe out the center of town is to permit no one to live there. No one then advocates for the area to be an agreeable place after work-hours, on weekends, and on holidays, and a downward spiral begins that may take years or decades to reverse. But need there be a center of town? That is a good and often debated question, given the dispersion of work and the availability of high-technology communications. Increasingly, however, members of the fifth wave consider small-town centers desirable and even find urban living appealing. A substantial number are choosing to relocate in the center of desirable cities, in the midst of stores and cultural sites, while many others migrate to micropolitan hubs. Large cities, such as New York, Seattle, Denver, and San Francisco, are attracting new residents from the suburbs. In general, those attracted have high incomes and seek a diverse lifestyle. Many elderly, single people, young couples, and empty-nest families are drawn to neighborhoods that feature a lively mix of cultural and consumer resources and unique housing opportunities.

Fifth wavers are attracted to town cores where housing is available because mixed commercial and residential neighborhoods are convenient and sensible. As Jane Jacobs pointed out more than thirty years ago, mixed use also means increased interest and vitality. Roadway, utility-line, and other infrastructure costs are reduced. Open spaces are used by more people more of the time with greater ease, increasing safety in parks and plazas and on sidewalks. Committed, invested stakeholders look after the area because it is home. Such a group can save the center of town and does so time and time again to the immeasurable benefit of everyone in the region.

Often, the rescue of a third- or fourth-migration declining commercial-center area hinges on the insertion into it of residential life, even though retrofit is expensive, time-consuming, and agonizing. The rescue mission is needed as a consequence of prior disinvestment, decay, social disarray. In growth towns, why not avoid these painful, expensive, and disruptive consequences of boom and bust and instead do it wisely in the first place by encouraging mixed use of land at the town's core? Older cities that have instituted mixed-use zoning and adaptive reuse of historic buildings have seen a steady influx of new residents downtown. Newcomers are drawn to traditional top-quality locations as well as to historic areas—such as those in Denver, New Orleans, New York, and Minneapolis—that feature stores, restaurants, offices, and entertainment venues alongside warehouses and factories converted into spacious residential lofts. Even in Phoenix, where rampant development of separate residential areas has long prevailed, an antisprawl backlash has set in. As a result, Arizona State University planners from the School of Planning and Landscape Architecture have been investigating core-area mixed-use development, although local skeptics abound, especially the builders of suburban housing.

RECOMMENDATIONS FOR TOWN CENTERS

In every growth town, apartments should be permitted within the central business district. These might be in single-purpose residential buildings. But housing must also be allowed above street-level commercial establishments. Most zoning ordinances still require, and many financing institutions still prefer, the outmoded separation of commercial, residential, and industrial land uses. Although the segregation of housing from certain types of industrial activity makes sense because of environmental, access, and aesthetic issues, this is not the case in downtown areas where residential and commercial uses are compatible. Indeed, at the town center or in shopping malls, the mixture provides suitable complementary habitation of land. Mixing uses affords convenience, which is increasingly appreciated, and reduces traffic congestion.

Smart growth towns, I believe, will be wise to strengthen identifiable centers with various types of uses that serve a public purpose, such as education, governance, or recreation. A center that has a public function is especially appealing. There public buildings may be mingled with private residential, office, and commercial buildings. A simple type of neighborhood center might be an easily accessible small park. In a mid-size town it might be a centrally located public space connected to major streets, commercial establishments, and public offices. Important community facilities such as houses of worship, day-care centers, headquarters of nonprofit groups, and schools should be nearby. Examples of small and mid-size towns with successful older centers are East Hampton and Santa Fe.

While there is still time, why not think more imaginatively about under-utilized, undifferentiated central places so as to expand their role and enhance their design? In edge cities, why not insist that shopping malls incorporate evening uses such as movies, restaurants, a motel, to take advantage of available parking areas that are otherwise desolate at night? Why not incorporate into the shopping mall or town center, as the case may be, requirements for playgrounds and day-care facilities so that families with children can be easily accommodated? Why not assert some aesthetic-design direction for such centers so that a place of quality and grace is created? At the mall, what better place to incorporate housing for senior citizens?

Access into and through any core area—whether it is a village square or a shopping mall—should be diverse and carefully planned. The automobile must be accommodated, but it must not preempt other means of transportation. In large places, frequent public transit will relieve congestion while making the center accessible to more people. Although it is difficult to accomplish, safe routes for bicycles—a multigenerational, inexpensive, nonpolluting transport option—should be provided. If bikeways are created and convenient bike storage is made available, they will be used.

When redesigning access to the town center, why not admit that accommodating freely flowing peak-hour traffic on traditional and conventional roads in a growth town will require paving over downtown? Instead, towns should offer ride-sharing incentives and endorse modified or staggered workhours in offices and departments of government. Large employers, including government, can institute car-pooling incentives that reduce peak-hour traffic by 20 percent or more.[1]

Making it convenient, agreeable, and safe to walk in the town center should be a basic goal. Pedestrians moving about create viable stores, parks, sidewalks, squares, arcades, and alleys. Because pedestrians follow the shortest path, their routes should be made as direct as possible and street-crossing locations should be carefully designed for safety. To avoid noxious exhaust, dangerous street crossings, and loud noise, alternative paths can be fashioned out of alleys and even building lobbies. If thought about creatively, safe shortcuts can be arranged through parking lots and parks.

In many older small towns and mid-size cities, the town center is too small to serve as the principal headquarters of commercial, residential, recreational, and civic activities. The biggest markets, the multiple-building government center, the spacious multifamily housing complex, big chain stores, bank headquarters, and principal parks have grown too large to be organized into a pedestrian-scale downtown core. So in spite of the longings of many planners and residents and wishful thinking about the new town-center paradigm, the successful, up-to-date small-town or mid-size-city downtown is likely to be a cluster of well-designed specialty shops and branch outlets of public and commercial enterprises, with headquarters and bigger stores outside the core.

Any town that wishes to attract the fifth wave should strengthen its center. If designed to appeal to the pedestrian and if filled with varied uses, it will attract patronage and residents. They will come for the amenity of scale and design. The personal, the intimate, the convenient, the aesthetically appealing are cherished by *émigrés* to fifth-migration growth towns, especially those who have abandoned suburban sprawl or center-city decay.

Examples of Revived Downtowns

Revived small-scale downtowns and main streets all across the country present evidence of the potential. The National Main Street Center in Washington, D.C., an organization devoted to downtown revitalization, lists more than 1,300 downtown improvement districts across the country, all established since 1980. Within these districts, which are supported by a local tax surcharge, property values are up about 90 percent, and vacancy rates are down from around 30 percent to less than 10 percent.

Somerville, New Jersey, provides an example of how such a transformation can be engineered. Its failing Main Street languished for years after the opening of nearby Bridgewater Commons, less than one mile away. This giant mall reduced patronage of downtown stores and so created many vacancies there, triggering a dramatic drop in downtown property values. To fight back, Somerville passed a law designating its downtown a business improvement district: an architectural review board was empowered to regulate renovation and construction; funds were allocated to the district from an extra property tax; and capital was raised through a bond issue. As work progressed, cracked concrete sidewalks were upgraded, light poles were replaced, plant beds and wooden benches were added, and a business-recruitment task force went to work to fill vacant stores. Slowly, downtown Somerville came back. It is in the process of becoming a regional center for the small, privately owned, one-of-a-kind store in which the personal taste of the owner is reflected in the merchandise and the owner is available to assist customers. Gift shops, antique stores, ethnic restaurants, craft stores, clothing boutiques are there now. And people are there too. As one patron said, "I like the personal experience. . . . There is a life that a town has that people like to be a part of." Commenting on the results of these efforts, Lloyd Silverman, owner of Lloyd's Furniture on Somerville's Main Street since 1950, remarked, "The atmosphere is just what they are looking for. It's away from the mall."[2]

Downtown Santa Monica is another place to look at to learn what is possible. Years of decline were capped off by the opening in 1980 of a new, peripheral, enclosed shopping center, Santa Monica Place. Today, rejuvenated Santa Monica Pier, two-mile-long Palisades Park, and the successfully revamped Third Street Promenade are all attracting people and commerce. Revitalization was based on the correct premise that a city's public spaces—its sidewalks, streets, parks, plazas—and its semipublic spaces, such as store entrances, courtyards, and lobbies, are the zones that most affect and most appeal to people. The city installed a thirty-foot-wide sidewalk to encourage strolling and to allow space for outdoor cafés. It planted dozens of trees, erected kiosks, and provided public space for newsstands, art displays, and seating areas. Zoning laws were passed to concentrate new cinemas on Third Street. Theaters and restaurants followed quickly, as did new businesses, including a number of specialty shops. A wise zoning incentive has attracted second-floor residential development. New shops, restaurants, and movie theaters are generating over $1 million a year in increased local sales taxes, more than enough to pay back the public investment. With the success of Third Street Promenade assured, Santa Monica is now turning its attention to adjacent areas in which, as Boris Dramov, the design principal for the project puts it, "pedestrians, not drivers, will get top priorty."[3] Santa Monica, as of 1997, was the only California municipality with an AAA bond rating, a reflection of its decisive attack on center-city decay.

Protecting Cultural and Historic Resources

A wise community will create special districts to protect its noteworthy historic and cultural resources. Special districts are usually subparts of downtown characterized by historic buildings, entertainment zones, or some other distinctive use or architectural quality. The first special district to be isolated for protection was the Old and Historic Charleston (South Carolina) District, which was established by an innovative zoning ordinance in 1931. Soon after, in 1937, the Vieux Carré in New Orleans was protected. To assure preservation of unique historic structures, each town disallowed development not in character with the special area. Since then a similar approach has been utilized in many places but not just for historic preservation. In New York City, for instance, a special theater district was designated in 1969 with rules to protect the legitimate theaters there and their distinctive, low-rise commercial surroundings. Since then, just in New York City, over thirty special districts have been formed. Santa Monica has used the device to stimulate and control its Third Street Promenade.

When intentions are announced early, before major contrary proposals are presented for public review, the special-district approach is successful. Once the boundary of a district is defined, a zoning ordinance or special-district legislation can be used to direct, encourage, control, and protect land uses. When private help is needed, the objectives set for each district and the ways they may be attained must make economic sense. Various incentives, such as transferable development rights, can be offered to developers if necessary in order to achieve public objectives.

Historic-district designation has also proven to be a successful strategy to promote wise economic development. Data from around the country—from communities as diverse in locale and scale as New Orleans, Philadelphia, Brookline (Massachusetts), Denver, San Antonio, and Savannah—are conclusive. As an example, in New Orleans three thousand people are now living in historic brick warehouse buildings converted into often stunning apartments; in the early 1980s these structures were mostly empty and decaying, and the neighborhood had no vitality. Today it is full of thriving restaurants, art galleries, entrepreneurial start-ups, and a weekly green market. The appeal of Denver's Lower Downtown, known as LoDo, like that of many central-city areas now attracting fifth-migration participants, stems from declining urban crime rates; rising congestion in the suburbs; the presence of clusters of restaurants, galleries, and other entertainment options; and the changing needs of more and more singles, childless couples, and older people. By 2010, 72 percent of American households will not have a child at home, a statistic that suggests the likely increased movement of more people with a choice into town- and city-center residences.

In areas like New Orleans's Warehouse District and Denver's Lower Downtown little or no displacement of former residents was required. This is the ideal situation but not the most common. When an older area becomes attractive to members of the fifth wave, economic pressures are likely to cause social disruption and displacement of those tenants already in place. A community intent on avoiding the wholesale transformation of a newly attractive district has options. Before the area begins to attract outsiders, certain units can be reserved through public acquisition as affordable housing. It is also possible to offer owners tax-reducing homestead exemptions based on household income or federal low-income-housing tax credits. But, at the same time, wise town managers are likely to share a view espoused by Ronald Fleming, president of the public-interest Townscape Institute in Cambridge, Massachusetts, who advised at an economic-development and historic-preservation conference, "It is not such a bad thing to have people with money move back to the city. European cities are so vital because the upper classes didn't leave." He added, emphasizing his point, "We need to have people of all colors and incomes working together to solve the problems of our cities."[4]

The movement into selective downtowns is not likely to produce an unmanageable cascade of new residents. A 1998 report by the Brookings Institution and the Fannie Mae Foundation documents a major reversal in a trend that started after World War II with the fourth migration. Rather than continuing to lose people living downtown, each of twenty-four cities investigated reported increases. However, even in Denver, which stands out for its rapid residential growth in LoDo, population has increased since 1980 by only 2 percent, or twelve thousand people, while Denver's suburbs added over 30 percent, an increase of over five hundred thousand residents. But many of the new residents in downtown are clearly members of the fifth migration, including the president of Coors Brewing Company, the president of Norwest Bank of Colorado, and many executives in high-tech industries. By 2010 Houston and Denver are each expected to add about 9,500 new central-city residents, while Chicago—larger to begin with—is projected to attract about twice that number.

Across the country the wise protection and continuing use of older buildings such as mills, warehouses, and factories has brought new benefits to communities. These historic artifacts provide space for existing businesses and may offer low-cost and distinctive accommodations to attract new ones. Tourism is often not just enhanced but begun, and local tax revenues increase. The ongoing process of rehabilitation and the new construction compatible with it create new jobs and support artisans.

To capture the maximum economic and aesthetic gains through a well-conceived historic-preservation program a community does not have to go it alone; but it must know where to look for help and be willing to take part in state and federal programs and meet their standards. Ever since passage in 1966 of the National Historic Preservation Act (NHPA), which was substantially amended in 1980, the federal government has exerted an immense and positive influence. NHPA established the National Register of Historic Places and made it government policy not to inaugurate federal programs that would undermine historic preservation. Well-informed local advocates will realize that the National Register, an ever-expanding listing of the most important cultural resources in the country that are considered worthy of preservation, allows for diversity; it recognizes five kinds of places: districts, sites (locations of significant events), buildings, structures (large buildings such as factories and warehouses), and objects (trains and ships). Listing in the National Register does not automatically protect a property. It does form the basis for binding local regulatory action, and it also triggers various favorable tax and assessment benefits for owners.

Other federal assistance to the cause of historic preservation is now available. The Transportation Department prohibits spending that would have an adverse impact on historic resources whether designated in the National Register or by state or local action. The successful Main Street Program, created by the National Trust for Historic Preservation, supports town-center revitalization. Facade easement donations to a non-profit or public entity can enhance the feasibility of historic-building renovation. The Internal Revenue Service typically approves a tax deduction equal to about 10 percent of the value of the entire property. Perhaps the most important stimulus to local developers and rehabilitators of historic properties is a federal income-tax credit calculated at 20 percent of the cost of approved rehabilitation. During the representative four-year period of 1982–1985, this credit stimulated an estimated $8.8 billion of investment in more than 11,700 historic buildings. The dramatic rehabilitation of many city centers and the rescue of decrepit but interesting older areas and structures were accurately praised during Congressional hearings when Louisiana Representative Lindy Boggs testified, "The rehabilitation tax credit has worked as has no other tool to encourage and facilitate the preservation of historically or architecturally significant structures and has contributed to reversing the downward trend in the older sections of our nation's cities. It has worked by making projects not otherwise economically feasible into reasonable, cost-effective investments. It has worked by creating jobs for people in construction, by putting derelict and abandoned houses and buildings back into commerce."[5]

The NHPA also set up the mechanism through which state and thereafter local participation in historic preservation has become increasingly efficient. Through the State Historic Preservation Offices (SHPOs), local and state proposals for preserving particular assets can be filtered, reviewed, and if found worthy sent up to the federal level. Today, every state has an SHPO. Although they vary in scale and presence, most do much more than simply review and direct National Register applications. This is another resource that a sensible local community will investigate and use selectively. SHPOs certify local programs, which makes them eligible for federal funding; they conduct surveys of historic resources, a valuable aid to a community in need of help; and they may provide technical, educational, financial, and regulatory assistance to advance local preservation activities. These tasks supplement the coordination of statewide historic-preservation plans, the management of National Register nominations, and the acquisition and management of historic properties of statewide significance.

At the beginning of any long-term historic-preservation program a wise growth town will create its own well-documented inventory or survey of cherished historic and cultural properties and resources. This survey, the foundation for all that follows, should be conducted and overseen by someone with appropriate professional training and experience—a local historian, a resident architectural historian, or perhaps a well-trained research-oriented landscape architect. Whoever it is should obtain assistance from the SHPO and representatives of the National Trust for Historic Preservation. Based on local wishes and vision, and taking into account owners' rights and economic interests, comprehensive plans and zoning regulations can be prepared that incorporate historic-preservation objectives; and a historic-preservation ordinance can be created that details the rules that must be followed locally with respect to historically significant assets. In general, the local historic-preservation ordinance focuses on terrain that is of great importance to local culture and history, whether or not it is ever considered for the National Register. The ordinance or ordinances establish a procedure and a standard to ensure that alterations and new buildings within historic districts are appropriate and compatible.

Usually the mandates of the historic-preservation ordinance are carried out by a local historic-preservation commission. The commission must have adequate authority to protect landmarks: to approve or forbid demolition, new construction, and exterior renovation. If the commission is only an advisory body, its power is lessened, and its community is denied a powerful tool with which to fashion an enhanced future. Members of the commission must include appropriate professionals, such as historians, architects, planners, and landscape architects. These members need to be energetic; sophisticated about relevant aspects of law, finance, and real estate development; imaginative enough to find ways to treat private owners equitably; and, at the same time, courageous and committed enough to be unwilling to allow dilution of the long-term objectives of the process.

Other programs for historic and cultural preservation will be created by wise growth towns. Through print and television publicity based on findings of the historic-district survey and through other means of publicly disseminating information—walking tours, publication of pamphlets, information meetings in schools and at community functions—community awareness can be enriched. Important buildings now ignored, an industrial heritage all but forgotten, a couple of blocks of intact warehouses or outdated commercial buildings—any or all of these can become the center of new interest, new care, new vitality, new tourism, new commercial success, new tax revenue. They can be transformed into vital community assets, especially if accorded property-tax benefits. By reducing the tax on approved historic structures being targeted for reuse or rehabilitation, as Austin and other communities do, towns can encourage owners not to demolish them. Agreeing to freeze taxes for a meaningful period after successful redevelopment attracts entrepreneurs. By granting tax concessions for renovated older structures, a wise town recognizes the long-term benefit of its own investment in the past.

Preserving Public and Semipublic Space

Communities contain various kinds of important open spaces. The most commonly recognized public and semipublic areas are playgrounds, parks, courtyards, malls, plazas, esplanades, and the sidewalk. Also important are the small, seemingly incidental spaces not commonly recognized as part of the public domain—spaces such as entrances to buildings, vest-pocket parks, transit stops, pedestrian paths. In such places residents meet and interact. Visitors, strangers, and outsiders are all permitted in these spaces too, and from them they obtain an impression of the community. These places are carefully and sometimes unconsciously evaluated by residents and visitors for amenity and safety. If they are not working, neither is life in town. People will leave. The appearance and mood of public and semipublic spaces are a measure of the quality of a place.

A smart growth town must protect and enhance its semipublic and public spaces. The solution is not to eliminate them. Places where people can mingle need to be thought of as an essential physical attribute. A smart growth town will lay out or reserve suitable public spaces at the same time that it plans streets. It will also enhance and expand those public areas already available.

Among the greatest and most successful social spaces in the world are innovative forms of streets—think of the Galleria in Milan or its namesake, the Galleria in Houston. A covered shopping plaza is a street, as is the central mixing space of New York's Grand Central Terminal, which is indeed a grand street for people—it permits no automobiles, and it leads to numerous rail platforms, to an enticing variety of shops, and right into the interior of numerous office buildings, all linked seamlessly to surrounding sidewalks.

On a much smaller scale, conventional streets devoted to increased amenity for pedestrians offer reclaimed public space. I think of the conversion of Nicollet Avenue in Minneapolis and other center-city streets into a lively mixture of recreational, commercial, and small-scale public spaces safe from intrusive automobiles. Other successful street transformations are San Francisco's palm-decorated Embarcadero and Los Angeles's Olivera Street. None of these transformed streets, however, quite replaces the appealing vitality of a busy conventional street containing shops, houses, and public spaces—streets on which people mix and along which the wares of commerce are displayed. Streets such as Madison Avenue and Canal, Mott, and Orchard in New York come to mind. Every successful town has one or several.

The appearance and safety of a town's public and semipublic spaces, including its streets and sidewalks, are a clue to its health and desirability. They stand as a symbol and as substance. The care taken in designing lights and light fixtures, trash baskets, street furniture, and landscaping, while rarely discussed except by well-meaning civic organizations, is noticed by everyone. Taken into account consciously or unconsciously, these features contribute to the overall impression and to the pleasure and the amount of use. Flower boxes and street trees may do as much to assure the future of a community as capital investment and police patrols. When sidewalks are filled with discordant signs, overloaded trash cans, flying refuse, and needy supplicants, people with a choice will stay away. Then the scene is set for decay, for subversive use of the street, for the familiar spiral down.

As a town grows, it can implement thoughtful and effective measures to ensure the increased scale and quality of its public spaces. In central San Antonio, the Riverwalk, revitalized in the late 1960s, provides a meandering oasis for recreation, shopping, and eating out. It has brought renewed vitality to much of San Antonio's downtown. A greenbelt surrounding a community and then penetrating into it or even through it—an area such as a natural watercourse, woodland swath, park, or a mixture of these—holds great promise. Where special environmental features already exist, such as natural wetlands, drainage courses, or open waterways, what could make more sense than to use them to make the town more attractive? Indeed most residents prefer a mixture of the natural and built environment to provide continuity with surrounding open lands. Greenbelts, stream courses, and linear parks are fine and logical places for trails and recreation corridors.

These kinds of amenities, which attract and hold people, are easiest to introduce when a place is growing. They are much more difficult and much more expensive to retrofit into overdeveloped sprawl. Before development proposals are considered and large tracts of undeveloped land are converted, public spaces—residential squares, linear parks, watercourses, wetlands, continuation of a greenbelt, a wide swath of forever-wild woodland, and so on—should be incorporated into a town's master plan. Doing so will create a successful, long-term pattern to town growth and a valuable one. The result will be an orderly and coherent development of public amenities and an enhanced quality of life.

If planning occurs early, a community can realize its public-space objectives at little or no capital cost. In James Oglethorpe's innovative 1734 plan for Savannah, for instance, residential squares and vest-pocket parks were reserved before development took place. In Pennsylvania, the Natural Lands Trust has been successfully sponsoring its Growing Greener program. Its sensible and logical approach is to map primary and secondary land-conservation targets before development occurs. Primary areas for conservation are the most severely constrained lands, such as wetlands, floodplains, and steep slopes; development there is legally restricted. Secondary areas for conservation include desirable land that requires modification of comprehensive plans, subdivision ordinances, or zoning maps in order to be conserved. Lands that might typically and legitimately be saved are mature woodlands, wildlife habitats, prime farmland, groundwater recharge areas, greenbelts, stream corridors, historic sites, and areas with scenic views. Once these desirable areas are mapped, a mixture of regulation and negotiation can be employed to conserve them as private development occurs. But little of long-term consequence will be achieved unless a community displays the wisdom and commits the resources necessary to prepare these crucial maps and coordinated regulatory mechanisms in the first place.

It is precisely when large parcels are first being developed that the private sector has the financial energy and economic incentive to comply with various public objectives. The only public cost is likely to be for the maintenance of dedicated public spaces. If these costs prove onerous, fifth-migration growth towns can make such areas the quasi-private responsibility of one or several homeowners' associations, or they can establish a taxed "improvement district" in which revenue generated from the private sector is dedicated to land and resource upkeep.

Safety and security in public and semipublic spaces are enhanced when they are actively used, when they are surrounded by involved neighbors, and when they are not so large or so densely planted as to permit nefarious activities. Actively used public spaces enjoy cost-free, continuous surveillance. It is a sad commentary that large open spaces in many communities, especially those in decline, are no longer safe and no longer well tended, an easy-to-read sign of a place that has fallen. When this occurs, a few people may exploit the opportunity. For many others, rising fear and increasing crime rates are an inducement to look elsewhere for a place to live. In the contemporary battle over public open spaces in declining communities, the few often prevail over the vast majority who pay the bills. Fear then sets in, and the community is in jeopardy. When the opposite occurs, when the parks and squares and sidewalks are safe and are enjoyed by all, a place is on the right track; it will thrive.

Integrating Roadways

One of the great mistakes made during the rush to build on open land during a boom, especially in residential areas, is the overbuilding of streets: roadbeds too wide, sidewalks and bike paths too narrow or nonexistent, and bad landscaping everywhere. Most modern suburbs look like paved airfields with dwellings set back from the runway. The dominance of the street as an independent and often greedy element in the landscape was first prompted by health considerations and later stimulated by romance with the motor car.

New ideas for interesting residential streets were part of Raymond Unwin and Barry Parker's 1904 design for Hempstead Garden Suburb near London. Rather than conform to the mandates of the Public Health Act of 1875 for wide through-street rights-of-way, Unwin and Parker proposed the creation of cul-de-sacs and argued that street widths of twelve to sixteen feet rather than the prevailing thirty-five feet would be perfectly adequate. As a result, the Hempstead Garden Suburban Act of 1906 made it legal to develop cul-de-sacs and hierarchical road types, which varied in curvature and cross-section. When completed, the streets of Hempstead Garden Suburb became influential prototypes for suburban planners in both America and England. Frederic Howe reported in *Scribner's Magazine* in 1912, "The roadways in Hempstead ignore right angles.

They avoid regularity in every way. They meander about aimlessly, comfortably, following the natural contour and advantages of the land. Nor are they of equal width. The residential streets are narrow. They are designed to discourage traffic and keep it on the main thoroughfares."[6]

The focus on ever wider and more plentiful roads as a newly significant ingredient of town design gained momentum with the mass production of cars. Between 1909 and 1930, in response to the enormous growth in auto traffic, thoughtful private architects and planners and newly formed nonprofit associations supported high-quality and innovative planning of streets. The First National Conference on City Planning and the Problems of Congestion was held in Washington, D.C., in 1909. Influenced by the English Garden City movement founded by Ebenezer Howard, of which Unwin and Parker were a part, twenty American planners and architects including Lewis Mumford, Henry Wright, Clarence Stein, and Clarence Perry in 1923 formed the Regional Planning Association of America. Following Unwin's earlier lead, Perry, together with Thomas Adams, devised principles for residential street systems in the New York region; they were published in 1929 in the first New York regional plan. Contemporary growth-town managers would be wise to review their main suggestions:

- Streets should be adapted to the traffic load and kind of use they are destined to have.
- Street layout should fit the land, for attractiveness and lower cost.
- For local streets, a pavement width of eighteen to twenty feet is sufficient, and the balance of the right-of-way can be devoted to sidewalk and planting.
- Staggered cross-streets, dead-end streets, and cul-de-sacs contribute to safety, attractiveness, and variety.
- Cul-de-sacs and dead-end streets should be used only as part of a complete subdivision plan integrating both pedestrian and vehicular circulation.
- If long blocks are used, pedestrian footpaths should offer shortcuts.[7]

At Radburn, a suburb in Fairlawn, New Jersey, Stein and Wright obtained a commission in 1929 from Alexander M. Bing, a progressive real estate developer, to design and build a community based on these principles. Curbs were not used, sewer and water lines were scaled to actual need, and a hierarchical street layout achieved a reduction in paved road. Compared with a standard grid plan, the plan for the development reduced street area and utility lines by 25 percent. Radburn was a great success and still remains an instructive model.

The demonstrated savings at Radburn had a major impact on the rhetoric about street design but unfortunately did not influence the great majority of engineers and bureaucrats who took charge of establishing road-construction standards and who, even today, continue to control that turf. For example, the Institute of Transportation Engineers *Recommended Practice for Subdivision Streets*, the basic manual still used by most communities and their consulting engineers to set street-design standards, proposes a minimum right-of-way of sixty feet, even in residential areas, and within it a paved width of thirty-two to thirty-four feet. Related standards, such as the width of parking lanes, the width of each traffic lane, and the recommended turning radii, are calculated to ensure a smooth, rapid, continuous flow of traffic rather than street variety and multiple users, including pedestrians.

Maverick jurisdictions that permit narrower streets than are commonly recommended today by traffic engineers include Bucks County, Pennsylvania, and Orange County, Florida. They have amended their ordinances to permit minimum street paving on local streets of sixteen to eighteen feet with two-foot shoulders on either side. This is a sensible standard for suburban streets expected to handle fewer than 250 vehicles a day. When more traffic must be accommodated, as in subcollector streets, a paved right-of-way of about twenty feet with two-foot shoulders is perfectly adequate and contrasts sharply with standards established in most communities still seized by traditional, engineer-dominated standards. An added bonus: narrower streets encourage slower automobile travel and safer driving, what is known in the trade as a "traffic-calming" effect. Speed bumps, roundabouts, occasional street narrowing, street trees near the right-of-way, and curves achieve the same purpose.

What a smart growth town will do, and has every right to do, is set its own standards and its own criteria for different types of streets. Most important, streets must be designed to serve a variety of functions, not exclusively and simply to be conduits for traffic. Streets have other clients besides cars, others entitled to a fair share of precious public space. Street rights-of-way should include sidewalks and paths or trails. Walkers, cyclists, joggers, children, and people socializing have a legitimate claim to this terrain. It is possible to integrate street design with potential abutting properties, to design streets as a locale of pedestrian action and social interaction, and to recognize their potential for aesthetic enhancement when combined with other public space in the community. Well-designed streets might include vest-pocket parks, good lighting and attractive landscaping, public bathrooms, and transit-service shelters.

In most places streets are designed in only two sizes, local and collector. A smart growth town will have eight, ten, even a dozen types, such as boulevards, courts, lanes, alleys, each with its own design standard and only wide enough for its intended purpose. Landscape, lighting, speed limits, and parking protocols will be established for each. Over time, a sensibly managed place will retrofit the public right-of-way, an area usually much wider than the paved roadbed, of each existing street so that walkers, bicyclists, and, when appropriate, users of transit are accommodated. The width of car lanes can usually be reduced without causing motorist inconvenience. The captured space, together with available shoulder area, can then be devoted to whatever makes sense, whether it be a bike lane in a city or a hiking path in an outlying suburb. A wise local community will look at contemporary innovations in street design in a place such as Robert Davis's Seaside in Walton County, Florida, planned principally by Andres Duany and Elizabeth Plater-Zyberk, or at some resourceful larger residential communities in Florida, such as Hunter's Creek, south of Orlando, and the Hummocks, southwest of Miami, which connect residential enclaves directly to their own community centers via shortcut pedestrian and bike paths separate from the road system.

What about the highway, the principal gateway to every American community? Its edges are usually exploited for commercial use without concern for social consequences or aesthetic impact. Direct access by motorcar from the highway to commercial areas, shortest and best from an advertising and marketing standpoint, creates delays and danger. Along the highway in town, signs and traffic lights proliferate, accidents multiply. Pedestrians are often injured amid the jumble of competing, confusing signs, signals, turning vehicles, and parking lots. Wherever houses are crammed in near the highway, the incessant hum of motors and rubber becomes the background noise of daily life, as traffic and pollution threaten inhabitants.

The federal government and some state governments have designated a limited number of scenic roads, whose edges and vistas are protected.

State implementation of their own programs has been uneven and unreliable. But a local community could designate its own scenic roads—perhaps the principal gateways into and out of town, the routes leading to the best local scenery and recreation or to the most beautiful views of characteristic landscape. Once the designation is made, as in Austin or in Hilton Head, South Carolina, a community can protect these roads in its comprehensive plan. Measures that entice the private sector while ensuring the intended results can follow if regulations and incentives are wisely balanced. In addition, once local scenic-road designations are made, local, county, state, and federal assistance becomes available.

A new way of thinking about open land along the ordinary highway is necessary in a smart growth town. This space should be recognized as premier public vista. It is one of the few strips of land whose view is most frequently seen and shared by all. Why not require along the right-of-way a reasonable setback of all commerce and its parking areas together with controlled access and carefully planned landscaping? Stores and offices would remain in an equal competitive position. The interest of the community is honored by respecting one of its most easily appreciated visual assets. And why not cluster residences far back from the highway as well so that the auditory impact of motors and the biological impact of carbon monoxide are reduced inside houses, while the visual delight of open land is increased along the road? There are other sensible uses for wide strips of land along the highway in developing communities. They are ideal for contiguous parcels reserved for farming. Where better to encourage the noise, chemical discharges, and dust stirred up by agricultural activities? Forest areas, zones of steep slope, and scenic vistas all make sensible and attractive highway neighbors.

Smart growth towns will incorporate into street or highway rights-of-way well-designed and physically separated paths for people who are not inside of cars. The popularity of bicycles reached a peak in 1877 with the introduction of the rear wheel–driven "safety" bicycle. The convenience, mobility, and low cost of bikes were so compelling that during the "bicycle-craze era" of 1890–1895, bicycle clubs in both England and the United States lobbied for road improvements that would incorporate the cyclists' needs. Today, the roadside is again teeming with people, not only on bicycles but also on skates and rollerblades, on cross-country skis, on horseback. A smart response can be seen in the expanding Colorado resort communities of Frisco, Breckenridge, Copper Mountain, and Vail, where a paved, multipurpose network of paths parallels the highway, including a connected perimeter trail around Lake Dillon. A similar paved trail well separated from Minnesota Highway 95 travels gracefully from Center City to Marine-on-St. Croix.

However it is achieved, the roadside should be recognized as a precious, highly visible, jointly experienced part of the public domain. Heightened attention to this particular aspect of community development will assure a much higher-quality and more appreciated environment and will lend a town dignity, which will become an enduring part of its appeal. The opposite, the trashing of the gateway and of the roadways within town, will lead to traffic jams, to visual blight, and, eventually, as the edge of the road becomes ever more disfigured, to deterioration of the community itself.

The road should be considered a servant of the landscape, the residents, recreation opportunities, aesthetics. Both traffic engineers, who traditionally delight in magnifying a road's width, and planners, who tend to abandon this crucial element of urban design, must understand the street to be an integral, multipurpose aspect of total land use, not an isolated corridor, the exclusive purview of big trucks and four-wheeled vehicles. As I have advocated since the 1974 publication of *The Future of the City*, once this general idea pervades the design of growing and expanding places, as it has in some places designed by advanced practitioners, communities will become more attractive to residents and to visitors.

Containing the Automobile

If any one piece of the whole puzzle is able to ruin a community, it is the car. The acreage consumed by the nation's two hundred million automobiles is enormous, more than all the space devoted to housing. The automobile's "uncapped appetite," says Jane Holtz Kay, "has made the city dweller a slave. ... Sidewalk and street tree vanish for driveway; walkability gives way to driveability."[8] Although proportions vary from city to city, from 30 to 50 percent of urban America is given over to the car. In Los Angeles and Houston it may even be more. A good average is about 35 percent of all land in settled places devoted to streets and parking. Close to 100 percent of the most annoying experiences in most communities can be traced to the car. Think of everything from noise pollution to air pollution to ozone-destroying gases to smog to strip commercial development to gridlock to traffic congestion to accidents and to the most serious of all, the loss of life.

There is no denying that the car is convenient and private and flexible—an appealing combination. How can we accept the car and yet make a town the better for it? That is a basic dilemma with which advanced urbanists and growth-town managers now struggle. Strange as it may sound, in town-planning circles this is a new problem. The more traditional problem was how to increase the urban space devoted to cars. Road-widening solutions were offered by the Italian futurists before World War I, and other destructive ideas were inspired by the images and rhetoric of the internationally celebrated architect-planners Mies van der Rohe and Le Corbusier. Only recently, beginning with Louis Kahn, the great contrarian, has it become repugnant to advanced thinkers to devote the bulk of public space in a town to the automobile. Since Kahn's Philadelphia diagrams of 1953–1956 thoughtful planners and town managers have slowly come to recognize that during growth periods there is simply no way to make local roads and access highways big enough to take all residents rapidly just where they want to go without destroying most of a community.

Designing roads in an enlightened way, as described in the previous section, is one way to reduce the dominance of the car. There are other methods. Underground and above-grade parking garages, although expensive, do remove the vehicle from the street. However, when such parking is inserted at the center of town, as under the Boston Commons, it only attracts more vehicles. How much more sensible to restrict automobile parking to the perimeter of central areas, as Kahn proposed for Philadelphia. Then, depending on the size of the community, people can walk or take shuttle buses to the center. Park-and-ride systems operate on this general principle. As examples, the town of Carmel, California, requires tour buses to park outside the central area, and Atlantic City, New Jersey, maintains closely regulated drop-off periods for buses entering the casino area.

Although in no way a substitute for the car, bicycles can be used for short trips if communities are organized to accommodate them. Safe paths and routes need to be set out as do specific, secure places to park and store bikes when they are not in use. Cyclists will be encouraged when a network of paths links homes to destinations such as schools, shopping areas, offices, recreation centers, and parks. The ten miles of networked, paved pathways for pedestrians and cyclists in the Hummocks, a rather dense 1970s' development in southwest Miami, for instance, is extensively used and relieves traffic on nearby streets.

The use of public transit is another obvious and too-often-ignored means of reducing the destructive dominance of the automobile. Many options exist, ranging all the way from shuttle jitneys in the street to a fixed-rail system on a separate right-of-way. In places such as Minneapolis and Seattle, where frequent and reliable shuttle buses have been put into service, use has been above expectations. In most larger cities where convenient, well-designed, areawide transit networks are available, they are used extensively and cut down on the need for automobile access into the city center. Buses are feasible in both small and large communities. However, only the most heavily populated, densely settled, and extended urban areas demonstrate favorable cost-benefit ratios from a rapid-transit rail or light-rail system. But sensible planning for such a network, ahead of need, is rarely achieved. If a public transit system is begun after a town reaches a density or configuration that merits it, as in Los Angeles in 1990 and as in Seattle in the late 1990s, the cost is much greater than it would have been otherwise. Costs become astronomical when rights-of-way are not reserved in advance. Also, condemning and clearing land through settled areas create embarrassing political difficulties. When advanced planning has not occurred, public transit systems are often not built.

Promoting Housing Diversity

A fifth-migration growth town, if it is to thrive over a long period of time, must contain housing for everyone from poor to rich. And it must have a strategy for increasing the availability of housing across the economic spectrum at a pace appropriate to its overall growth. This is a difficult undertaking, and getting it right is a delicate task.

At the top of the economic ladder and down into the middle, the free market takes care of housing supply based on demand. But in a dynamic, growing community, housing for the working poor and for not-well-off retirees is likely to be scarce. As new low-wage jobs are created, workers often have difficulty finding an adequate place to live. And as older low-income residents age in place, they often cannot find housing that is safe and affordable.

What is to be done? The record of public-assisted housing is not especially good. Production has been meager. Management is notoriously neglectful. The level of building maintenance by people in residence is close to scandalous. This bleak picture might change some day. But I am not optimistic. What about the genuinely indigent, the structurally unemployed and unemployable, the infirm and the insane who refuse institutional care? These social-policy issues stray outside the purview of this book. But surely local, state, and federal programs should at a minimum provide a genuine safety net. Federal, state, and local collaboration— through low-income housing credits, federally insured mortgages, tax-abatement programs, housing vouchers, and direct subsidies—seems to provide the only options. Burden sharing for all taxpayers in the country is more appropriate than the current situation, in which particular towns such as Chicago, San Francisco, and New York, which possess large-scale public-housing projects, become havens for a disproportionate share of the needy. The necessity of providing for them, in turn, accelerates a community's potential for self-destruction. One sure way to fail at becoming a self-sustaining growth town is to allow the local working and taxpaying population to become the financial and social guardian of disproportionately large numbers of people who do neither.

Neither housing experts nor legislators are certain about the best way to conduct the nation's publicly assisted housing program. Some federal authorities are now promoting a program to allow more working families to rent apartments currently reserved for the very poor, although advocates urge protections for the poorest tenants, including guaranteed priority. The optimistic goal is to open up public housing to 5 to 10 percent per year more working families and at the same time to create incentives that might encourage very poor residents to find jobs. Since the early 1980s the federal government has also required housing authorities to give preference to the homeless, people spending more than half their income on rent, victims of domestic violence, and people displaced by government action. As a result of these mandated preferences, in 1995 in New York City, as an example, 77 percent of new admissions to the city's housing projects were people in the lowest income category. One of the promising work-incentive ideas is to repeal a requirement that links rent increases to income increases.

For those who can afford modest monthly payments, free-market solutions exist. Private initiatives supported by wise town regulation can provide needed housing at little or no public expense. One of the most direct and effective ways is to permit an independent apartment in a single-family residence. Besides advancing a specious argument about manageable density, advocates of the current restrictions on this type of housing contend that an apartment in a residential neighborhood will bring down property values. But one apartment can be provided within many single-family residences without diminishing the appearance and character and real estate values of residential neighborhoods if the apartment is skillfully designed. First, the apartment must appear from the exterior as an integral part of the house. This way the "look" of the neighborhood is not compromised. Second, its entrance and parking area must be planned and landscaped in a discreet and tasteful way. And it is critical that the construction quality of the apartment be regulated by town laws and standards.

Although this suggestion may seem radical to some and will surely be rejected in many places, consider the advantages of this approach. A place for older people at ground level becomes available, perhaps even in their own family house or with neighbors who are able to assist when necessary. Young working individuals and couples obtain a choice of places to live. Those with meager incomes are able to find affordable housing. For all those who own homes and find their upkeep a financial drain, such apartments, or "echo housing," which stands for "elder cottage housing opportunity," become a source of supplementary income. This new income makes it more likely that houses will be maintained, especially in marginal neighborhoods. Such arrangements avoid spot blight, a fungus that can bring down the whole neighborhood.

Another workable approach is to allow apartments over stores in the central business district; such zoning can provide less expensive accommodations just where older people, some working people, and a lot of single people might in fact prefer to live. Towns can also require that each private developer of a large-scale residential subdivision contribute a pre-established and prorated amount of money to a community-managed fund used exclusively to build affordable housing. In a growth town this fund will build up rapidly. Another proven approach is to require developers of large residential projects to incorporate a fixed percentage of moderately priced housing within the new development itself, perhaps in exchange for a reasonable density bonus that offsets the cost of this requirement. In this way subsidized, moderately priced housing is provided along with open-market new construction at no direct public cost for land or construction. In Montgomery County, Maryland, for instance, most residential projects larger than fifty units must include 15 percent moderate-cost housing, which is allocated to eligible low- and moderate-income applicants. In exchange developers are awarded a 20 percent density bonus above the number of units they would otherwise be entitled to build.

Certain lessons have been learned from prior public-housing experience that are applicable to subsidized housing. Any financial inducement offered the private sector must be consistent with profitability, or nothing will be built. To assure care of the housing, units should be owner-occupied, not rented. To be equitable, if a house built with public funds is sold at a profit, the owner-occupant might participate in a share of the profits, but the initial investment plus a portion of any appreciation should be returned to refresh the town's affordable-housing revolving fund. Construction should be undertaken by a private contractor working to strict standards and overseen by an independent, private housing-construction manager. In general the public sector and in many instances even the not-for-profit sector have proven to be woefully inept at getting construction completed well, on time, and on budget. When construction of such projects goes wrong, the waste is immense, the political fallout is considerable, and the public's willingness to authorize more affordable housing is often decisively diminished.

Another way to ensure housing diversity over the years is to zone for it and to promulgate subdivision regulations that become the blueprint for it. In this way appropriate locations can be zoned for small lots or high-density residential development. Rental or ownership costs can be reduced if the town elects to subsidize development by providing roads, utilities, drainage, landscaping, land preparation, and sewage treatment. These then become a shared community expense, a contribution by all property owners toward the goal of diversity in housing.

A wise growth town will also calibrate the production of lower-cost housing to avoid unmanageable traffic, overwhelmed schools, and a town government expanded into inefficiency. In many fourth-migration suburbs fear of these consequences is now causing resistance to rowhouse developments. In places such as Prince William and Prince George's counties outside Washington, D.C., for instance, which in the 1970s welcomed town houses as sensible and affordable starter homes for young couples or as step-down homes for empty nesters, a rebellion is brewing. Now, as town-house projects proliferate in these and other suburbs, and as many become rental units, complaints about higher density, cheaper housing stock, and increased numbers of children have become loud. Fear of the devaluation of single-family houses is taking hold.

Encouraging Home Offices

Over thirty million Americans now work at home at least part of the time. More join the movement every day. These workers are in large measure fifth wavers. There are two distinct groups: the self-employed and corporate home-office workers. Many people who work in home offices no longer wish to commute. Many want to combine quality time at home and consistent childcare with the workday. Part-time work or working for several enterprises or working on several projects at one time becomes feasible. A person can produce an amazing amount of work at home using small, inexpensive, and powerful new technologies. Indeed, the home office and telecommuting are reversing trends that began with the industrial revolution, the basic force that propelled the third migration. Corporate-sanctioned home offices are becoming so prevalent that large companies such as Merrill Lynch have set up rigorous training programs to prepare workers. Its "telecommuting simulation lab" teaches people to work at home the Merrill Lynch way.

A smart growth town will find ways to accommodate people working at home and will benefit from doing so. Home offices should be permitted in every residential area. It makes sense to capture productive activity right in the community. If able to work at home rather than having to commute to another town, people spend more of their money in town and become more integrated into their community, more responsive to its variety, and more interested in its destiny. A wise growth town, however, will define "home office" in such a way that the quality of residential neighborhoods is not diminished. It will clearly delineate the types of permitted activities, restrict the number of workers, limit visitation, and enforce strict parking requirements. Requiring community approval for home offices taps a potential public income stream. In Tacoma, Washington, residents must purchase a license to conduct business at home. The city of Tampa, Florida, depends on home-office license revenue for about

$8 million per year, or roughly 2 percent of the city's general operating budget.

A community is much more attractive to fifth-migration participants if it is legal to work at home. Aggressive smaller towns are so aware of the importance of attracting "lone eagles" (a term created by the Denver-based Center for the New West to describe individual entrepreneurs) that, as a key development strategy, many send brochures to likely out-of-town candidates. Kerrville, Texas, with a population of nineteen thousand, solicits individuals by promoting its local telephone company's digital switching capacity and the ability of residents to receive the *New York Times* daily. As another example, on its web page Eureka, California, with a population of twenty-seven thousand, welcomes newcomers to a "Victorian seaport where lone eagles soar" while listing business incentives targeted to the small-office and home-office entrepreneur.

Insisting on Environmental Impact Statements

The National Environmental Policy Act (NEPA) of 1969 may not be familiar to growth-town residents, but it ought to be. NEPA is surely the most significant piece of federal land-use regulation since comprehensive zoning was legalized in 1916. Its basic requirement: public disclosure of the environmental impact of any federal land-use initiative. Prior to 1969, the physical and biological environments within a community remained unprotected as long as a new proposal was in compliance with local zoning and the local comprehensive plan.

NEPA set forth, for the first time, a national policy on the environment that is of great importance to communities. It also established the Council on Environmental Quality to supervise implementation. The core of NEPA is contained in these requirements:

> All agencies of the Federal government shall ... include in every recommendation or report on proposals for legislation and other major Federal actions significantly affecting the quality of the human environment, a detailed statement by a responsible official on (i) the environmental impact of the proposed action, (ii) any adverse environmental effects which cannot be avoided should the proposal be implemented,

(iii) alternatives to the proposed action, (iv) the relationships between local short-term uses of man's environment and the maintenance and enhancement of long-term productivity, and (v) any irreversible and irretrievable commitments of resources which would be involved in the proposed action should it be implemented.

The detailed document that must be prepared to address these concerns is known as an Environmental Impact Statement (EIS); it has become the fundamental NEPA compliance device.

Once NEPA became federal law, interested groups obtained similar legislation to require review of large state and local public and private projects. By 1997, twenty-nine states had an environmental review law. Now, if a major development or redevelopment is proposed in aware communities, most regulatory agencies require an EIS. At its best, the EIS procedure is one of the most important safeguards available to communities interested in a healthy future.

To work optimally, the EIS must be seriously prepared. The local government reviewing agency must have the courage and the expertise not only to review what is presented but to bring up relevant issues ignored or omitted in the document and to declare the EIS incomplete if indeed it is. When a reviewing agency has the capacity and the will to genuinely scrutinize proposals, projects are much more likely to be consistent with wise long-term growth policies. When the opposite is the case, the EIS more often than not becomes a fat collection of boilerplate and platitudes.

CHAPTER EIGHT

Resource Preservation and Enhancement

J UST AS IN A FAMILY, if a community depletes its resources, in time there will be ruin. Nothing can poison and ultimately destroy a settlement more rapidly than the despoliation of its natural resources. When the air is noxious, people want to leave. When the land is ruined, its productivity is compromised and its beauty no longer attracts. When the water is fouled, the consequences are genuinely dire: the watercourses are no longer a healthy source of food; recreation in and on the water is halted or much reduced; and the lack of safe, fresh, easily accessible, and inexpensive drinking water becomes a major limiting factor. In all the civilizations of the world and all across the North American continent, towns have been abandoned because the water was destroyed or depleted. In years past, the environment as a whole had no constituency. And various parts of it, like poor, inner-city neighborhoods, are still underrepresented in the halls of power. But today leaders in a wisely managed place realize that they must search for ways to protect its natural resources.

Wise growth towns will protect their own water, air, open lands, and recreation areas. Each must be spared overuse and surreptitious exploitation. If use begins to overwhelm the terrain, then reasonable methods to limit use are justified. Permits, passes, and rationing may not be popular, but they do reflect long-term care of precious and irreplaceable resources.

I propose here a wider and a deeper definition of community resources than is commonly accepted. My view is that the visual, aesthetic, and environmental attributes of a community are assets owned by inhabitants. The word community, in fact, suggests a commonality of ownership and interest in the basic resources of a place. Based on this collective interest, every resident is a stakeholder in the maintenance of scenic vistas, critical parcels of unique lands, watercourses, the exterior appearance of high-quality historic properties, the view from the principal roads, rail lines, and harbors. If recognized as collectively held assets, each of these will become subject to careful scrutiny, design, and management by resident individuals. When planning occurs in advance of excess growth, protection of these assets will be possible at reasonable cost and with reasonable regulation in ways that are extensions of citizens' private rights.

Protecting natural resources begins at the most mundane level. When the ditch next to a house is polluted by an irresponsible act, its fouled contents travel on to stream, to river, ultimately to the groundwater. Air pollution works the same way. A poisonous discharge at one location reappears as acid rain hundreds and thousands of miles downwind. So each community, and in fact each individual, is inextricably part of an environmental, ecological continuum. Soon after anyone spoils his or her immediate physical environment, a negative impact is likely felt elsewhere. Seen in this way, resource preservation is much more than a means to wise and successful community management. Aberrant social behavior, in which a few people or companies destroy the quality of life for the majority, is characterized as crime precisely because such behavior does enter the ethical and moral realm. Protecting the immediate natural environment, such as the driveway drainage ditch, is the key. And this domain is under local control and, even closer to the bone, is the responsibility of individuals.

Fertile Soils and Farmland

Protecting fertile topsoil is essential, and not just for efficient crop production. Topsoil erosion, caused by excessive cutting of woodlands, careless property development, and irresponsible management of agricultural areas, clogs streams, pollutes reservoirs, debilitates irrigation canals, and silts harbors. In times past, agricultural practices that destroyed the topsoil caused the collapse of civilizations. Today individual communities are still harmed when their productive soils are either ruined by overuse or lost by conversion to other uses. Although soil productivity has been greatly increased by scientific advances, including the intense use of chemical fertilizers and pesticides, eventually, if enough top-quality soil is lost, the foundation for producing abundant, safe, and reasonably priced food is destroyed. And chemically enhanced soils present their own danger—pollution of groundwater as the fertilizers and pesticides leach into the groundwater system below. Soil, once lost or destroyed, takes generations to replace, if it is replaced at all. How much wiser to avoid decisions that either degrade the most productive and fertile agricultural soils or cause the loss of soils in ways that produce dysfunction or contamination elsewhere.

In a wise, developing growth town, farmland will be maintained along major roads. How can this goal be achieved and the rights of those who own large parcels of land along such a right-of-way still be ensured? It starts with zoning. In most sensible towns, development is guided by area zoning. The zoning ordinance specifies the minimum amount of land required for each dwelling. It also details the percentage of each site that must be left as open space or as agricultural reserve. Let's assume, as is true in many such ordinances, that half the agricultural soils on any developmental site must be left as agricultural land. The maximum number of houses that may be built is based on the total size of the overall parcel, but the location of these dwellings is not specified, nor is the location of areas within the parcel that must remain as open space. Thus, what has been ignored in this otherwise progressive zoning ordinance is priority planning of the spaces to be left open. So the parcel is cut up into patches of houses, stores, and parking lots, with the 50 percent open space left as odd bits of agricultural land scattered about. The wrong part of the checkerboard has received all the attention.

If the location of contiguous spaces to be left open along the road had been mandated on one large property after another in the first place, economically viable farming could continue. Development of the same number of houses and buildings on each parcel would be allowed without destroying the agricultural vista from the road, a precious community resource, or the ability to farm a viable stretch of terrain. Conserving these lands enriches a place by retaining diversity. It offers the practical advantages of jobs and locally produced agricultural products. And it maintains for the local community, as well as the region, the varied landscape that in many instances attracts newcomers and pleases residents.

In growth areas much more farmland than just the terrain visible from the road must be preserved. For farming to be an economically viable activity that colors the character of a town, significant surrounding acreage on the best soils must be retained—enough to sustain a local agricultural economy, which includes suppliers, storage facilities, and market-distribution mechanisms. Proven local growth-management strategies, such as agricultural district zoning, cluster zoning, development-rights purchase programs, and differential property-tax initiatives, facilitate the long-term maintenance of a thriving agricultural economy, even one in the immediate vicinity of a growing community.

However, to make a real difference these programs must be started early, and they must be fair to farm landowners. The task of preserving land that produces relatively low per-acre economic returns within an escalating real estate market is not easy. Such preservation is somewhat easier in rural areas where farming properties are situated beyond a town's growth boundary. Such efforts in places as diverse as Boulder County, Colorado; Black Hawk County, Iowa; Hardin County, Kentucky; King County, Washington; and Lancaster County, Pennsylvania, benefit entire regions, the national economy, and growing local communities within their areas.

Whether local, county, or statewide measures are involved, a hazard of all agricultural-protection programs is not so much soil erosion as determination erosion. In expanding and desirable communities, when market forces encroach, attempts are inevitably made to undo previous commitments, to revise protective zoning, to invalidate prior easements. Strong town and county management backed by determined and insightful citizen support will be necessary to preserve prime agricultural soils and the basis of a vigorous, local agriculture.

Many types of land other than high-grade agricultural soils need to be protected. As discussed in detail later, land resources can be protected in many ways other than the most obvious and most expensive, purchase. But most of all it is crucial to protect against the kinds of wanton land spoiling that occurred routinely in the past. For instance, because of a single industry, coal mining, land and environmental destruction became so lurid that a federal bill, the Surface Mining Control and Reclamation Act of 1977, was passed to try to force states to control and, where necessary, to repair the damage. The bill's preamble lucidly states the case against surface mining operations and other types of land despoliation:

> Many surface mining operations result in disturbances of surface areas that burden and adversely affect commerce and the public welfare by destroying or diminishing the utility of land for commercial, industrial, residential, recreational, agricultural, and forestry purposes, by causing erosion and landslides, by contributing to floods, by polluting the water, by destroying fish and wildlife habitats, by impairing natural beauty, by damaging the property of citizens, by creating hazards dangerous to life and property, by degrading the quality of life in local communities, and by counteracting governmental programs and efforts to conserve soil, water, and other natural resources.[1]

Water

Water is, of course, precious beyond compare. Any smart growth town must pay particular attention to its supply and quality. Unlike the air, the other critical ingredient of human and community life, water is generally obtained only with effort and expense, even after a reliable supply is secured. I believe water will be the natural resource most contentiously fought over in the twenty-first century, certainly west of the 100th meridian, which slices the country in half through the Dakotas, Nebraska, and Texas; there annual rainfall is entirely inadequate to support the burgeoning population. Whereas at one time the U.S. Army Corps of Engineers and the federal Soil Conservation Service were both staffed by experts dedicated to water protection and sound resource management, policy in those agencies now displays an engineering bias that is often indifferent to conservation objectives and local community needs. As a consequence, decisions at the local level are critical. At times, local government must ignore or overrule permissive federal mandates in order to protect sources of water and to conserve its use.

Protecting water supplies depends on knowledge of how water is obtained and stored. Other than prehistoric water trapped in below-ground reservoirs, most of the North American water supply comes from the annual snowpack in forested water catchments. As Chris Maser, an expert on the natural history and ecology of forests, points out, "A curious thing happens when water flows outside the forest boundary: we forget where it came from. We fight over who has the 'right' to the last drop, but pay little attention to the supply—the health of the forested water catchments."[2] Water used locally can be stored in only three ways: in the snowpack above ground, which eventually feeds streams and river; in subsurface streams, aquifers, and lakes; and in above-ground reservoirs. Each of these sources can be spoiled within the local community, although the first may also be impaired anywhere along the way. Even though water is a renewable resource, its quality and quantity in many regions are being negatively affected because of unrelenting demand. As Maser details, "Water . . . is increasingly degraded by soil erosion, increases in temperature, and pollution with chemical wastes, salts from irrigation, and overloads of organic materials." Is it any wonder, he asks, that "the hydrological system is under stress?"[3]

There is a great difference between any water and water safe for humans to drink. More than half the United States relies on groundwater supplies for drinking water. Contamination is already pervasive. The federal Centers for Disease Control and Prevention estimates that almost a million Americans get sick each year from contaminated water. The Environmental Protection Agency estimates that twenty-three million septic systems and over one million underground storage tanks pose threats to groundwater. Even though more efficient equipment and delivery systems have managed to reduce average per capita water consumption by about 20 percent since 1980, before 2010 in some growth-town areas clean, safe drinking water is likely to become expensive and scarce.

The availability of water—locally, nationally, globally—is a concern to many policymakers. But on the practical level, until a shortage occurs, little is done to conserve it. Indeed, as Professor D. J. Chasan has observed, "One might suppose that people would automatically conserve the only naturally occurring water in a virtual desert, but one would be wrong. Land and farm machinery have capital value. Water in the ground, like salmon in the sea, does not. Just as salmon are worth money only if you catch them, water is worth money only if you pump it."[4] If water is used in an undisciplined manner, eventually a self-inflicted shortage will occur. If the shortage is not managed wisely, community deterioration is inevitable.

In fact, the shortage of potable water has long been a development constraint in most of the western part of the United States. Phoenix, unlike most of Arizona, enjoys a large supply. In 1911 Roosevelt Dam walled off the Salt River sixty miles to the east. The combined watersheds of the Salt and Verde rivers became a 13,000–square-mile catchment—an area larger than Maryland—that keeps Phoenix supplied with a reliable flow of water. In neighboring Colorado, Denver is also an exception. The city continues to grow because of a massive water sluiceway and piping system that reaches as far as Dillon Reservoir, more than sixty miles west in the Rocky Mountains.

Only a small portion of the water used in the United States is consumed within communities. The largest single use of water is for crop irrigation. In water-short states, such as Utah and New Mexico, over 80 percent of water withdrawn is diverted to irrigation. Water rights tied to western agricultural lands are now so valuable that urban speculators, led by Fort Worth–based Edward and Lee Bass operating through their Western Farms company, bought forty thousand acres of Imperial Valley farmland between 1995 and 1997 to capture its plentiful and valuable water rights. By right they are able to purchase water for about $12 per acre-foot from the Imperial Irrigation District, which controls a large amount of the flow from the Colorado River. They offered this water to Los Angeles, Las Vegas, and San Diego at close to $400 per acre-foot. San Diego, desperate to expand and dependent otherwise on the Los Angeles–controlled Metropolitan Water District of Southern California, was interested. In the area ever since, the game of water enterprise and politics has been played for ever higher stakes.

Smart growth means recognizing ahead of time that when water availability becomes questionable, its price will escalate based on both shortage and fear. To avoid this possibility, community leaders must pay attention to the quality and quantity of the local supply. Water is, after all, a resource that can be reliably managed. However, the old way of obtaining more water for a community, augmenting supply by acquiring water rights and developing surface or groundwater sources distant from the location of use, is becoming all but impossible. The rights are not available; the cost of dams, reservoirs, aqueducts, tunnels, and pump stations has become enormous; and the environmental impacts that must be mitigated present an awesome obstacle. As Rutherford Platt, professor of geography at the University of Massachusetts, told the International Symposium on Water Management for a Sustainable Environment, "The era of new large-scale, out-of-basin diversions to augment urban water supplies has virtually ended."[5]

Instead, in a wise growth town, in-ground catchments, from which water flows into wells or is pumped through a municipal system, will be protected. Water catchment areas make ideal growth-limit boundaries. They can also double—on the surface—as locales for light, communitywide recreation, such as hiking, bicycling, and walking. Used in thoughtful ways, water-protection areas enhance the quality of life within a community, protect the value of local real estate, and insulate the settled area from potential massive deterioration and devaluation.

These benefits can be derived in a self-supporting way. Purchases of open-space water catchment areas can be financed from tax receipts or revolving funds supported by tax receipts. Municipal water is routinely billed. When a private water company is involved, payments to the community can be required to offset related public expenses. To subsidize the public expense of acquiring, leasing, and maintaining water catchment areas, an annual private-well fee can be charged to households.

Aesthetics

America's acceptance of aesthetic elements as a significant aspect of town building has always been limited. Evidence of aesthetic care goes back only as far as the 1893 World's Columbian Exposition in Chicago. The "White City," a mixture of classical architecture, urban landscaping, and monumental public art, intrigued the nation. Its extraordinarily talented and influential creators, the landscape architect Frederick Law Olmsted, the architects Daniel Burnham, Charles McKim, and Richard Morris Hunt, and the artist Augustus Saint-Gaudens, produced a popular vision for an appealing townscape at a time when many American communities were expanding out of control. Within a few years, a basic revision of Pierre Charles L'Enfant's 1791 plan for Washington, D.C., was authorized, and with its acceptance aesthetic civic improvement, focused particularly on parks, landscape, and civic spaces, became the hallmark of planning in progressive places such as San Francisco, Seattle, Denver, Kansas City, Dallas, and Philadelphia.

For a brief time in America, ambitious, aesthetically based town design even enjoyed broad political, social, and economic support; it was characterized as the City Beautiful movement. During the first ten years of the twentieth century this coalition movement united civic reformers, community volunteers, business leaders, and municipal politicians, who were eagerly joined by those who might most benefit, architects and landscape architects. As the high point of the movement's success, in 1906 Burnham and his associate Edward H. Bennett were commissioned by the Merchant's Club, a Chicago business association, to produce a visionary plan for the city. The text, photographs, diagrams, plans, sketches, and a beautiful series of colored views of the envisioned city (drawn by the New York painter and illustrator Jules Guerin) were influential stimulants to communities across the country. But the City Beautiful movement, at its best a serious inquiry into the economy, transportation options, and design of the city, was short-lived. Yankee expediency and short-term enterprise reasserted their primacy.

And so today, when talking about communities, it is again not fashionable to focus on aesthetics. In America, *aesthetics* as a concept is still tarred with the pitch of effeteness, irrelevancy, superficiality, subjectivity. And yet, unpopular as the topic may be, the appearance of a place—its spaces and buildings—has an undeniable impact on people. A city, wrote Lewis Mumford with seasoned insight in 1938, is a "conscious work of art, and it holds within its communal framework many simpler and more personal forms of art. Mind takes form in the city; and in turn, urban forms condition mind."[6] People enjoy the center of Santa Fe or the Vieux Carré in New Orleans because each in different but relevant regional ways displays a measure of aesthetic care and uniformity. People feel a sense of openness and appropriate hierarchy in Washington, D.C., because rules enacted nearly a century ago require that building heights be calibrated in relation to adjacent street widths, and no building in the center of town may be higher than the Washington Monument.

I am not suggesting—nor do I endorse—any particular aesthetic regimen. I am suggesting only that attention to the issue, difficult and allusive as it may be, will impart a valuable and appreciated quality to any community. To ignore the potential is to overlook an important way that a place can both distinguish itself and bring its future a subtle grace and harmony. In the 1990s professional investigators discovered that "a community's aesthetic qualities, its livability, and its quality of life are far from merely a matter of luxury and taste, but are important factors in retaining existing businesses and attracting new ones, particularly in the most dynamic sectors of the economy, such as health care, electronics, and professional services. ... The third most important location factor (after labor-climate and proximity to markets) is an area's attractiveness to managers and skilled workers."[7]

Aesthetic regulation is most often achieved through design-review requirements, which vary enormously in level of insight, level of scrutiny, and level of enforcement. In scattered locales, architectural and aesthetic design requirements have been a feature of local zoning since 1925, when the city of Santa Barbara, after a severe earthquake destroyed much of its downtown, established uniform design guidelines reflecting the city's Spanish/Mediterranean heritage. In Santa Barbara an architectural board still reviews all renovation and construction plans. As mentioned previously, early historic-district ordinances in Charleston and New Orleans pioneered and popularized the idea in America of influencing and preserving in a historic area the *tout ensemble*, a term that translates roughly as "the whole impression of things that go together." Few newcomers to any community graced by a recognizable *tout ensemble* fail to admire it. Think of central Paris, the Vieux Carré in New Orleans, an unspoiled New England village, a seaside town in Normandy, or a medieval hill town in Italy. These are vastly different locales, but each is loosely unified architecturally and spatially. As new-urbanist architect Elizabeth Plater-Zyberk correctly observed, "Good design has a healthy respect for history, understanding that some experience transcends time and can be beneficially applicable under new circumstances."[8]

Aesthetic guidelines, however, are difficult to establish. Who is to say what the right criteria are? Are local regulations able to relate a changing community to its built history, to its climate, to its region through the materials used, to local traditions, and to the terrain? Should general considerations such as these be converted into design guidelines for the bones of a structure: window details, door types, balcony and porch height and scale, the massing and pitch of roofs, column placement, the materials used? Local aesthetic guidelines, if implemented, must also be able to evolve. Places that are alive and growing are not museums. They need to breathe and flex. Inventive design must be welcomed.

Two communities that were developed fairly recently by master plan from raw land apply design-control precepts on a townwide basis, a controversial undertaking that raises many questions. At Seaside, Florida, exterior colors, materials, and overall design must meet strict criteria. In Celebration, the successful neotraditional community near Orlando owned by the Walt Disney Company, every new house must be selected from a pattern book containing distinct and varied options prepared by Disney's master-plan architects. Although some people (including understandably some architects who feel constrained and frustrated) find this kind of aesthetic regimentation objectionable, these places are popular permanent-home destinations. Most communities will not find it practical to go as far as Seaside or Celebration, particularly as they have a prior history, but aesthetic care will go a long way toward distinguishing one place from all others, toward avoiding the non-place-related homogeneity that is enveloping so many American communities, and toward leaving individual designers ample room in which to produce distinctive pieces of architecture.

Robert A. M. Stern, a student of Vincent Scully and now a leader among influential American architects seeking a thoughtful basis for place-related but still innovative design, argues and quite wisely advocates an architecture that respects but is not trapped in the past: "Architecture should be an affirmation of place—that is, the physical product of a truly environmentally responsive approach. The widespread acceptance in local communities of fresh versions of time-honored styles is gratifying. To work with the place and its traditions is not to be trapped in a dull set of conventions. The tension between timeless ways and the all-too-timely circumstances that call a new building into being should lead to a vital architecture. The tension between the past and the presence of the past should foster an architecture more culturally resonant than one that is either all about the past or all about the present." Making his point even more succinctly, Stern asks, "Why hold on to the past? Because tradition is a gift, not some onerous weight. In this technological era of placenessless, perhaps our greatest challenge is to build up, not destroy, our relationship to the natural and built past."[9]

When aesthetic standards are imposed, public buildings must be required to conform, even though they are technically exempt from local planning and design-review controls, an odd and regrettable situation. In every community, some of the least appropriate and least attractive twentieth-century buildings have been erected by local, state, and federal agencies. This was not always the case: look at many older courthouses, statehouses, post offices, libraries, and other municipal structures. Among all the layers and levels of jurisdiction, I believe the local authority should have the final word on land-use control, and this means that all agencies of government should be required to comply with its mandates, just as private individuals are. In this way, interstate highways and state roads would have to comply with local landscape and zoning ordinances. The design of the federal post office and the state office building in town should pass local muster, as should all local-government structures. As it stands today no agency of government is required to comply with local planning, design, and development ordinances.

Most local design-review legislation has been instituted since the mid-eighties. The number of places imposing some form of design review is increasing by about 5 percent a year. And design review is no longer limited to historic districts. A 1994 national survey found that among 373 cities polled more than 83 percent had some form of design review. Although historic preservation was frequently an important concern, only a small portion of the cities surveyed limited their regulations to historic considerations. More than 85 percent of communities with design controls regulate nonhistoric development projects.[10] In an increasing number of informed towns, some sort of design-review procedure must be followed to obtain a building permit within particular districts.

Design review, quite understandably, often stirs strong reaction. Those who oppose it frequently point to the subjectivity of the process and complain that individual freedoms are violated, particularly those associated with private-property rights. Architects, of course, frequently criticize design review as a restriction limiting their personal, professional, and aesthetic freedom. Nevertheless, design review, while controversial, has been upheld in the courts against a broad range of challenges. Only when design-review standards are judged unnecessarily vague, as in *Pacesetter Homes, Inc., v. Village of Olympia Fields (1968)* and *Morristown Road Associates v. Borough of Bernardsville (1978)*, have they been ruled illegal, based exclusively on failure to prescribe adequate guidelines for reviewers. Public protection of aesthetic resources is now well established as a proper use of a community's power to regulate general health and welfare.

This body of legal opinion also enables local communities to control commercial signs, roadside advertising, billboards, and homeowner signs placed along public rights-of-way. Roadside in-town billboards are resented more than any other intrusion in the public environment. They create traffic-safety risks and degrade the appearance of a community. As a result, many aware and ambitious places have worked on the basis of federal and state legislation to eliminate outdoor off-premise commercial signs. By now the list is long of fifth-migration growth towns that have successfully and adamantly banned billboards.

Aware places also increasingly recognize that establishing and protecting scenic roads is a legitimate option. Associated with it is a growing effort to protect not just the road corridor but the view from the road, a scenic vista. These possibilities were first explored in the parkway movement of the 1930s, when the Blue Ridge Parkway and the Skyline Drive were created in Virginia and North Carolina. Today, local roads and views cherished in individual communities are garnering attention. Many of the most attractive towns have as part of their distinctiveness special vistas or corridors or prospects that, if destroyed, will diminish their quality and special attributes, even their uniqueness of place. These may be views of natural and cultural features, such as mountains, watercourses, bluffs, and farmland, or of historic buildings and public landmarks, such as a state capitol, city hall, or important monument. Through various regulatory measures, including condemnation, zoning, overlay zones, design review of designated corridors, and transfers of development rights, aware local communities such as Denver, Austin, and Seattle are moving to protect their aesthetic context as seen on and from the road. In some corridors, new subdivisions must cluster houses. In other places building-setback requirements also include specific landscape treatment within the protected area. To protect views, other communities place height limits on buildings within particular areas or along important vistas.

Resolving aesthetic issues is by no means an easy task. The question of what constitutes good design opens up a can of worms. Good design has frequently been interpreted to mean design that is consistent with overall community character. In Santa Fe, New Mexico, for example, where historic character has been protected since 1912, the community has always had a clear idea about how streets and buildings should look, valuing its Pueblo Spanish Revival architecture as a matter of civic identity. In 1957, when Santa Fe passed its Historic Styles Ordinance, it affirmed the need for design review within a historical context not just to protect old buildings but to ensure that new ones conformed to the historic character of the community. However, it is also quite simple to design a mediocre building using these criteria.

When Phoenix decided to establish design review in 1991, it had no established community character on which to draw. The city had grown so fast (it was the ninth largest city in the United States by 1990) and spread out so far (one-third as dense as Los Angeles) that its defining characteristics were the automobile and the commercial strip. To resolve the problem of community character, the city developed two sets of design guidelines: one broadly defined set of standards for the entire city and another targeted at establishing neighborhood character in numerous "urban villages" scattered around the city. A similar approach was undertaken in San Francisco in 1985, when a series of special area plans focused on establishing "contextualism" through specific design requirements for individual neighborhoods.

Aesthetic stewardship is difficult. But, if handled deliberately and wisely, it is also a low-cost way to protect and enhance a town. Once thoughtful and flexible aesthetic standards are in place long enough for residents to see and to feel the results, enthusiasm tends to mount. After enthusiasm comes pride in the appearance and specialness of a town or a part of town where some kind of aesthetic regimen is employed.

Every would-be wise growth town should ponder the potential of aesthetics as a planning priority. What principles make sense locally? What qualities are worth attention within a specific community or any part of it as it evolves over time? Whatever the details settled on, certain broad principles occur to me. First, everything that is seen from public places and spaces has an aesthetic component that exerts a direct impact on individuals. These views include not just the skin of buildings but the spaces between them as well as lampposts, wastebaskets, street trees, parking lots, lighting, commercial signs.

Second, everything visible in the public environment is the collective aesthetic property of all the citizens of a town. This principle is increasingly recognized in certain residential subdivisions in which the external maintenance of houses, including fences, gardens, lawns, and even roofs, is turned over to a service that is bound to specific aesthetic and maintenance standards. In this way, subdivision residents are assured that their aesthetic experience of the public aspects of their private housing enclave is not diminished by the habits of a particular neighbor. The same approach is visible in the best-maintained central business districts and suburban shopping malls. Design options are specified for landscaping and colors. Inside the store, inside the house, or in the back garden, in the private domain, anything goes. These are not a part of the collective aesthetic property. Wise community managers will make a clear regulatory distinction between what is in the public visual domain and what is not.

Third, wise growth towns will take responsibility for controlling and maintaining the public domain in an aesthetically enhancing way. If this principle is given priority, many once-complex decisions become easier to make. Consider the issue of the regulation of land use along major streets and highways. If the view from the car is the public domain, maintaining pleasing vistas, open spaces, farm fields, and landscaped buffers becomes a legitimate regulatory obligation. If it is consciously determined, for instance, that a bright, neon-lit townscape is sought along the highway, as in Las Vegas, or along streets, as in Times Square, then that becomes a controlling aesthetic idea. Go with it. The issues of historic preservation, which raise many policy questions for town government, are also more easily resolved by asserting the primacy of the public visual environment. From the collective point of view, the appearance of an older neighborhood or streetscape is the aesthetic business of the stakeholders in the community. Recognition of this principle helps town management know which preservation regulations and inducements ought to be extended and where they are needed.

As locally agreed on, distinct aesthetic goals evolve, criteria will emerge and will be revised from time to time. Except in historic areas, evolutionary change is to be expected. What matters is that the assertion of an aesthetic component in town design not be forgotten.

Landscape

The landscape within a town and at its periphery is an important part of the shared aesthetic experience in every community and a crucial component of many towns' economies. The setting of a growth town, its context of woodlands, farm fields, mountain slopes, meadows, and watercourses, helps define it and is a part of the reason the town attracts.

Depending on the nature of the community and the capacity of the land itself, a town's landscape serves critical and diverse functions. On the most pragmatic level, open space may provide a number of important economic benefits. The most obvious uses in this regard are for agriculture, livestock grazing, and forestry—viable economic endeavors in many parts of the country and essential industries nationally. Local undisturbed watersheds, wetlands, marshes, and watercourses are vital to fisheries and to maintaining at low cost high water quality. Scenic beauty attracts tourists and offers enduring pleasure to residents. There are also direct health, safety, and recreational benefits. Undeveloped hillsides and unbuilt-upon floodplains protect against the loss of life and property while contributing to the diversity of the open landscape. Open land is the essential ingredient of parks, preserves, greenbelts, trails, and access to waterways. Archaeological preserves, historic and cultural sites can be ruined if not set amid enough distinctive open space.

As a growth community expands, its collective values and land-development practices alter the characteristics of the surrounding environment. A smart community will protect and guide this evolution of the landscape. The regulations by which it does so will reveal its values and priorities. Green spaces are "part of what keeps a city going from week to week—just as much as transit and good police protection," Tony Hiss, author of *The Experience of Place*, recognizes. "They speak to something deep within us, some need to feel like members of the same human community."[11] As the landscape is altered abusively or wisely, so the future quality of the settlement is diminished or enhanced.

Within each community, street landscaping attracts and pleases people. But, regrettably, it is ignored in most places. In those selected spots where it is done well, as in parts of Alhambra, California; Blacksburg, Virginia; Salt Lake City, Utah; and Tucson, Arizona, it draws attention, acclaim, visitors, and new residents. I think of the majestic oak trees that line both sides of St. Charles Avenue in New Orleans. Visitors ride the streetcar along this stately street partly to enjoy the nineteenth-century building museum spread along its edges and partly to experience the sensation of being in the midst of a well-landscaped linear park running through a completely urbanized corridor. In San Francisco palm trees along Dolores Boulevard create a distinctive Mediterranean flavor to imposing Victorian buildings that seem worlds removed from harsh contemporary living. And in Boston the trees and greenery that adorn Commonwealth Avenue provide a civilized, appealing identity to one of the city's main thoroughfares.

Whether a street and its overhanging canopy of branches is wide or narrow, tree-lined edges impart weather protection, shade, beauty, and a reminder of nature that appeals to almost everyone. A tree-lined, well-landscaped street is more sought out as a place to live than one that is barren. Indeed studies in communities as diverse as Rochester, New York; Athens, Georgia; and Austin, Texas, find that street trees add 5 to 19 percent to the value of single-family houses.[12] The same is true of a community. In Coral Gables, a carefully planned community first developed by George Merrick in the early 1920s, the trees are the element that makes the place distinctive.

Within developing areas, a wise growth town will require the planting of appropriate trees along all new roads. As part of the approval process for commercial buildings, wise communities should require an approved landscaping plan, even if just to assure an evergreen screen for parked cars. Providing an adequate public budget for a communitywide landscaping program will pay off handsomely in citizen satisfaction and in increased revenue from higher property values.

The Purchase of Open Space

Through the tax on real estate, each local community has a source of income that fluctuates but does not stop. In every smart growth town, as gross revenue rises, a portion should be devoted to an open-space acquisition fund. Obtaining the right open space early enough so that it need not be purchased later at a premium is fundamental to assuring the livability, stability, attractiveness, and in some instances the environmental health of a place. When visitors to places of scenic beauty in Colorado were polled, over 90 percent said that rural surroundings, meadows, fields, farms, grazing cows and horses added immensely to their vacation enjoyment. Nearly half warned "that if ranch land continued to be converted into golf courses and condominiums, they would not return. 'The value of scenery far outproduces the value of livestock and hay,' said C. J. Mucklow, a state agricultural extension agent who worked on the survey."[13]

A wise town will do exactly what individuals do when they want to buy something expensive: open a savings account to make the down payment. Several revenue-generating options are available other than using a portion of annual tax revenue: a surcharge can be levied on real estate transfers or a local sales tax can be initiated or increased. These options are politically possible as long as the funds are dedicated to real-property acquisition because the majority of residents in most fifth-migration places are willing to pay for the protection and enhancement of the public realm.

The crucial steps are making the decision, setting the policy (determining not just the objective or goal but the functional mechanism), and getting on with it. In Boulder, Colorado, as a vivid example, residents imposed on themselves in 1967 a 0.4 percent sales tax increase to finance open space. Pleased with the results but dissatisfied with the revenue stream, in 1989 the public reaffirmed the program, voting four to one to raise the levy to 0.73 percent of the sales tax. Now over $13 million a year is generated from this source. Over twenty-five thousand acres of mountain vistas, recreational lands, riparian corridors, wildlife habitat, and conservation easements on farms and ranch lands have been acquired. When U.S. West sought a new location and Boulder was selected, Jim Crain, director of the city's open-space program, observed, "Other communities offered them every incentive under the sun. In the end, they said it was Boulder's amenities that drew them here."[14]

New Jersey and several townships within it serve as current examples of what is possible within a single state. As the fifth migration spread, many people moved from city and suburb deep into the New Jersey farm belt. Simultaneously, people in those areas grew increasingly adverse to sprawl. They responded all across the state by imposing a conservation tax on themselves to purchase open space. By 1998, thirteen counties and fifty-three towns had approved open-space taxes, believed to be the largest number in any one state. The tax takes the form of a 1– to 5–cent levy per year on each $100 of assessed property value. In the middle of that range, a house valued at $250,000 would pay an additional $30 on top of the regular town, county, and school taxes. As mandated by state law, the funds are then segregated into a dedicated trust fund for open space and parks, farmland, development easements, and historic preservation. County programs use tax-generated income to acquire farmland and parks outright and also donate money to towns and nonprofit land trusts for preservation purchases. Throughout the country, to supplement a limited number of state programs, over one hundred perceptive local and county governments endeavored in two years in the mid-1990s to win voter approval for tax increases or bond referenda to buy undeveloped land and to curb urban sprawl, and most succeeded.

In New Jersey the state itself also supports land-preservation purchases. It offers 2 percent loans and matching grants to growing communities through its Green Acres bonding program. Between 1961 and 1997 New Jersey voters approved $1.4 billion for state land-preservation bonds. In 1998 the state's governor, Christine Todd Whitman, for the most part a tax-cutting, staunch Republican, pressed to raise gasoline taxes and car-rental fees statewide in an effort to preserve half of New Jersey's remaining two million acres of undeveloped land. In November 1998 voters approved the governor's plan to raise an additional $1 billion for a land-conservation fund to save vanishing New Jersey farmland and to protect open space from commercial development. Although none are as advanced as New Jersey, other states are moving forward. Georgia legislators are testing a real estate transfer tax to establish a $36 million conservation fund. Minnesota has approved a $140 million bond measure to create parks, hiking trails, and recreation areas and to preserve open space.

Local politicians in New Jersey are beginning to campaign on a platform of saving open space. They marshal the accurate argument that raising taxes slightly for the purchase of open space is a prudent fiscal alternative to the higher property-tax increases that will occur if bigger schools, wider roads, and more police are required. As Phyllis Myers, president of State Resources Strategies in the State of Washington, has said, "There is no question that the governors and the state legislators are listening to the people. When they see that people are willing to tax themselves for this, they recognize that this is an issue that they need to address."[15] Michael Catania, executive director of the Nature Conservancy of New Jersey, believes the open-space taxes are popular because voters view them as voluntary investments that protect a town's character and quality of life. "I think it's a reaction against overdevelopment and mismanaged, or runaway development that doesn't go in the right place," he says. "These taxes give towns control over their own destiny."[16] Reinforcing these remarks, in November 1998 voters approved nearly three-fourths of all land-conservation and environmental proposals in states as geographically and ideologically diverse as Maryland, Florida, Arizona, Georgia, Minnesota, Oregon, Michigan, and Rhode Island.

In individual communities across the country voters have wisely elected to use revenue from real estate taxes, sales taxes, or other types of surcharges to protect their own environment. As early as 1984 residents of Nantucket (Massachusetts) agreed to impose a 2 percent real estate transfer fee to finance a nonprofit local land bank whose twenty-year objective was to purchase critical parcels amounting to 15 percent of the island. The land bank is also able to accept tax-deductible donations of property and cash and is accorded the powerful right of eminent domain as long as two-thirds of the community supports the acquisition. Because of generous community support, when suitable properties become available, the five-member commission that administers the program is able to compete in the Nantucket real estate market. The commission is supplemented by a local land trust, the powerful Nantucket Conservation Foundation, and by private owners who donate local property to other recognized nonprofit, land-focused organizations such as the Nature Conservancy and the Massachusetts Audubon Society. Well over one-third of Nantucket Island has been preserved through the combined efforts of these organizations supported by the wise and thoughtful resident stewards of this fifth-migration growth community.

If it is not already an available option, far-seeing growth towns should join with one another within each state to lobby the legislature for the right to impose a special fee or tax for a dedicated land-acquisition fund, as Nantucket did in 1984. Growth towns on the eastern end of Long Island, including Southampton, East Hampton, and Shelter Island, succeeded in late 1998 in obtaining the right to levy a 2 percent tax on real estate transfers, which was expected to raise $120 million to preserve farmland, open space, and historic places over the next twelve years.

The expenditure of public funds for open space cannot be casual, haphazard, or directed toward the settlement of political debts. Rather, public funds should be devoted to acquiring property that serves one or several compelling functions: protecting the communal water system; conserving critical plant or animal habitat, wetlands, and sensible growth boundaries; providing recreation; maintaining or enhancing the community landscape. Any one of these will benefit all residents in many ways, including adding value to the built environment that far exceeds any expenditure for open space.

Among the largest and most fundamental areas that a wise community will consider for acquisition or control are its critical riparian areas and floodplains, usually referred to as wetlands. Riparian areas, the most productive habitats for plants and animals, are located in the landward vicinity of streams, bays, and estuaries. Here, 60 to 90 percent of spawning and nursery grounds are located for many fish and shellfish species. They are also essential to wildlife, critical zones of eco-diversity, and a bulwark that protects bodies of water from pollution and erosion. Riparian strips along rivers and streams, which should be preserved at least 150 feet back from the water edge, are the most productive of all land corridors. These various uses make riparian areas uniquely valuable as open space rather than as terrain to be built over.

Floodplains, wider than the riparian fringe, are wisely kept uninhabited because they do indeed flood from time to time. In doing so they help to dissipate the energy contained in seasonally high water flows, thereby protecting built-up settlements farther back from the watercourse. Building within a floodplain is always at risk and never sensible. Floodplain land, if maintained as open space, can also be used for seasonal recreation. Beyond a floodplain boundary, upland buffers of no less than fifty feet should be established to shelter plant and animal habitat and to protect wetlands and bodies of water from erosion and nutrient overload.

There will never be enough public money to protect all the forest, farmland, scenic and recreational lands, water catchments, floodplains, and the like that any community might wish to preserve. But public and private funds can be wisely used by targeting key parcels. They can also be leveraged by purchasing easements and development rights rather than the property itself. Regulatory assistance is warranted through restrictive zoning and subdivision regulations. In addition, once the public sector is committed, corporations, foundations, individuals, and local and national conservancies are likely to help with both cash and property donations. For instance, the Audubon Society, working on a national scale, has acquired over five hundred thousand acres, predominantly of wetlands, to preserve bird habitat. The Nature Conservancy, in fulfillment of its broader mission, has acquired or arranged for the preservation of hundreds of thousands of acres of ecologically and environmentally prime property.

Once it has its open-space objectives clear and its priorities worked out, a wise growth town will follow several approaches simultaneously to assure success. It will create an income stream from annual tax and surcharge receipts coupled with the bonding power of local government to ensure a funding basis within sensible debt limits. It will tap county, state, and national public and private programs. It will bring landowners and developers into the process before their plans are hardened into inflexible, publicly released proposals.

In addition to standard vanilla environmentalists, a tremendously valuable, broad constituency supports prime open-space and wetland conservation; this constituency is composed of a wide cross-section of citizens way beyond the expected recreation enthusiasts such as fishermen, hikers, canoeists, and birders. At the local level little will be done to move toward wise community enhancement through open-space and wetland preservation until this broad-based, informed, resident constituency becomes active. The participation of private and nonprofit groups is crucial. Especially effective are nonprofit regional organizations dedicated to open-space conservation. Successful efforts by the Brandywine Conservancy operating around Chadds Ford, Pennsylvania, the Housatonic Valley Association in Connecticut, and the Platte River Greenway Foundation in Denver show how much can be achieved.

Growth Boundaries

The town boundary is an old concept whose formal twentieth-century genesis goes back to Ebenezer Howard's Garden City, first proposed in 1899 in *To-morrow: A Peaceful Path to Real Reform*, republished in 1902 as *Garden Cities of Tomorrow*. Howard's ideal was a series of communities based on a human scale: compact and diverse groupings of thirty thousand people living on sites of a thousand acres, each surrounded by and consequently embedded within a natural or agricultural greenbelt of five thousand acres.

Even if such idealized, well-planned, compact, continuous, and contiguous development can never be achieved, I believe that a well-managed place must decide where building stops and open space begins. If a community acquires an edge, a limit, it will become a more desirable place. It will also be able to build, support, and sustain a recognizable center, as vividly illustrated by the successful experiment begun in 1979 in Portland, Oregon, and more recently continued in Seattle. In Portland, two basic strategies were implemented. With notable help and pressure from 1,000 Friends of Oregon, an effective, progressive statewide group, a state-mandated Urban Growth Boundary was drawn. The Urban Growth Boundary is a mapped circle around the city center. Beyond it a preponderance of open space is required—forest, farms, and open land of various sorts. Then, a light-rail transit system and supportive zoning were created to guide development of a well-planned, relatively dense centralized community inside the circle. Even though over 250,000 people moved into Portland between 1980 and 1997, the designated urban area expanded barely 1 percent, and the adjacent areas remained generally open. Two percent more of the town's total area was open for development in 1997, a concession to local developers. Portland is widely recognized as one of the few cities in America that has tried since the 1970s to constrain and direct its own growth, to avoid sprawl, and to ensure continuation of a dynamic and healthy central core.

The Portland initiatives have worked. With the most aggressive growth-management measure in the country, Portland found a way to limit sprawl without reliance on costly land-acquisition programs. In spite of lawsuits, political pressure, and predictions of impending disaster from developers and commercial interests, the city and its region have been healthy. People and employers who give prime importance to the quality of life are attracted. Commenting on Portland and Oregon, where they have over nine thousand employees, Bill Calder, a spokesperson for Intel, the pre-eminent computer-chip manufacturer in the world, observed, "This is where we are headed worldwide. Companies that can locate anywhere they want will go where they can attract good people in good places."

Development boundaries serve multiple desirable purposes, especially if regionally coordinated. A network of parks and natural spaces can contain bicycle and hiking trails, wildlife refuges, and animal migration corridors, all linked while simultaneously separating nearby communities. Linear corridors once devoted to rail lines or currently reserved as utility rights-of-way may be enveloped within nondevelopment boundaries. The rails-to-trails movement, spurred by the Rails to Trails Conservancy, is making great strides in several areas, including reuse of an abandoned twenty-mile rail spur from the Maryland suburbs into Rock Creek Park at the edge of the Potomac River in Washington, D.C. After tortuous acquisition negotiations mediated by the U.S. Department of the Interior, Columbia, Missouri, has turned a 4.3–mile abandoned spur of the Missouri-Kansas-Texas railroad into a heavily used community asset. Regional water retention and recharge are also protected by nonbuild zones. Economically potent uses of the landscape become viable when large-scale forests, contiguous agricultural fields, or livestock-grazing allotments are accorded a place to thrive. Growth boundaries make it possible to incorporate the built community within the most valuable aspects of the aesthetically pleasing and commodity-producing landscape.

CHAPTER NINE

Smart Public Policy

MANY DIFFERENT INITIATIVES of the sort already discussed stimulate the thoughtful evolution of a smart community. A relatively few underlying policies can tie them
together. These general policies sound simple. And they
are. But following them in the midst of the tumult raised by competing
interests in many growth towns is not.

Rationalize the Planning Process

The federal government used to appeal to voters by cutting taxes without
cutting expenses. Inevitably, gigantic deficits occurred. This was "solving"
one problem by creating another. The national government has come to
realize that this is exactly what ought not to happen. Managers of a smart
community will come to the same realization. They will not attempt to
solve one problem by creating another. An example of such a misguided,
shortsighted approach long endorsed by quick-fix advocates is trying to
alleviate center-city traffic by widening streets. Another example is trying
to reduce traffic congestion in town by building more highways. Wise
towns can avoid these kinds of common mistakes by being more rational

in the enactment of comprehensive planning and then by monitoring the process.

THE PLANNING BOARD

In most places, planning-board members are, at the end of the day (literally), volunteers who devote long evenings to meetings. They are usually residents appointed by the town's chief executive. They may or may not possess appropriate qualifications. There is a problem when the political party in power uses these jobs as rewards. There is an even greater problem when members of the planning board possess conflicts of interest, especially when a conflict is undisclosed.

A smart town will have at least minimal criteria for appointing or electing planning-board members. Each member should reside in a different geographical area so all sectors of town are represented. In addition, each member should bring some relevant expertise to the table—not necessarily professional training, but at least some related knowledge and awareness. Ideally, there should be diversity of age, gender, race, social background, and economic status to reflect the makeup of the community.

The term *planning board* is itself a misnomer. This board, a review body, is generally not empowered to make communitywide planning decisions. Rather, it simply reviews applications to assure compliance with existing regulations. As a result, odd as it may seem, in most places, no one is really planning. Even when a paid staff of government employees works as a planning department to support the planning board, this staff may or may not include anyone responsible for thinking about a town's future and planning for it. In many locales, especially fast-growing ones, the planning department is preoccupied with processing paperwork. As a consequence, it is the rare community these days that has a fresh, up-to-date plan produced by thoughtful local people and supported by reasonable and relevant research. Reform of community planning is needed across America. The system that has evolved no longer serves most places well.

Imagine what could be accomplished if the planning board formed a committee on future directions and if this committee reached out to obtain private-sector knowledge. A new kind of committee composed of local private architects, planners, landscape architects, environmentalists, lawyers, civil engineers, academics, and allied professionals might be asked to conceive, monitor, and update periodically a wise blueprint for community evolution. Members would join with town officials such as the mayor, the director of planning, the superintendents of highways and parks, and the chairs of the planning board and the zoning-appeals board to develop an outline of town goals. Based on these goals relevant policies could be initiated, rules agreed on, laws proposed, and perhaps even a comprehensive plan derived for citizen scrutiny and eventual approval.

Most towns have a valuable reservoir of qualified help among residents not serving on the planning board. Local planning can be greatly assisted by borrowing their skills. A wise place will not ignore the private, volunteer expertise that will be eagerly devoted to assisting town government if requested in a serious and sensitive way. Overlooking this asset is wasteful, a mistake made by unwise public leaders. Wherever such a special group is assembled, as one has been from time to time in various communities including East Hampton, it contributes meaningfully. Most professionals who are residents are willing to contribute time to and be involved in the management of a town's land resources.

Community Planning Teams

A wise community, if it has the funds available, will also tap into nonresident expertise available through professional organizations. Expert panels need not be invoked only by planning boards or other agencies of government. In numerous places they have been convened by foundations, private interests, and partnerships between local government and the private sector. As a service, each of the three major national professional organizations most concerned with the quality of the built environment—the Urban Land Institute (ULI), the American Institute of Architects (AIA), and the American Planning Association (APA)—organizes short-term, intensive studies on behalf of requesting communities. Specialized nonprofit organizations such as the Sonoran Institute in Tucson have also responded to requests for expert planning services and "visioning sessions." The first ULI volunteer team was assembled in 1947; the AIA sponsored its first expert panel study in 1967; and in 1995 the APA began offering its version of expert planning panels, "community planning teams."

A typical community planning team, which usually convenes in a town for three to five days, is composed of out-of-town planners, architects, landscape architects, and other relevant volunteer professionals as well as interested local citizens with diverse backgrounds. The formal charge of each team includes (1) identifying the broad range of local groups whose cooperation is needed for a successful planning effort, (2) helping those groups formulate a common vision, (3) working with the groups to develop a multiyear work program, and (4) evaluating the work program as carried out over the next two to three years.

This laudable process, if tackled by the ULI, AIA, or APA, usually costs $50,000–$80,000 over the study and evaluation period. If funds are not available, it may be possible to complete a similar job right at home using local talent if it is available. Local people know what is feasible, what some of the ancillary issues are, who the important players are, and what ideas have already been rejected. To be optimally effective as a local endeavor, this process must involve the right capable people in the first place. Participants should not be only the obvious professionals and appropriate town officials. Commercial and entrepreneurial interests within the private sector should be represented by community leaders in finance, retail trade, and residential and commercial development.

The most successful format for a local communitywide planning effort may be to engage a broad spectrum of public, private, and nonprofit organizations and individuals under the guidance of an experienced, informed but nonresident facilitator. Organizations such as the Conservation Fund, which has an ongoing "successful communities program," offer organizational guidance and advice and will even supply a facilitator. At a Conservation Fund workshop in Jackson Hole, the agenda included the following relevant items: an economic and demographic profile of Teton County, values and assets worth preserving (what participants appreciated about Jackson Hole), vision statements about Jackson Hole's future, shared values (common themes among the vision statements), steps toward the future (action items for converting visions into reality), other voices (those who felt excluded), and how participants could get involved in shaping Jackson Hole's future. A community affair, the Jackson Hole workshop, like those held elsewhere, was sponsored by many local businesses; time was contributed by many local residents; and the process was endorsed by most divisions of local, county, and regional government, trade organizations, and media and educational institutions. This format, a publication, and the essential follow-up were dedicated to one proposition: the future should be decided by those who live in the community.

As a result of the Jackson Hole workshop, and in spite of inevitable clashes in viewpoint, participants realized they shared essential common ground—a wish to protect the community's small-town flavor, beautiful scenery, abundant wildlife, and easy access to outdoor recreation. As a result they agreed on a new county and town land-use plan that was adopted five years later; the plan combines local updated regulations with financial incentives to induce landowners to conserve their undeveloped property and to reward developers for clustering houses, setting aside open space, and building affordable housing. The conversation about smart growth goes on in Jackson Hole, as some residents seek more aggressive restraint while others would like to unravel some of the controls. But out of the process have come ways to communicate, ways to change, ways to avoid the unbridled and potentially damaging growth induced by the fifth migration.

The emphasis on local decision making is a hallowed tradition in American community development. But in the past a handful of politically empowered people and financially powerful interests have usually been in charge. Wise growth communities will struggle to achieve a widening of dedicated participation in the process, despite the hazards and complexities involved. Help in reaching this goal is found in new and useful journals such as *Chronicle of Community*, first published by Northern Lights Institute in 1996, the "Partners in Community Stewardship" pamphlets produced by the Sonoran Institute, and the Conservation Foundation's 1990 book, *Creating Successful Communities*. Achieving communitywide planning is a daunting task. It takes time, patience, and determination just to engage a significant portion of private residents and community leaders. Authentic public involvement requires notification through mail and in the newspapers; it entails a public education program and ideally announcements in schools, at religious services, in citizens' organizations, and at public meetings. Only after substantial public interest is aroused can a meaningful "visioning process" take place.

A wisely conceived, successful workshop will produce more than a feasible direction. Its ancillary objectives, right from the outset, must include moving projects forward, bringing otherwise indifferent constituents into the planning process, convincing political leaders about a course of action and emboldening them to follow it, and engaging the local news media. Community planning teams, then, are not only about planning but also about garnering publicity, influencing politics, gathering insight, collecting wisdom, and harnessing expertise.

Monitoring Mechanisms

Monitoring the planning process is different from conducting it. In an astute community, a variety of citizens and citizen organizations will serve as watchdogs of planning and development. Monitors are most often citizen volunteers. At the formal end of the spectrum, these are members of not-for-profit organizations, environmental groups, historic associations, good-government associations, and the like. At times these monitors are also advocates, an ambiguous role of which all concerned must be aware. If formal monitoring is undertaken by an organization, a community report card should be prepared periodically that details noticeable trends and measures them against locally set benchmarks.[1]

The local press and sometimes regional publications are also effective formal monitors of the planning process. Planning is news, and planning is political. It always affects substantial numbers of people and their assets. However, the local press is not necessarily an objective or even reliable monitor. As much as any lobbying group, it may be an advocate, even on its news pages.

There is good reason to monitor the planning process: as an understandable professional predisposition, planners tend to favor growth and are likely to automatically identify the public interest as consistent with growth. Just as architects and engineers benefit from new development and the growth that it brings, most members of the planning profession work in a political and economic context that aligns them with what might be called the growth machine. Most planners' métier in recent years has been formulating regulations that stimulate growth, often in the most unappealing ways, such as promoting freeways and overpasses, high-density development, and the expansion of water and sewer mains out into the open landscape. A carefully constructed San Diego study conducted in 1989, for instance, revealed that although professional planners are eager to draft ordinances that regulate growth, they are less inclined than the general public to endorse these measures. Planners' key role for the most part is to accommodate growth and to facilitate new development and redevelopment because they recognize that "job prospects, security and advancement and also consulting contracts depend upon the continuous expansion of developed space that typically results from increases in population and economic prosperity."[2]

Outside the planning profession and, I believe, in large measure in response to the beginning of the fifth migration, a wider perspective has developed. As citizens in selective fast-growing communities began to seek growth limitations to protect their environmental and fiscal resources, the 1973 Rockefeller Task Force on Land Use and Urban Growth discovered that "today the repeated questioning of what was once generally unquestioned—that growth is good, that growth is inevitable—is so widespread that it seems to us to signal a remarkable change in attitude in the nation."[3] While this environmentally and socially advanced task force was coming to its own conclusions, specialists in tracking the attitude of planners concluded that "the planning profession's response to the idea of limited growth was slow and cautious, if not outright hostile."[4]

Recognize That Infrastructure Precedes Development

Often in growth towns sprawl subsumes the land and overbuilding inundates established areas before adequate infrastructure—roads, utilities, public facilities—and open spaces are even planned, much less created. When the problems are finally noticed by disillusioned residents, it is often too late or too expensive to correct them.

To deal with infrastructure properly, a town must wisely manage its capital budget, while making appropriate demands of developers. Five-, ten-, and even twenty-year financial plans need to be set up and then, as prices change and revenue fluctuates, periodically revised. Each town must determine its own safe level of public indebtedness, just as a sensible family manages its own budget. Too much debt makes a place depend upon high-volume growth, a sure formula for boom and bust. Planners must accurately and honestly forecast new development and the net revenue that it will cost or relinquish to the public purse. They must then correlate these figures with wishes for future growth and set a desirable pace, rather than letting the pace be dictated by unwisely assumed debt, as discussed below. Developers, too, must be required to carry a reasonable share of the infrastructure burden before being awarded the right to proceed. Giving away the store to appeal to private interests that request fast growth is a sure way to increase the probability that eventually few customers will be around—and maybe no store.

Ignoring existing infrastructure maintenance and upgrade is another folly. As a single example, consider Massachusetts. In the early 1990s, 74 percent of road miles in the state were declared "deficient" and 47 percent of the bridges "substandard," with over 19 percent classified as "functionally obsolete."[5] As with deferred home maintenance, eventually the cost of repairing infrastructure will be high, or abandonment will be necessary.

As the timing of growth is crucial in a wisely managed town, controlling infrastructure is the best mechanism for ensuring that growth takes place on the community's own schedule. Pioneering efforts were made in managing growth through timed infrastructure planning in Ramapo, New York, in 1969, and in 1972 in Petaluma, California. These significant first initiatives in this thorny but crucial aspect of community management paved the way for later, less cumbersome efforts. As these first excursions into timed growth are innovative and instructive, I will describe the Petaluma initiative in some detail.

When Highway 101 was redesigned and rerouted in 1956 as a freeway, Petaluma became a suburb of San Francisco, forty miles to the south. In 1969–1970, 2,280 people moved to Petaluma, up over 100 percent from the previous year. In 1971, 891 housing units were built, a large increase from 59 the year before. The next year nearly 1,000 units were proposed. The town was alarmed at the consequences of this sudden spurt of growth: double sessions in schools, large classes, inadequate parks and playgrounds, insufficient sewage-treatment capacity. As a result, Petaluma's planning department organized moratoriums on rezoning and land annexation.

In 1972, after a year of public discussion and considerable controversy, the town limited new housing construction to five hundred dwelling units a year for each of the next five years. Through this plan Petaluma hoped to retain its small-town character, to create a permanent greenbelt, and to encourage infill of undeveloped land in central areas. The unusual methods selected to control growth came to be known as the Petaluma Plan, which is still in effect and still popular. Each year housing developers compete for the right to supply the five hundred units. Proposals are judged by a residential-development board. Each application has to conform to the city's comprehensive plan and to its environmental-design plan. Each submission is then rated with regard to specific criteria in two general categories: (1) availability of public utilities and services, and (2) quality of design and contribution to public welfare and amenities. I list below several of the Petaluma criteria that would be useful in the management of other growth towns. Any community can incorporate some of these into its own planning, zoning, and development procedures. Here's what is evaluated with respect to utilities and public services:

- The capacity of the water system to provide for the needs of the proposed development without system extensions beyond those normally installed by the developer
- The capacity of sanitary sewers to dispose of the wastes of the proposed development without system extensions beyond those normally installed by the developer
- The capacity of the drainage facilities to adequately dispose of the surface runoff of the proposed development without system extensions beyond those normally installed by the developer
- The ability of the fire department to provide fire protection according to the established response standard without the necessity of establishing a new station or requiring additional major equipment at an existing station
- The capacity of the appropriate school to absorb the children expected to inhabit a proposed development without necessitating adding double sessions or other unusual scheduling or classroom overcrowding
- The capacity of major streets to provide for the needs of the proposed development without substantially altering existing traffic patterns or overloading the existing street system
- The availability of other public facilities (such as parks and playgrounds) to meet the additional demands for vital public services without extension of services beyond those provided by the developer

These are the criteria for quality of design and contribution to public welfare and amenities:

- Harmony of the proposed buildings in terms of size, height, color, and location with respect to existing neighboring development
- Amount and character of landscaping and screening

- Efficiency of traffic circulation, on- and off-site traffic, safety, privacy
- Provision of public and/or private useable open space and/or pathways along the Petaluma River or any creek
- Contributions to and extensions of existing systems of foot or bicycle paths, equestrian trails, and the greenbelt
- Provision of needed public facilities, such as critical links in the major street system, schoolrooms, or other vital public facilities
- Orderly and contiguous extension of existing development as against "leap-frog" development
- Provision of units to meet the city's goal of adding 8 to 12 percent low- and moderate-income dwelling units annually

To be approved, each proposed development must attain a minimum score on these criteria. The top-scoring proposals are further analyzed to ensure that every part of the community receives some new development.

This system established a level of bureaucratic control that was understandably resented by many land sellers and housing developers. The construction industry had little sympathy for a plan that forced a reduction in annual housing starts and that also involved a lot of red tape. The industry went to court—and came out the loser. After long hearings and one court reversal, the Petaluma Plan was upheld. The main thrust of many differing state and federal court decisions regarding the legality of controlling growth is this: the ordinance must attempt to meet anticipated problems and must not be deliberately discriminatory.

The Petaluma Plan's impact on both housing and land values was not surprising, but it is instructive. When it became difficult to obtain building permits, many fine Victorian houses in the older parts of town were rehabilitated. With the annual supply of new housing limited, the value of existing houses increased more rapidly than it would have otherwise. It became easier to sell a house and at a higher price. At the same time, bureaucratic procedures and administrative delays raised development costs by as much as $3,000 to $4,000 per new house.

The impact on the use and value of undeveloped land was equally clear. Suddenly, development of open land became linked to public expenditures, design analysis, and social priorities, all filtered through a review and planning procedure. As total annual development was cut back by about 50 percent, there was roughly a 50 percent reduction in annual land consumption. The accelerated land conversion of prior years was reversed. When much of the vacant land could not meet utilities and public-service criteria, scattered building activity beyond the greenbelt was curbed. Since 1972 the community has grown in a fairly compact way, while government expenditures for infrastructure and community facilities have been minimized. However, by late 1998 Petaluma had attracted fifty thousand residents and was plagued by sprawl outside the growth-limit area. As a result, city officials are determined to establish a new twenty-year plan for an expanded urban growth boundary and at the same time to promote a mixed-use redevelopment of the still-languishing central area spanning both sides of the Petaluma River.

Other innovative growth-town experiments relate infrastructure availability to the right to develop raw land. Boulder, Colorado, for example, protects its scenic vistas through a 1990s' plan designed to cluster growth near existing infrastructure. In Maryland's affluent Montgomery County, planners have established a program to manage new growth by transferring development away from scenic agricultural areas. More and more frequently, wise community policymakers understand that population growth must be accompanied by wise infrastructure, open-space, and other relevant policies or the quality of community life will be diminished. Although no single approach is dominant, the short review course on the subject is this: within a desirable community, if infrastructure is extended, population growth will follow, so plan in advance for it. New development first follows the roads and the electric wires. Later, if sewers and underground water lines are built, much greater density will result. Because utility companies and sewer and water authorities profit as more people are put on the system, they will be relentless in arguing for extension, for greater supply, for stimulated development. To resist requires substantial coordination and education.

Coordinate Efforts of the Private and Public Sectors

Community planning as a battle—between the public and private sectors, between maverick individuals and special-interest groups—is outdated and yet is still prevalent in many growth towns. Difficult as it is, in the wisest growth towns, public officials, nonprofit organizations, and private residents must make every effort to collaborate. Like the managers of a successful business, a community must develop a shared vision of its future if it is to have an optimal one. To arrive at this vision, which ought to incorporate community priorities as varied as promoting a growing economy, protecting natural resources, and preserving historic character, public and private power orbs must figure out how to adjust and to integrate their aspirations.

The private sector cannot build a successful town without considerable and continuous help from the public domain. The converse is just as true. The Central Park Conservancy in New York City provides a good example of how citizens' groups and municipal agencies can work together. Thanks to the financial and managerial efforts of the not-for-profit Central Park Conservancy, working closely with the Parks Department, Frederick Law Olmsted's and Calvert Vaux's scenic walkways, playgrounds, and natural areas have been revitalized. The Conservancy has been so effective, in fact, that management of Central Park has been turned over to it by the City of New York. In San Francisco, community groups and nonprofit organizations together with city agencies are responsible for the revitalization of the Yerba Buena Park area.

Such collaboration has also succeeded in numerous other places. In California the State Coastal Conservancy has worked with citizens' groups and small nonprofit agencies to realize projects that benefit the environment along the California coast. In one instance, the Conservancy created a partnership with a local PTA to open a small coastal park. In numerous other instances state and local governments have worked with local land trusts and residents to protect the environment by establishing private conservation easements over sensitive lands.

Business improvement district (BID) organizations are perhaps the most common and well-tested formats for public-private partnerships. There are approximately 1,200 BIDs in the United States and Canada, and the number is growing. A BID becomes guardian of a specific physical area, usually located within a city, whose property owners have a common interest in, at minimum, supplementing typical government services. Private leaders produce a plan for the area that usually involves enhanced landscaping; more frequent street cleaning; better lighting; more thorough maintenance; greater and more visible security achieved by hiring additional, uniformed personnel; and sometimes a range of promotional services such as marketing, advertising, and tenant recruitment. This group also works out a management and personnel structure, usually by founding a nonprofit corporation that the city government designates as the operating agent for the BID's area. The municipality, for its part, generally agrees to increase property assessments within the designated area, thereby raising property taxes, and then, as a conduit, turns over all or a large part of the enhanced revenue to the BID organization to support its operations. As a special, limited-purpose property tax is involved, most communities require agreement by one-third to one-half of affected property owners. Some BIDs are even authorized to incur debt by borrowing for capital improvements. Although the manager of the BID is often a professional, and workers who carry out the agreed-upon tasks are paid, there is much volunteerism. Typically board members of the parent nonprofit group contribute their services, as do members of various committees authorized to oversee activities. Nor, these days, are BIDs found only in their original locale, the central business district. Edge cities are now sprouting BIDs, such as the 1,800–acre commercial center along Mercury Boulevard in Hampton, Virginia. Elsewhere, as in the University City District of West Philadelphia, a variety of educational institutions, neighborhood organizations, and businesses have gotten together. And some industrial zones are also testing the waters, as in the Bunker Hill Special Improvement District in Paterson, New Jersey.

In a wise growth town, I would not be surprised to find BIDs becoming a big idea. They are applicable in small and large places alike, in commercial centers, residential neighborhoods, and institutional settings. They accommodate a wide variety of hybrid financing techniques, all the way from traditional municipal support through tax assessment to complete private support. And they allow for many types and many levels of volunteer efforts by citizens who wish to get involved.

Institute Innovative Tax Policies and Sound Economic Forecasting

A wise town can be identified by the taxation policy it applies to undeveloped land. In a wisely managed community, the real estate tax on open space should be low. This policy announces the objective of maintaining open space and offers public support to do so. The correct rationale is that open space requires no public expenditure for schools, social services, fire service, infrastructure, policing, and the like and is thus reasonably entitled to a low annual tax bill. A further reason for a town to tax its open space at the lowest possible rate is to preserve undeveloped land in its natural state for as long as possible.

The viability of farmland and woodland as productive terrain is prolonged in places that levy real estate taxes based on current rather than future use. In growth towns, when farmland and woodland are taxed as if they had been already converted to housing tracts, shopping centers, or industrial sites, you can expect the potential new use to appear before long and the former owner to take up residence in Florida. A relatively high real-property tax alone may induce a landowner to sell his or her farm, forest, or meadow, thereby accelerating its conversion. Wise tax-assessment practice encourages the economically viable continuation in private ownership of open space, farmland, and forests.

Wise growth towns use a range of other enlightened real estate tax programs to preserve private, undeveloped property at minimal public cost. One well-proven idea is the acceptance of a donation or the purchase by local government of a restrictive easement, a much less expensive approach than acquiring the property itself. If the easement is donated, the owner obtains a federal tax deduction. An easement is nothing more than a clear description of what can and what cannot be done on the property in question, how long this restrictive requirement is to remain in existence, and who is to be holder and enforcer of the easement. The easement "burdens" the property. Title to the property need not change hands. At the very least, in exchange an astute local government will reduce the real-property tax on the burdened land in order to reflect its lower actual market value. As an example, an easement over a one hundred–acre parcel of farmland in the middle of a fast-growing residential area might stipulate that the "burdened" land must remain in agriculture for thirty years. In exchange for the owner's agreement, a well-managed town will assess the property as farmland rather than as more highly taxed developable residential property. At the end of the easement period, the matter can be reviewed.

What is achieved by such an arrangement? For thirty years no houses will be built on this significant parcel of land. The space remains productive. If the land is beautiful and strategically located, perhaps a benefactor will be found to preserve the land in perpetuity. This benefactor might even be an individual or a group of residents who live nearby. Over the thirty years the original owner-family may decide to donate the property to a not-for-profit land custodian, a local land trust, or the town. The arrangement exemplifies the immediate creative use of a sensible, low-cost tax strategy for potential long-term benefit at nominal public expense.

A related incentive aimed at protecting forests and farms is available in a few jurisdictions across the country. Land dedicated to an approved use for a stated period of time, usually at least five years, qualifies for inclusion in a special-land tax district. In this district, real estate taxes are held steady or reduced in acknowledgment of the economic limitations placed on the land. As a result, for example, in an area under pressure to be developed as suburbs, farmland placed in a special district would be assessed and taxed based on farmland values not on its higher potential value as a residential enclave.

Another program with the same goal that is gaining adherents around the county is the public purchase of the development rights associated with targeted types of strategically located private land. Suffolk County, New York, pioneered this concept in the 1970s in its effort to preserve meaningful amounts of top-quality agricultural land within its fast-developing boundaries. In 1994 Peninsula Township, Michigan, became the first Midwest community to embrace a new tax to purchase development rights. Peninsula residents sought to protect farmland, cherry orchards, vineyards, and a farm economy. The tax increase on already-developed property, which amounts to about $80 a year on a $130,000 house, will raise nearly $3 million over fifteen years, enough to purchase development rights to thousands of local productive acres.

Now such programs are even penetrating into the traditionally laissez-faire western states. Routt County in northwest Colorado, near the resort town of Steamboat Springs, became in 1996 the first county in the intermountain West to approve a property-tax increase intended specifically for purchasing agricultural development rights. The county expected to generate about $360,000 a year, and during 1996 it succeeded in leveraging its program by obtaining an additional $430,000 in federal funds. Colorado has created a state-administered entity called Great Outdoors Colorado, which obtains $20 million a year from lottery funds to support the preservation of land.

About twenty-five similar programs exist, all begun since the mid-1980s. Of these, five are in Maryland, six in Pennsylvania, four in New

Jersey, and the rest are scattered principally on the East and West Coasts. The American Farmland Trust, a lobbying group based in Washington, D.C., that charts farmland losses and advocates methods to halt them, estimates that five hundred thousand acres have now been protected in eighteen states by public purchase of farmland development rights. The relative and unfortunate insignificance of this achievement is evident when the acreage protected is compared with the one million acres a year being consumed by urban sprawl.

The time-limited reduction or abatement of real estate taxes (typically for a period of ten to thirty years) for facilities built or renovated in conformance with community objectives is a final example of innovative tax policies. Renovation within a historic district can be covered by such programs, as can warehouse and loft conversions and the construction of corporate office buildings that might otherwise not have been built or expanded. Tax-abatement programs acknowledge the large private capital expenditures involved, the operating profit required, the jobs created, and the leadership offered when parts of the private sector decide to build new facilities in town or to remain in it. Eventually the property returns to full-tax status.

In addition to tax policies, new economic formulas can be used to promote community objectives. One of the best ways that the natural environment can be protected, and will be so increasingly, is to apply innovative economic formulas to questions of feasibility and risk assessment. The economic value of air, water, land, wetlands, forests, agricultural soils, and their ecological balance and contribution to human life should be factored into modern development-feasibility economics. When that happens, the feasibility equation changes. The "replacement value" of a wetland, forest, or watercourse must be appraised taking into account its real present and its future value. When the special value of such areas or resources is converted to conventional economic terms prior to any permitted intrusion, a proposed new development is likely to be forced to shift to a more feasible, more appropriate site.

Plan for and Control Tourism

Tourists, like well-off older residents, spend money in town and don't require most expensive public services; they are, on balance, a big plus. But tourism can have a downside: overcrowding and unbridled commercialism. In addition, a tourism boom may not last; tourists move in waves, sometimes even tidal waves. When tourism is high, demand for housing for service workers may drive up prices and drive out long-time residents. Jobs are often seasonal and low-paying, attracting not family wage earners but transient labor. And whatever tourists come to see may be damaged, especially if it is the natural environment.

Ecotourism, recreational travel to places of special environmental interest, is a major growth industry in America. Many places that qualify as fifth-migration growth towns attract in the first place because of their outstanding natural and environmental resources. The fastest growing counties in Colorado, Montana, and Wyoming, for example, are adjacent to Yellowstone and Grand Teton National Parks. Since the mid-1970s annual visits to these and other national parks have increased by forty million. Recreational use of wilderness areas has increased sixfold since passage of the Wilderness Act in 1962.

The economic contribution of such high-volume tourism will be recognized by a thoughtful community. Consider these random indications. Wildlife-related tourism now attracts over one hundred million people a year and generates $60 billion a year in revenue. One subsector, bird watching, brings half a million to several million dollars to every community with a nearby national wildlife refuge. Fishing alone, the favorite recreational activity of American men, brings in over $25 billion annually.

However, in places with great tourist appeal, if seasonal gridlock and overdevelopment are not controlled, tourists will eventually go elsewhere. This outcome may be considered desirable in some communities, by some residents. But unless there is a communitywide consensus on the matter and unless declining tourism becomes a recognized objective, a wise growth town will set guidelines to monitor and to regulate tourism.

What are possible and proven ways to handle the damaging aspects of successful tourism? All involved know that access is crucial if attraction is to continue. But those responsible have seen the ravages of overuse time and time again, as at the Grand Canyon, Blowing Rock Preserve on Jupiter Island, Florida, and Phantom Canyon, Colorado. When crowding is a problem, in order to restrict access to comfortable and safe numbers of people, daily use limits can be instituted. The visitor obtains a higher-quality experience, and the community is not overwhelmed. In addition, user fees and taxes on local sales can help to defray public costs for site protection and maintenance. And limits on population and commercial expansion can smooth out a town's growth process. A smart growth town will not allow tourism to drive out significant local enterprise or compromise local resources such as a beautiful landscape.

Tourism driven by interest in the past has the potential to stimulate town growth on a year-round basis. Historic districts attract not only visitors but also new residents who appreciate the quality control gained through district regulation, including the setting of design standards. Property values within designated historic areas generally increase at a rate of 1.5 to 5 times those in comparable areas outside the district boundary. At the same time, community preservation is achieved, and the tourist economy is augmented.[6] Consider the experience of Fredericksburg, Virginia, the site of four Civil War battles. In the early 1970s Fredericksburg was beset by an economic slump and a deteriorating downtown. In 1972 the downtown was declared a historic district. New incentives were offered for businesses to relocate there and for owners to restore historic facades. Since then a complete renewal has occurred.

For tourism to be a long-term boost to the local economy, specific policies must be set. Regulating tourist-oriented commercial development with a sound land-use plan is crucial. Building-height limitations, scenic-vista protection, sign control, and thoughtful illumination standards all help protect the community's appearance. The types and pace of development of overnight accommodations must be calibrated. The site—building, river course, trail, battlefield—must be sensibly protected if a community wishes to maintain its appeal to visitors and residents, its economic diversity, and its cherished specialness.

Coordinate Growth Management with Regional and State Initiatives

A smart town will coordinate its growth with other communities in its own region. Regionwide issues such as tourism, parks, transit, and water supply benefit from intergovernmental collaboration. Local control is not threatened. Most regional governmental agencies in the United States are strictly advisory. Smart growth towns recognize that sustained cooperation with other communities in their immediate region will go a long way toward reducing pollution, preserving open space in critical areas, defining community boundaries, enhancing water quality, planning for transportation and communication infrastructure, and reducing overlapping, wasteful, uncoordinated spending on each of these initiatives. Like the Salt Lake City–Provo corridor or the area surrounding the Raleigh–Durham–Chapel Hill research center, new growth regions are finding ways to attack relevant issues on a regionwide basis, as are their trade associations, nonprofit organizations, bankers, and private companies. Within such areas, for instance, highways are no longer simply concrete links; they are the new Main Street of enterprise-clustering entrepreneurial regions. In the wisest places these economic corridors are treated as a shared regional asset with coordinated land management and sensitive planning.

Related and interrelated new business enterprises tend to locate near one another within a particular region. In the past, natural resources dictated enterprise location; today, many firms rely on related technologies, university clusters, or similar manufacturing processes, and so they locate and expand in close proximity to one another. Their spin-off ventures remain nearby too. Think of Silicon Valley and the massing of digital-technology companies there. The Institute of the Future South in its white paper *The Entrepreneurial Opportunity* identified other emerging regional clusters that are growing up across the United States: optics in central Florida; digital technology around Austin, Texas; film and television production near Orlando, Florida; computer software around Portland, Oregon; and banking services in the Charlotte, North Carolina, region.[7]

This kind of interrelated regional growth in the private sector should be paralleled by new ways of managing within the public sector. Minneapolis–St. Paul, perhaps the most advanced area in America with respect to intergovernmental regional links, serves as a model of city-centered regional cooperation. The Metropolitan Council's mission is to coordinate the planning and development of the Twin Cities area, with more than five thousand square miles, 275 local government units, and over 2.4 million people. It focuses on physical development, transportation, and social programs.

To the despair of many in the suburbs, it is increasingly evident that the interests of suburb and core city are also intertwined. Upper Darby, Pennsylvania, just outside west Philadelphia, serves as a typical example. There the drastic decline in the city has seriously affected the near-in suburb's schools and real estate market. "I guess you could say Philadelphia's problems are moving in," laments District Justice Mary Alice Brennan. It's the same story all across the country. As Myron Orfield, a Minnesota legislator and keen observer of suburban issues, has accurately pointed out, "The irony is that as social and economic problems cross particularly into blue-collar and middle-class suburbs, they tend to pick up speed."[8] As Upper Darby and countless other near-in suburban communities struggle, they come to realize that they do not possess basic resources such as downtowns, historic districts, universities, and cultural institutions, which are so often used to help revitalize failing districts within big cities. A growing number of policy and economic-development experts now recognize that near-in, middle-class suburbs have more in common with core areas of their nearby central cities than their first inhabitants, who fled the city, ever wished to be the case. Efforts are under way in many metropolitan areas to achieve regional cooperation, although resistance within the suburbs to this "new regionalism" is substantial. For their part, the cities have little or no power over the suburbs nor a strong constituency in Congress devoted to regional solutions to urban-suburban problems.

However, a wish to be included in regional-management opportunities is increasingly evident in alert fifth-migration growth towns. These communities recognize that their own interest is at stake and that they will likely benefit from thoughtful control of a regionwide resource such as a national park, a watershed, or a significant river valley. Consider, for example, the stunning sweep of the Hudson River valley, which extends from Waterford in upstate New York to Battery Park at the tip of Manhattan island. Within these three million acres are twelve counties and hundreds of communities. Not until the late 1980s, however, did small-scale coordinated efforts begin. Genuine regional cooperation did not occur until 1991, when the Hudson River Valley Greenway Act was passed by New York State. Today, as a result, the Hudson River Greenway, operating through the Greenway Communities Council (for planning) and the Greenway Conservancy (for implementation), is making an enormous difference in community after community along the Hudson River. Advocacy for their collective interests has attracted significant funding from both New York State and the federal government, which has designated most of the Hudson River valley as a National Heritage Area, a new type of National Park Service entity. From these two sources, it is expected that in the first decade of the twenty-first century as much as $25 million will be made available to local governments and not-for-profit organizations for trail development, waterfront planning, open-space purchase and protection, historic preservation, tourism promotion, and agriculture protection.

Through its contacts in all the contiguous communities involved and its reach into the myriad agencies of government with jurisdiction in the area, the Hudson River Greenway, besides assisting individual communities, is enabling many types of related multiple-town and joint community efforts. A two hundred–mile walking-hiking system is evolving. A bike trail is winding its way from Manhattan to Albany. Linked campsites and boat launches are emerging. In addition, the Hudson River Valley Landmarks Alliance has been formed and recognized by the National Trust for Historic Preservation. It coordinates private, local, state, and federal activities and opportunities at fifty-six different historic sites.

As a result of another sensible form of regional coordination, relief may be on the horizon from gridlock in some national parks and the development assault on fast-growing gateway communities along their edges. Under the National Parks and Recreation Act of 1978, each national park was required to assess its capacity to accommodate visitors overnight comfortably and to provide parking for day and extended-visit vehicles. Each of the 375 national parks was expected to develop a general management plan that includes goals for visitor accommodation and preservation of natural resources. By the end of 1997, twenty years later, only half the parks had completed their plans. Apologists for the National Park Service, including private planners working on this mandate, claim that budget and staff constraints explain the long delays. However, the good news is that in many instances the plans include growth-management initiatives for adjacent areas outside the boundaries of the parks, especially in the nearby gateway communities that are so heavily affected by tourist interest and real estate development pressure. Increasingly, gateway communities are viewing themselves and being recognized in regional planning operations as an integral part of the park experience. Today, most gateway communities embrace this coordinated approach. Others, less wise, may be unwilling to adopt design standards, growth limits, water-conservation programs, or land trusts to protect their own physical environment.

Work going on in the vicinity of Estes Park in Colorado illustrates the cooperation that is now gaining momentum between some national parks and their surrounding fifth-migration communities. Planners for Estes Park have identified and mapped the most environmentally important parcels all along the park's edges. They are working with neighboring communities to fulfill goals within these various places such as maintaining scenic vistas and wildlife corridors, preventing fire, retaining access to trails across private land, and reducing pollution. These sensible measures are possible because Estes Park and surrounding Larimer County agreed in 1996 to unify their zoning and density regulations regarding the park boundary, thereby enabling adoption of a comprehensive plan for the thirty-two-square-mile Estes Valley.

Other promising efforts have been initiated around national scenic treasures such as Yellowstone, Yosemite, Rocky Mountain National Park, Mount Rainier, Zion National Park, and Alaska's Sitka National Historical Park. One of the most extensive collaborations, the Greater Yellowstone Coalition, founded in 1983, promotes coordinated planning for the park as a single ecological area by sixty community organizations and conservation groups within its eighteen million–acre region. Included in the purview of this enormously ambitious example of coordinated regional planning are three national parks, seven national forests, the Wind River Indian Reservation, and about 3.5 million acres of private land. Inside this territory, as a result of the Coalition's work, energy, and good public relations, ranchers and others have donated conservation easements on 250,000 acres.

Statewide mandated planning has also stimulated regional coordination. To improve transportation, environmental quality, or land-development practices, since 1970 fourteen states have adopted some form of growth-management policy. Coordination within each region usually requires a new overview organization, which unfortunately creates another layer of government. Mandated statewide planning has an uneven record. But it is surely here to stay, and it does further interjurisdictional collaboration and cooperation.[9]

Promote Job Diversity

Throughout the history of settlements in America, reliance on a single employer has led to a bitter experience. In the worst case, communities fail. Mill towns, mining towns, company towns, and single-industry towns, as proven by long experience, are each at risk. In less dramatic instances, after the primary employer collapses or moves away, a long, harrowing struggle to diversify follows. Consider the impact when Louisiana-Pacific closed its waferboard mill in Kremmling, Colorado. The consequences seemed so dire that residents could not at first envision a future. Town manager Bill Koelm observed that the shutdown was "kind of equivalent to the Martians landing in town square."[10] This shock eventually led to new long-term plans. Residents formed an economic-development committee that conceived a plan intended to nurture an environmentally sound, diversified economy. The result was Kremmling's Vision for the Future, an ambitious set of twenty-one projects ranging from a new motel to a ranching museum to scenic bikeways.

Anaconda, Montana, had to deal with another legacy of a single-industry economy: the need to clean up after the company leaves. Once known as the "richest hill on earth," the town was designed to serve what was then a state-of-the-art copper smelter. When the last copper-smelting operation closed in Anaconda in 1980, it left behind, in addition to thousands of unemployed workers, a giant smokestack and a landscape strewn with a century's worth of hazardous waste. Nowadays, the town is placing its hopes on attracting tourists. The key attraction is a $10 million golf course owned by Jack Nicklaus and others that will have an industrial smelting theme and feature sand traps that are actually slag traps containing black, granulated mining waste.

Smart towns will learn from places like Kremmling and Anaconda and decide to promote job diversity. Town managers will structure incentive programs after determining which jobs and industries are desirable and should be targeted for recruitment. To appeal to new businesses, towns must ask logical questions and answer them candidly. What natural assets within the community are attractive? What community policies, such as tax incentives and relevant zoning, will make recruitment of new entrepreneurial organizations possible? Is the communications infrastructure up to date? Is the cost of living in town reasonable, and how many new people is it desirable to accommodate over a period of time with new residential construction? Are local financial institutions and private entrepreneurs interested in helping? What regional assets are available? What types of new companies have been already successfully recruited or expanded in the region? What community benefits above and beyond future tax revenue should be sought? Desirable companies will be attracted through town-provided public-relations efforts, tax-incentive programs, infrastructure preparation, and maintenance of a state-of-the-art communications system.

Provide and Support Recreational Opportunities

One of the greatest attractions of a place these days is the availability of recreation above and beyond near-by obvious natural amenities such as beaches and mountain slopes. Smart growth towns will incorporate into their planning the widest imaginable range of recreation. Available but often unexplored sites include neglected lots that can be converted into sports fields or community gardens, old rail lines that can be converted into trails, waterfront areas abandoned by industry that can be redeveloped for multiple uses, coastal estuaries that are preservable as wildlife sanctuaries, and unkempt and crumbling park facilities that just need upgrading.

Ambitious towns will also seek to promote themselves and attract citizens through the draw of organized sports. Teams on all levels, from professional franchises down to informal seniors' leagues, will be given priority. Failing as well as prospering communities have long recognized the attraction of professional sports and their importance as an instrument of city growth and development. Think of the numerous stadiums, rinks, superdomes, and professional golf courses built in recent years in and around cities, often as a part of community public relations and economic development.

Smart growth towns, however, also recognize the appeal of casual, amateur sports. These activities are so important to residents that citizens voluntarily organize the events on their own. Adult leagues for soccer, touch football, baseball, and basketball are pervasive. Tennis and especially golf, while less widely popular, are nevertheless enjoyed by increasing numbers of people. What is needed—almost all that is needed—for amateur sports to become a part of community life is a place to play. Well-located terrain set aside for the use of amateur sports enthusiasts is a critical amenity that wisely managed and well-planned communities provide.

In the traditional planning of American communities, adequate space for public recreation has usually been neglected. Even the commons or central square in eastern-seaboard colonial towns was intended for the grazing of livestock rather than for use by people. Although prior to the fourth migration a few communities, such as New Orleans, New York, San Francisco, and Chicago, allocated generous space to large, public recreation areas, even the most advanced communities no longer find it possible to plan and develop big parks that offer playing fields, skating rinks, carousels, swings, slides, zoos, arboreta, and golf courses. In one of the most pitiable comments on our time, large-scale open municipal spaces have become too hospitable to criminals, incubators of trouble, and therefore dangerous.

At the more intimate scale of the small park, most towns—even those now growing rapidly—are equally deficient and shortsighted but for less credible reasons. When large parcels of undeveloped land are being approved for conversion to new residential neighborhoods intended to house hundreds of people, subdivision regulations rarely require land to be set aside for parks. A limited number of wise growth towns, however, including those designed by practitioners of the new urbanism, are beginning to place neighborhood parks, gardens, and trails in the midst of residential areas. The wisest communities will acquire or reserve through regulation well-located, attractive recreation areas in the path of and in advance of new development.

Wherever small parks exist in either residential or commercial neighborhoods, they tend to be appreciated and successful. With London's many residential squares as a model, places like Philadelphia's Rittenhouse Square and New York's Bryant Park, Washington Square, Union Square, and Gramercy Park delight, enliven, and add value to their neighborhoods. Residential neighborhood parks perform an especially valuable social function. Within them, neighbors meet, children socialize and play safely, casual adult conversations are initiated during long summer evenings, people of all ages engage in informal sports activities; small parks do wonders to enhance the quality of life for all nearby residents. The potential for creative use of these spaces is without limit. Sports fields can serve multiple purposes. In some places communal vegetable gardens make sense. Others contain flowers and paths for walking. Elsewhere, small-scale children's recreation areas with swings and slides are mixed in with a basketball court. The use of the space can be changed as the neighborhood changes. But once the space is lost, the option is foreclosed, usually forever. Wise fiduciaries of a growth town's future will be increasingly on the lookout for opportunities to create small parks.

Recapturing neglected areas for recreation need not be expensive. And it is generally not controversial. At the center of many growth towns (and all other communities) are neglected, vacant lots that can be purchased or leased and refurbished at reasonable cost. With little capital and a lot of cooperative volunteer effort, these spaces can be transformed into much used and much appreciated community gardens, play areas, social gathering places. Wise community managers will offer financial assistance to obtain and preserve open space in neighborhoods. Neighborhood parks also attract the support of private foundations and residents' donations. They may even be self-supporting. A nominal neighborhood surcharge attached to the property-tax bill can pay for refurbishment and upkeep. Alternatively, a private property owners' association might take over management, and volunteers can be recruited to maintain the area. When neighbors take responsibility, they become part of a new social group. Shared responsibility is a bond that holds those involved together and intricately committed to their community.

Many other kinds of public recreation spaces ought to be available if a town wants to be attractive to a wide variety of people. Cross-country skiing, skating, bicycling, running, and walking along roadsides attest to the ever-increasing American devotion to outdoor exercise. Elsewhere I have advocated providing walking, bicycle, and multipurpose skating paths as a normal part of road rights-of-way, separated from automobile traffic but going along the same course. Stimulated partly by a new interest in health, youthfulness, and longevity, walking and running are the least expensive and most accessible forms of recreation. And next comes biking, one notch up on the scales of cost and skill and way up there in the fashion department. Americans are looking for safe and pleasant public places in which to stretch out, to limber up, to be aerobic, and to feel the energy surges that accompany consistent and vigorous exercise. This quest occurs right across the age span deep into elderly territory. A smart place will not just take notice; it will figure out ways to create outdoor paths and trails.

There is also an ever-growing quest for year-round, active indoor recreation. At one time the YMCAs provided indoor tracks, basketball courts, and swimming pools. That network is no longer expanding. In many towns facilities are obsolete or even closed. Here again, the schools—expensive facilities strategically located in every community—can play a major role as ideal indoor recreation centers. Hours for public use of the track, basketball court, swimming pool can be set aside. Leagues can be organized by volunteers. After-hours yoga and exercise classes could convene in the gym.

At all levels, the sharing of public spaces for passive and active recreation reinforces the reality that a community is a commonly owned habitat. Using public spaces actively and constructively makes people aware of these areas as their own precious asset. A psychic privatization of public space occurs, an internalized event that assures its quality, presence, protection, and support.

In addition to public recreation opportunities, private nonprofit and for-profit recreational and sports assets are a critical if rarely discussed aspect of growth-town appeal. Private recreation encompasses many activities including club life, sports events, ballet, symphony, and theater. All these opportunities make a place attractive to fifth-migration participants. Private nonprofit clubs are the least discussed and least obvious outlets but are very important. Country clubs, tennis clubs, private golf courses, health clubs, equestrian centers, and the network of men's, women's, and mixed social and business organizations, such as Lions, Kiwanis, Masons, are a part of the reason that wealthy families, business owners, corporate executives, and affluent retirees visit or settle in or remain in a place. Not to be forgotten are special clublike facilities built into sports arenas and now occasionally into theaters and opera houses. The contributions made by these organizations to a town's overall appeal, indeed the public purpose served in the broadest sense, is correctly acknowledged in the real-property tax exemption offered to private nonprofit civic and recreational organizations.

CHAPTER TEN

Private and Nonprofit Initiatives

UNLESS PRIVATE INDIVIDUALS and nonprofit organizations in a town commit energy, time, professional expertise, and financial resources, wise growth is unlikely. In fact, their level of involvement is a key indicator of the progress a particular community may be making toward becoming a smart fifth-migration growth town.

Institutional Contributions

The programs, determination, and leadership of a town's nonprofit institutions reveal a great deal about its capacity to grow wisely. How is the future being conceived in the town's schools, hospitals, and cultural facilities, and who is in charge of them?

EDUCATION

For a place to attract all echelons of the fifth wave from kids to retirees, good schools are essential. Nothing is more crucial to families. Even in Celebration, Florida, it is not design and planning but its state-of-the-art school in central Florida, where quality public education is so hard to come by, that has been the prime attraction for families, who pay a 25 to 40 percent premium for houses there. A wise community will not just attract skilled fifth wavers, it will learn to grow its own.

A wise growth town will have a congenial attitude toward learning at all levels and for all purposes. This attitude alone will help to ensure a satisfied and educated population. Such a town will focus on obtaining good-quality schools, both public and private. It will endeavor to attract community colleges and vocational training centers managed by qualified people. Adult-education programs will be encouraged within the schools and colleges, as well as within nonacademic settings such as museums, libraries, religious institutions, and hospitals. A smart community with a clear vision of contemporary priorities will recognize continuing education as recreation, as an attraction, and as a fundamental service to residents.

An informed, skillfully trained and retrained citizen body is essential if a growth community is to function in a sustained, competitive way. Although much fifth-wave adult education is recreational, there is a basic need in growth towns for continuous job retraining as careers evolve in the fast-changing work scene. A smart growth town will therefore incorporate within its schools good-quality facilities for adult education and specialized evening and after-school vocational programs.

To ascertain how seriously a town views education, various questions must be asked. Are educational institutions planning for the future, and have they adequate financial support and land reserves to carry out these plans? What is the attitude in town toward the first twelve years of school? Do townspeople appreciate and support quality primary and secondary education as a prelude to more advanced education for their children? Or is the school system a perfunctory youth holding tank fulfilling mandated tasks without enthusiasm? Even worse, is the school system rife with discipline problems, indifferent faculty, and even possibly contempt for serious learning on the part of significant numbers of students, staff, and parents? Are the schools overcrowded, out-of-date, and, even more devastating, places in which learning is not respected?

In an enlightened educational program, children will be taught the economic, social, and physical history of their own town. They will learn something about significant community values. The ideas of economic restraint, sound design, and environmental care will be explained in various ways all through grade school and high school. These lessons can be conducted in imaginative ways through participation in town meetings, work days at the town hall, junior committees of nonprofit and public-private entities, field trips, policy briefings, and so forth. A special focus on local issues related to the environment, economics, and government could be used to teach broad principles while exposing young residents to the inner workings of their own community and its relationships to the surrounding landscape. Students may even be encouraged to perform some kinds of community service as a part of the curriculum. The nation's third largest school system, Chicago, requires each student to perform forty hours of public service in order to earn a high school diploma.

Why the local community is so often ignored as a learning laboratory is a mystery to me. If such an opportunity were not overlooked, young people could begin early on to understand the impact they can make as adults in determining the destiny of any place in which they choose to live. Just as important, they would begin to understand a range of view-points about community growth, to encounter some of the inevitable conflicts, and to enjoy some of the positive feelings associated with partic-ipating in the democratic matrices that hold a place together. The out-come would surely be, at minimum, enhanced environmental, economic, democratic, and community literacy. If young people began to imagine themselves as trustees of the environment and as strategically and politi-cally empowered guardians of their town's future, deep social, ethical, and moral values might be shaped sooner and more clearly, at least among those who become interested.

Emphasis within schools and adult-education courses on community-wide issues related to growth, the environment, resource protection, and future development is also a proven way to reduce misunderstanding and friction within the adult population. People from the most diverse back-grounds and with seemingly conflicting interests are brought together in a setting where information and assumptions can be shared.

LIBRARIES

In the ancient world libraries were the repository of all civilization; these invaluable assets were nearly destroyed in Europe during the Dark Ages. In America, until recently libraries were as important to neighborhoods and to communities as religious institutions and schools. Every dignified, proud town made sure it had a well-designed, well-equipped, prominently located library. The library served as an important cultural symbol as well as a necessary adjunct to the school system and as a repository of information sought by ordinary citizens, local businesses, and cultural organizations.

Today the efficacy of libraries as physical establishments is being questioned. Vast amounts of information are available on the Internet or on computer disks. To compete, many libraries are joining the technological age by putting their own resources on computer files and sometimes on line. They are also trying to become user-friendly and appealing to a wide audience, often expanding into lending compact disks, audiotapes, and videotapes.

In a smart growth town, I believe the library will again come to be recognized as a critical community attribute. Books are not going away, and library computer workstations are popular. Much older printed material is not being made available on computers and is increasingly difficult to find in bookstores. And not everyone can or likes doing research on the keyboard and screen or has a quiet place at home to undertake thoughtful writing and reading. In addition, libraries function as a special type of democratic social center where people from all parts of town and from different schools find one another. Wisely managed libraries will be able to serve these functions even more effectively in the future as cyberspace becomes less novel.

In the design and redesign of contemporary library spaces, it is wise to create appealing community meeting places. The library is a natural gathering place for younger and older people who seek a secure but socially neutral environment in which to study or interact. Wise public libraries may begin to offer coffee and light food, much as museums learned to do as they increasingly recognized their role as much more than being a repository of visual material. Barnes & Noble has already figured all this out to great advantage, attracting record numbers of visitors and increasing sales by offering a quiet, safe mini–community center in the midst of its book-lined commercial spaces.

CULTURAL FACILITIES

Cultural facilities and planning for them offer another clue to the quality and viability of a place. More than ever before in America, migration is targeted to places where inhabitants can enjoy art, music, literature, theater, and all the other enriching fare provided by cultural organizations. Traditionally considered nonessential to town growth, in the competition among places for fifth-migration participants today, quality cultural organizations and programs provide communities with a distinct edge, as corporate relocation experts will tell you. So will retirees looking for a place to spend the winter or a place to move to. Entrepreneurs who envision an energetic, agreeable future for themselves, their children, and their employees seek to supplement the ordinary with the promise of the arts. Take the Santa Fe Opera as a case. Its productions draw sell-out houses. It attracts not just visiting and local opera lovers but discerning new permanent residents. New fifth-migration residents of Sarasota boast that their town offers the most and the best live cultural fare in Florida, which is why they moved there. There is a yearning in the spirit of many fifth wavers for a place to live that offers the amusement and enlightenment and pleasure found in cultural pursuits. A community headed for sustained attractiveness will find ways to foster and to satisfy these yearnings.

People also like to participate in the arts on the amateur level. Amateur theater, choral and chamber music groups, and small orchestras spring up in growing places; casual art classes are found in the schools, museums, and private studios. These and many other types of informal cultural offerings for amateurs are manifestations of the vitality of a place and its inhabitants.

Bozeman, Montana, a picturesque fifth-migration growth town of thirty-five thousand residents including the ten thousand attending Montana State University, illustrates this thirst for the arts. With little government support and almost no organized private philanthropic or corporate backing, Bozeman manages to sustain a diverse and vibrant arts community. Its ballet company has operated for more than fourteen continuous seasons and runs a school with 150 students; its Intermountain Opera Company was started in the mid-1970s; the Bozeman Symphony, staffed by seventy-five professional and amateur musicians and an equivalent size choir, plays five concerts a season to nearly eight hundred subscribers; the Museum of the Rockies displays a world-class collection of dinosaur bones; and the Vigilante Theater, now in its seventeenth season, produces only original work. In 1992, with the support of local contributors, the Emerson Cultural Center was inaugurated. It purchased and refurbished an old school building on Main Street. Now its art galleries, seven hundred–seat theater, work space for forty artists, and two cafés create a lively cultural hub. The arts organizations and cultural activities in Bozeman are the fifth largest employer in town. Situated amid awesomely beautiful terrain, Bozeman is far better known as a gateway to the Big Sky ski area and Yellowstone National Park. But its appeal to new fifth-migration residents and second-home buyers is grounded, in addition, in its special nurturing of cultural activities and creative lives.

In urban redevelopment, the arts are now a recognized growth engine. The model for this accelerating movement is New York's Lincoln Center, which broke ground in a blighted neighborhood in 1959. This bold initiative now anchors vibrant entertainment, commercial, and residential revitalization way beyond its immediate West Side neighborhood. This experiment occurred, of course, in a laboratory where a large susceptible population provided ready, built-in demand and where world-class performance organizations such as the Metropolitan Opera, the New York Philharmonic, and the New York City Ballet were capable of providing high-quality and reliable programming.

Since the establishment of Lincoln Center, many communities have found that the arts hold special promise for reinvigorating older urban areas. Even as federal funding for the arts diminished during the 1990s, states, municipalities, foundations, corporations, and private sources rallied. Between 1985 and the late 1990s, towns such as San Jose, Newark, San Francisco, Kansas City, Chicago, Providence, Tucson, Rock Island (Illinois), Cleveland, West Palm Beach, Escondido, Charleston (West Virginia), Miami, and Pittsburgh came to recognize the power of the arts to simultaneously attract and hold people while providing a central focus for successful urban-center revitalization.

The diverse and often imaginative methods used to finance arts-related development in older communities offer instructive precedent to any smart growth town. Foundations, corporations, and individuals are willing to finance not-for-profit cultural, educational, and sports endeavors. In many cases the municipality provides the land or low-cost financing to obtain the land. In some cities, such as San Jose, where 2 percent of the annual municipal operating budget is devoted to public art, a reliable stream of financial assistance is available. In most places, some form of joint public-private organization is created to coordinate public regulation and finance with private programming expertise, experience, and knowledge of the arts.

MEDICAL FACILITIES

All along the human life span, medical facilities are needed. Yet in most places medical services are rather rudimentary. When a community has the good fortune to be the site of a quality medical center or the foresight to create one, it is on the path to continuous incremental growth and to sustained attractiveness. In the complex mixture of attributes sought by fifth wavers, high on the list is quality medical care supported by quality medical institutions. Consider as potential residents of a town just the elderly population of America. People over sixty-five, a group of some thirty-one million, constitute roughly 13 percent of the national population, and the proportion is growing. And further consider that this group possesses a large portion of the discretionary income and private capital in America. On top of that, this is a fluid part of the population, more easily able to and more likely to move than any other group except the young.

A town gains numerous benefits from medical institutions. In jobs and education, medical facilities offer sound opportunities for growth. Research and information spill out into the community in a beneficial way. A quality medical facility creates a sphere of influence through which the place where it is located gains a competitive edge. Some communities have found medical services and distinguished medical facilities their most reliable economic armature. I think of Houston. Without its impressive medical institutions, boom and bust would have taken a more drastic toll when the mid-century oil bonanza collapsed. Throughout the 1980s, as Houston lost thousands of jobs, its massive multifacility medical establishments took up some of the slack, emerging as the largest employer in town and a sustaining economic force. Houston medical institutions serve a vast client population that extends into Central and South America, along the Gulf Coast of the United States, and up through the heartland of the central plains.

CREATIVE USES FOR SCHOOL BUILDINGS AND RELIGIOUS FACILITIES

The schools of America are the largest single consumer of local real estate tax dollars. In the average community, over half of all property-tax receipts are devoted to operating and financing the school system. These taxes are paid by all property owners, including those with no child in school. Tax revolts have been mounted in many growth towns with sharply rising expenditures, and bond issues for school expansion are being defeated in more communities than ever before. Beneath the surface resentment, I believe, is outrage that use of these often expensive facilities is restricted to such a narrow band of the entire citizen base, and even at that they are underutilized. In many places, school is over by mid-afternoon. Then the buildings and grounds become quiet except for selective after-school programs. In the evenings, except in unusual circumstances, schools host no activity whatsoever. In summer months, during long winter vacations, and usually for a period in the spring, school is dark. How have the most expensive facilities in town, the schools, which are supported by the entire resident population, become, in effect, exclusionary institutions, the private domain of a limited number of children and their instructors?

As an alternative, the wisest towns, I believe, will increasingly view their schools—replete with well-kept and sturdy buildings, large grounds, institutional kitchens, extensive athletic facilities, equipped art studios, theaters, workshops, and laboratories—as a community resource. Great advances in public relations and practical management gains will be achieved in places that share these well-equipped and costly-to-operate public facilities with the people who are paying the bill.

A few enlightened programs address the woeful underuse of school buildings. The U.S. Department of Education has made available $40 million in grant money to help set up hundreds of after-school programs in rural and inner-city public schools. In New York City, the Children's Aid Society has inaugurated a program to see that a number of new experimental, prototype school facilities are designed as community centers and places for neighborhood outreach. In other towns, after-school adult classes are held, and in various places the gym and swimming pool and even some of the workshops are shared evenings and weekends with town residents. The YMCA of Greater New York, in partnership with the New York City Board of Education, is working to bring extended services to ten thousand public school children by turning two hundred of the city's underserved public schools into Virtual Y's from 3 to 6 P.M. each day. The Unified School District in Elk Grove, California, has developed Twilight Centers at four large elementary schools. These schools are open year round and offer a variety of evening activities for young people and adults.

Since 1994, the Lighted School Program in Waco, Texas, has kept schools open until 7 P.M. Monday through Thursday to provide activities and services to students and the community. And the St. Louis system uses public schools as evening community education centers that serve forty-four thousand residents each year by offering tutoring, arts courses, recreation, adult classes, and drug-prevention programs. These initiatives, while rare, point the way to great opportunity in every community and should certainly send a signal to alert growth-town managers.

Instead of using their school buildings in imaginative ways, most communities unnecessarily duplicate these facilities. Senior-citizen centers, youth centers, community theaters, and the like are often contained in separate public or quasi-public places with duplicate custodians, duplicate power plants, duplicate bricks and roofs, duplicate insurance, duplicate parking lots, duplicate kitchens and heating plants. Why not, instead, incorporate a senior-citizen center as a wing of the school or encourage sharing of the facility when school is not in session? Why not open up—perhaps even lease space in the summer—to community theater and arts groups? Why not charge the public to see high-quality films on weekend evenings in an otherwise empty school auditorium? An entire alternative forum for public entertainment could evolve right at school, one that would supplement the limited commercial fare available on the outside in many towns. School boards that recognize these potentials will contribute to the wise growth of their communities. It might even come to pass in such places that the tax bill and the next school-expansion bond issue will be greeted with good cheer rather than resentment.

In both schools and local colleges, the opportunity for evening adult education is too often overlooked. And yet there it is: the facilities, the faculty, ample parking right at the door. A trained cadre of teachers who have dedicated their lives to education, who often feel underpaid and under appreciated, would be given a chance to supplement their income and to become involved with adults in town. Every school and every college in America should set up some form of continuing adult education, perhaps bringing in as adjunct faculty experts living in town who would be eager to teach a course, participate in a seminar, or get involved in some other way.

The same approach makes sense for religious institutions, and indeed around the country many have recognized both the need and the opportunity to share their available human and physical resources. A study by

Partners for Sacred Places, a national nondenominational group dedicated to the preservation and effective use of older and historic religious buildings, found that nine out of ten churches housed in pre-1940 buildings provide space for some community program. These range from food pantries to donated-clothing shops, soup kitchens, shelters or other support for the homeless, child-care centers or after-school programs, tutoring centers, summer camps, and sports and art, music and drama activities. The study determined that four out of five people benefiting directly from these programs are not members of the host congregation. The Partners for Sacred Places study attempted to assess the monetary value of these shared services, spaces, staff, overhead, and volunteers. It estimated that each facility provides a community with more than the equivalent of $140,000 per year. As with schools, this kind of community participation is an appropriate use of facilities and a reasonable exchange for the privilege of real estate tax exemption.

Citizen Involvement

Even the most enlightened public authorities cannot do all the work and all the thinking required to convert an ordinary place into a smart community. The private sector must be predisposed to help. A town must be populated by individuals with enough vision and enough courage to lead rather than resist, to lend energy and initiative. The committed and multi-tiered involvement of private citizens is essential.

It is not easy for the private individual who wants to help. Substantial time and energy are required, a good deal of it in the evenings, when most community meetings take place. Surface familiarity with the functioning of the local real estate market is extremely helpful, and genuine familiarity with the rules and regulations that guide local development is essential. Some knowledge of innovative ways to manage growth, such as floating zones, tax credits, conservation easements, and transfer of development rights, can help one suggest ways to move beyond impasses.

To be effective in all but the most unusual instances, individuals must overcome the temptation to be self-righteous and uncompromising. Planning and land use are intensely political endeavors, and, as in all political activity, negotiation, compromise, and trade-offs are routine, although compromise on the most crucial standards should not be tolerated. An interested individual will soon realize that lone-wolf tactics may be fun, but they are not particularly influential. To achieve significant results, building a coalition is much smarter. It then becomes easier to arrange meetings with public officials and with developers in private before the public fireworks. Early discussions can lead to improved development proposals or wiser draft regulations as less posturing is necessary and less face saving is required than in later public meetings.

Citizen participation is not automatically effective or helpful. It can be a waste of time or lead to irrelevant controversy. When individuals or groups assert a narrow self-interest, their contribution may be counterproductive. When a variety of opposing groups insist on vocal promotion of their own limited objectives, one force may cancel out another. In the long run, private participation will be most constructive when it is devoted early on to hammering out a shared vision and agreed-upon goals.

In a public hearing, private individuals, coalition representatives, and advocates of every sort should make a well-prepared, rational presentation, not a long-winded, personal ramble. The information presented should be accurate, up to date, and to the point. Irrelevant personal asides are worse than unnecessary; they sour decision makers. A short, carefully drafted statement should be submitted into the record at the end of the meeting.

Elected leaders of smart growth towns will figure out how to obtain the help of resident executives, economists, engineers, land-use experts, real estate managers, social scientists, and artists. Think of all the talent assembled in medical, educational, and cultural institutions, all the trained, skilled working and retired residents who possess a lifetime of experience. Small, inadequately staffed government agencies in growth towns under tremendous development pressure are especially needy. And even in larger towns government is so busy with the day-to-day that it doesn't have time to ask the right questions about the future, much less begin to prepare for it. Local government might start by setting up a coordinating office staffed by volunteers. This group could create a registry of useful resident talent. Most town administrations don't even know the professional capabilities of potentially useful residents.

A whole sequence of benefits follows from citizen involvement, some direct, some not so obvious. When enough residents get involved, public officials become accountable. And once citizens become involved in policy formation and in monitoring programs and projects authorized by elected officials, they often produce constructive ideas. In addition, involvement affords the committed individual a community presence. Not infrequently, the engagement reveals to individuals something new about their own vision and special interests. As they dedicate time and energy, they come to feel like—and to be—owners, stakeholders in the destiny of a place. Out of the cauldron of citizen organizations, dynamic public leaders often emerge.

Homeowners' associations, which are nothing more than private citizens acting to self-govern the neighborhoods and districts in which they live, are now the fastest growing form of political organization in the country. These associations control the area in which one of every eight Americans resides. Some newly developed communities have so many different private neighborhood and district associations that nearly all local town management is carried out with intense citizen involvement. In Celebration, Florida, a company town in which the last word belongs to Disney, all operational details of town government are under the direction of a homeowners' association, which serves as a surrogate lower-level governing body.

In the future, in the most progressive growth towns—if out of nothing more than self-interest—citizen involvement will infiltrate deeply into town planning and management. More qualified people will be willing to serve on boards; greater attention will be paid to public hearings; and a growing constituency will become involved in long-term planning and resource allocation. Eventually every important public space, roadway, scenic vista, trail system, and watercourse is likely to have its own citizen advocates. The same goes for the historic properties and natural resources in town. In this way, these attributes will be represented and protected by the town's own residents. With attentive involvement by the private realm, important but underrepresented public assets obtain a private constituency, a guardian that understands, advocates, and supports their unique value.

Whatever the specific format for citizen involvement, it constitutes an unusual and valuable means of continuing education. People involved inevitably keep learning and keep teaching one another. They also provide a public forum from which, in the best instances, collective, up-to-date wisdom can be distilled into proposals and action. A thoughtful citizen group is able to transform an individual member's naivete into genuine understanding. Voluntary networking forges links between people across the social, economic, and political spectrums. A free and open exchange of viewpoints from the bottom up is the opposite of citizen apathy, in which people complain of political impotence while idly watching shortsighted, top-down decisions diminish their town. As increasing numbers of residents become interested, community apathy gives way to learning, understanding, and widespread participation. This is the specter that some political leaders fear. And some will argue that it is a prescription for decision gridlock. But I have more confidence than that in the good judgment of the people who get involved.

Nonprofit Resources

Nonprofit organizations dedicated to community improvement have a long history; and they continue to be instrumental in the development of wise public policy and in the protection of community resources.

COMMUNITY-IMPROVEMENT SOCIETIES

Well-meaning matrons inaugurated the first nonprofit community watchdog and enhancement organizations in the United States. Some of these organizations go back deep into the nineteenth century. The Laurel Hill Association, which began in 1853 in Stockbridge, Massachusetts, may be the prototype. By 1880 Massachusetts had twenty-eight associations and Connecticut between fifty and sixty, many in small towns eager to emulate Stockbridge. The original charge was town beautification: planting flowers in prominent locations and caring for trees visible in the public domain. These societies also served to forge patrician, public-spirited social networks for ladies. Teas were addressed by interesting speakers. To help pay for programs and good works, these organizations often sponsored well-attended annual fairs, such as the one the Ladies Improvement Society in East Hampton has sponsored for over one hundred consecutive years. These fairs in and of themselves promoted a feeling of joint interest in the community. Men's community-improvement societies include organizations such as the Lions, Rotary, and less openly the Masons, although these are not commonly thought of as such. Both men's and women's groups serve an important additional function: they provide mentors, models, and an introductory social network for people who move into town and for young men and women growing up there.

These citizen organizations are well positioned to be successful advocates of public space, of civic improvement, of enhancement of the public realm, of doing the right thing. Knowing that all these well-intentioned, well-established, and not easily intimidated people are watching the store can make a big difference in the precise policies that public officials may pursue.

LAND TRUSTS

The land trust is a modern hybrid of the older civic-improvement society crossed with the more recent environmental protection organization. Its focus is typically the preservation of open space, the protection of precious community watercourses, woodlands, and farms. In some cases land trusts not only conserve and preserve but also manage significant open spaces. Trusts may own property outright or purchase or accept development-rights easements over property. Just since the mid-1980s, private conservation groups have protected 2.7 million acres from development—an area about the size of Connecticut—with nearly half protected by easement. During this same time the number of local land trusts in the rural Rocky Mountain region has increased by over 100 percent, with Colorado the clear leader as home to twenty-nine of the fifty-two local land trusts in the Rockies.

At the national level, the Nature Conservancy, the Trust for Public Lands, and the Sierra Club are the well-known newsmakers of the movement. Since the 1940s the Nature Conservancy has been responsible for the protection of 7.5 million acres of especially precious land in the United States and Canada. A community in which one of these nationally prominent land trusts obtains property is being endowed with an enduring, enhancing gift.

However, the big national organizations cannot afford to pay attention to any but the most ecologically significant stretches of terrain. The local land trust and local conservancy must focus on the locally significant in order to step in rapidly, flexibly, and with the resources necessary to protect local parcels of pivotal visual and environmental importance.

The first local land trust was founded more than one hundred years ago in New England, where more than a third of the nation's land trusts presently operate. Hardly a dynamic movement before the 1960s, local land trusts now number more than twelve hundred in America, double the count in the 1980s. Locally managed land trusts are forming at the rate of about one a week. Most possess property that might otherwise have been developed. Some take on an even broader mission. The Vermont Land Trust, founded in 1977 to preserve Vermont's settlement pattern of small villages and hamlets surrounded by farms and managed woodlands, will, for a fee, give towns technical and legal advice and undertake open-space design and land-use planning; it is also available to advise local and regional land trusts. Over time, a successful land trust can make an enormous difference in the quality of its community. Ask anyone who lives on Nantucket or Martha's Vineyard about the most important force that assures the continuing desirability of these islands.

A land trust is a must for any smart community. It serves a crucial function in town besides the direct protection of precious property. It promotes awareness and sometimes even provides direct education through sponsored lectures, conferences, and events. It offers technical assistance and information to landowners about private, voluntary actions they can initiate to conserve all or a portion of their land and still achieve financial goals. Land trusts raise capital to purchase worthy endangered lands outright, or they alert a conservation-minded buyer when inappropriate development threatens. Aggressive local trusts take an interest in the planning for any land to be developed within their jurisdiction. They may also intervene during the land-development approval process to try to protect environmentally precious acreage.

Once a local land trust becomes moderately successful, it is not unusual in growth towns for it to become fashionable. Prominent board members and managers are then more easily recruited. In time, because of its social appeal mixed with its undeniably significant mission, finances improve. Eventually, sufficient assets will be available to purchase property or partial interests in property, such as easements, without depending entirely upon grants.

Land trusts are effective because of their legal status as not-for-profit organizations, a format that allows any individual to make a tax-deductible contribution of cash or another asset, such as appreciated securities. Landowners may make a donation to the trust of property or easements in return for a charitable-gift tax deduction. To trigger the deduction for an easement, the donation must be to a qualified nonprofit organization or public agency for conservation purposes. Donating an easement also allows the owner to maintain title and to use the property in conformance with the easement conditions—for instance, as a ranch or farm. The donor's heirs obtain an estate-tax benefit in the marked-down appraised value of the burdened land. As estate taxes can be as high as 55 percent of value, this considerable benefit is sometimes the primary reason a large property holding, such as a farm or ranch, is kept intact rather than incrementally sold to satisfy estate taxes. If property owners elect not to donate an easement during their lifetime, they may do so by will at death, thereby conserving property and reducing estate taxes. Although land or easement donations to government agencies might accomplish the same purpose, many private owners prefer to work with land trusts and other locally based, nonprofit private organizations. This preference, especially with respect to outright land grants, is based on a fear that government agencies might devote property to unspecified uses, and it would be impossible to stop them from doing so or to regulate them locally. The local land trust is correctly perceived as community-oriented and more likely in its stewardship capacity to adhere to a donor's conditions and wishes.

The growing popularity of land trusts, even in terrain where anything but laissez-faire private enterprise was until recently abhorred, is illustrated by a transaction in Clark, Colorado, fifteen miles north of the tourist-oriented growth town of Steamboat Springs. Pressure from Steamboat Springs for land was gnawing away at ranches and farmland nearby, with developers paying twenty times the underlying economic value of property devoted to ranching. Jay Fetcher, whose still-living father and uncle had bought a ranch many years ago, decided to save it by donating to a land trust the development rights to the 1,300-acre spread. Future estate taxes were cut in half, and use of the land for ranching was assured without potentially opening up family property to public use. The experience proved to be so satisfactory that Fetcher proceeded "to form the nation's first land trust by and for ranchers, the Colorado Cattlemen's Agricultural Land Trust. The idea of ranchers donating development rights to land trusts managed by fellow ranchers spread like wildfire."[1] Since then the National Cattlemen's Beef Association has endorsed conservation easements. Attesting to the popularity and viability of the land-trust notion, cattle raisers and farmers are now openly cooperating with land trusts all across the country to help preserve their productive property and their way of life.

The extraordinary opportunity for local land trusts is apparent if one considers, as an example, the situation in Colorado, where agricultural land is being converted at the rate of some two hundred thousand acres a year. Easements of various sorts, including those donated to land trusts, protect only 3 percent of the ten million privately owned acres. Yet more than half of that acreage is owned by ranchers, farmers, and others who are over fifty-five years old. "We are going to see a major intergenerational transfer," says Lynne Sherrod, the executive director of the Cattlemen's Agricultural Land Trust. "Without estate planning, it could really change the face of Colorado."[2]

Residents of any town who want their community to thrive through the next century must inaugurate a local land trust or, if one exists, must support it. In every wise community people will be interested in participating. In every community leadership is available. And currently operating trusts will provide information about how to get started. Once formed, the local land trust will become an increasingly significant direct and indirect force in setting community planning and development policy. It will also become an important part of the community's social and political network, through which constructive influence is exerted and enlightened town leadership emerges. And the difference in the appearance and quality of a place, looking back from a vantage point of let us say fifty years, will be immense.

ENVIRONMENTAL ADVOCACY GROUPS

Beyond the land trust, other types of community and regional advocacy groups are dedicated to wise use of the natural environment. They usually focus on environmental concerns more broadly defined than land protection. The help of these groups should be solicited by any area struggling to achieve wise growth.

One prominent example is 1,000 Friends of Oregon, a statewide public-interest group formed in 1975 to resist efforts to repeal the state's land-use planning program. Lawyers and professional planners form the core of this nonprofit organization. Today, the organization, whose budget is over $750,000 a year, has a membership of over six thousand, an independent board of directors, a ten-member advisory board, and a sizable professional staff. Funding is obtained in about equal parts from membership dues, gifts, and foundation grants. The organization's work has made a substantial difference all over Oregon, and it has served as a model throughout the country. In part because of its constant presence and professional competence to intervene, the comprehensive plans and zoning of over 36 counties and 241 cities in Oregon have been revised to comply with state goals, which include establishing a growth boundary around each city. The staff provides free legal assistance to citizens in addition to conducting planning research and public education.

Other well-known and effective statewide and regional environmental advocacy groups include the MSM Regional Council, whose domain is Middlesex, Somerset, and Mercer counties, which surround Princeton in New Jersey, and the Vermont Land Trust. The MSM Regional Council, in its role as an advisor to various state agencies, has been especially instrumental in advocating and obtaining an effective regional open-space program and various growth-management initiatives. A locally based, nonprofit environmental advocacy group, such as the Group for the South Fork on eastern Long Island, may be large enough, and well enough financed, to retain trained, science-based staff professionals to assist in review of all large local as well as regional development proposals and to advocate environmental care, going as far, at times, as joining in legal challenges.

The contribution by such groups of ongoing professional scrutiny, as a supplement to a town's resources, is an incalculably valuable gift. The very presence in town of a not-for-profit environmental advocacy group is likely to affect and improve large planning and land-development applications. And environmental advocacy groups provide additional benefits. Jobs in them attract sophisticated, trained specialists to a host community. In this way, a town might become home to professional biologists, archaeologists, environmental scientists, hydrology experts, agronomists, and others able to contribute, as interested citizens, to its destiny.

IV

A Resident's Guide

CHAPTER ELEVEN

How to Evaluate a Growth Town

IT IS POSSIBLE TO KICK-START an evaluation of the future prospects of any growth town by boiling down the ideas, policies, and initiatives already discussed to rock-bottom essentials. No matter what the size or character of a place, it is necessary to be sure it conforms to four basic principles, described below, and that it initiates as many as possible of the sixteen strategies that follow. These principles and strategic initiatives are practical, possible, and powerful measures that can guide any community—growth town or not—toward a wise and sustainable future. The principles are meant to ensure long-term planning. The strategic initiatives, distilled from Part III of this book, involve more immediate steps and then require sustained action. When accepted as guiding precepts, taken together these principles and strategies will transform the potential for boom and bust into a wise approach to community development—a transformation that anyone who is contemplating relocation to a growth town will want to be assured of.

Basic Principles

Before any specific initiatives can be fruitfully pursued, managers and residents of a growth town must accept four general principles.

Think Long Term

Private investment and public policy must be based on a long-term view. Long term means at least ten years. At the pace towns evolve, ten years is not a long time. Yet it is rare that a community plans that far ahead. Unless at least a ten-year perspective is adopted, daily policy decisions, investment commitments, and land-use changes may turn out to be unwise and unhealthy. In a smart growth town, public and private organizations must reserve time and resources for long-term planning rather than remain caught up exclusively, as they generally are, with the immediate.

Think of the Consequences

Actions taken should not exchange one problem for another. In community development, today's solution is rarely measured candidly against tomorrow's consequences. Why? In part, this is the traditional way government and business operate, and, in part, planning is political, and officials hold office for relatively short periods. Members of citizen groups that monitor government often view town officials as shortsighted, timid, perhaps laden with conflicts of interest, and unable to see beyond the next election or even the next edition of the local newspaper. In evaluating any plan, people in charge or involved must consider not just the primary but also the secondary and tertiary impacts, those that are less obvious and often more enduring.

Ensure Private-Public Collaboration

Local government officials and private citizen experts must collaborate not just in planning and in grand gestures of publicity and resolution making but in the gritty process of implementation. Local private and nonprofit talent must be incorporated from the outset into decision making about town growth. A more streamlined and fruitful set of results will follow. Conflict will not cease, but conflict resolution will more likely occur.

Link Population Growth
to the Desired Pace of Development

Realistic future population estimates must be factored into growth-town finances, plans, and enhancement programs. A fifth-migration growth town must monitor both rates and absolute numbers of population growth. It must then continuously relate this actual growth to its own planned and selected pace of development. Its strategy must be to coordinate the two, even to the point, if necessary, of restricting the rate of population growth. When population changes are forecast accurately and their expected impact is frankly revealed, a town can plan realistically for traffic, schools, parks, and all the rest. A smart community will continuously update projections and decide how much growth it wants and when. Rather than react too late or hastily, with inadequate or poorly conceived responses, by using modern measuring and analytic systems a place can anticipate growth, plan for it, and control it.

Strategic Initiatives

Sixteen strategic initiatives collectively provide a framework for smart growth. The initiatives cross the traditional disciplines of design, law, and finance, just the way every important activity actually does in town development. These initiatives do not apply equally to any particular town. Because of a town's size or stage of evolution, some may even be inappropriate. Each must be tailored to local circumstances. Used selectively, these strategic initiatives will get a growth town where it wants to go.

Protect the Natural Environment

A wise growth town will protect the most significant parts of the natural environment, including forests, steep slopes, wetlands, watersheds, aquifers, floodplains, scenic vistas, watercourses, and the most productive farmland and forests. It will understand that unacceptable levels of noise as well as pollution of water and air are intolerable in a successful community, and it will invoke standards more rigorous than operative federal, state, or regional regulations.

Natural systems running through and around the community must be recognized as essential to and part of the built-up areas inserted among them. The interface between the natural and the artificial world is a sensitive, delicate domain, and intervention into it must be thoughtful. Certain areas such as fresh-water and salt-water wetlands, coastlines, aquifers, lakes, rivers, and wildlife habitats are more fragile than others. They benefit the entire population and need the entire community as a constituency to ensure their protection.

Preserve Historically Significant Places

A wise growth town will preserve historically significant buildings as well as streetscapes, open spaces and vistas, and entire districts. A smart community will value its past and its innate attributes. These are a part of its distinctiveness, its individual appeal, its uniqueness as a place. These attributes include the special ways in which the natural environment has become entwined with the built environment. Modernity and historicity are not in opposition unless forced there by the poorly informed, the narrow-minded, the shortsighted.

Control the Automobile

The car need not be accorded the most direct route, the closest parking, or the most prime property. It is capable of rapid movement over large distances in a short time. People are not. To prevent congestion, especially at the town center, parking should be strategically but not intrusively located. Adequate and well-landscaped parking can be made available at the periphery. If the community is large enough, frequent and free bus service should circulate from peripheral parking to the center. People, as pedestrians, should be given priority: the shortest routes, protection from adverse weather, and direct links to transit or parking through interesting and attractive spaces. When the density and scale of a place allow it, some form of public transit focused on the center will help to relieve traffic and reduce costly reliance on the car. When designed into the town-center physical plan as a convenient and safe way to move around, cycling and walking will be popular and will greatly reduce congestion, pollution, and the deadened land use produced by oversized streets and pervasive parking lots and garages.

Enhance the Town Center

A wise growth town will enhance the appearance of the town center and ensure that it is a dynamic, pedestrian-oriented commercial locale as well as a viable mixed-use residential enclave. Mixed-use zoning, which encourages a combination of retail, office, commercial, and residential activities, is essential. Special attention should be paid to allowing residential accommodations suitable for young people and older residents. Well-maintained and well-landscaped open spaces must be set aside for public use and recreation. A quality landscaping, maintenance, and lighting program in the town center will contribute to making pedestrian rights-of-way and public areas appealing.

Reserve Rights-of-Way in Advance

In parts of town targeted for growth, rights-of-way must be reserved or planned before development occurs. These conduits include streets, transit routes, walkways, trails, bicycle paths, and utility, power, cable, and water lines. During the long future life of a smart growth town, utility demands as yet unrecognized will require a feed into each private property. Both nuisance and high cost can be reduced substantially if these requirements are anticipated. The well-thought-out accommodation of movement, whether it be human, transit, digital, molecular, or pulse-energy, is the armature of a successful settlement. The extension of these rights-of-way needs to be economical, timed to desired changes in land use, and coordinated with older links without continuously disturbing the public environment.

Expand Recreation Areas

Areas dedicated to active and passive recreation must be selected early and with great care and scaled to future residential and commercial development. Through zoning or acquisition these spaces must be secured in advance of new development. They must then be maintained and protected as a part of the public trust. The use of each area should be consistent with the patronage it is capable of sustaining without harm. Overuse must not be allowed. A fragile wetland should not be converted into a soccer field.

Zone for Accessory Apartments, Home Offices, and Affordable Housing

A smart town will use zoning, and where necessary zoning incentives, to encourage the private development of accessory apartments, home offices, and affordable housing. In far too many residential areas, accessory apartments and home offices are illegal or barely tolerated. Affordable housing is such a touchy issue that communitywide battle lines are drawn whenever the subject is raised. But in a smart growth town all three types of zoning will supplement standard residential zoning.

Clear Policy as to Who Pays What and When

A smart growth town will plan for neighborhood parks, schools, and infrastructure before private development occurs; it will pay for these, where appropriate, through charges to private developers or by the levy of applicable user fees. Expanded schools, extended roads, increased road maintenance, additional social-welfare programs, another public medical facility—all are predictable needs that will occur as a consequence of new development, depending upon the type and scale sanctioned. These and other inevitable costly impacts of community population growth must be candidly detailed in a developer's Environmental Impact Statement. As part of the approval process, an agreement should be worked out that describes who is to pay for these inevitable public—and too often neglected—consequences of growth. The adequacy of such impact fees must be routinely examined and updated periodically.

Invest in and Control Infrastructure

The public sector must continuously invest in and upgrade existing infrastructure, including roads, water, sewer, power, landscaping, and communications, on a controlled basis related to both predetermined community growth targets and new technology. State-of-the-art communications lines and satellite receptors are more important than ever before. But infrastructure must also be limited as part of an overall growth-management strategy. It is crucial, in advance of growth, to decide where population-expanding infrastructure, such as sewer and water lines, will not be allowed. Only in this way will a community ensure the integrity of its low-density areas, forever-wild buffer zones, watercourses, and wetlands.

If infrastructure is allowed to deteriorate, real estate prices will decline, and inevitably property taxes as a percent of value will climb. When this cycle revs up, tax-collection problems soar and delinquencies become common. Basic utilities must be expected to provide up-to-date, reliable, and safe service. Otherwise, the long-term quality of the entire community is at risk. Most local public officials pay insufficient attention to this matter.

Ensure Safety and Security

All citizens are concerned about their own personal security, the safety of their children, and the protection of their property. Residents seek a sense of general well-being in their town. These concerns know no social or economic boundary. They are pervasive on the grittiest inner-city street, within the lushest gated suburb, and throughout the fastest growing community.

The long-term answer is quality education mixed with a feeling among all residents of being part of a shared community of interests. But in most places this answer is a fuzzy dream rather than a current reality. The more immediate remedy is an alert and informed local police organization that knows the spoilers. Only a small group of people creates trouble. An honest, locally based, experienced police establishment must determine who the troublemakers are and deal with them. A local court system, observant of all due process rights, must be willing to back up the action of alert law-enforcement officers. Private citizens can be of help too. Neighborhood associations take responsibility for a block. Parent patrols walk the streets before and after school. Citizens join night patrols to supplement the police staff.

Certain land-use and design strategies also promote safety and security. Compared with an empty street, a pedestrian-filled, well-lit street is a self-policing entity. At the town center a lively mixture of residential and commercial activity promotes safe streets and sidewalks day and night. In low-rise apartment buildings, a common stoop will dissuade predatory behavior at the entrance; and kitchens that overlook mid-block play areas provide communitywide surveillance at the rear. Large store windows along the sidewalk also create free, community-based vigilance.

Provide Incentives for Religious, Medical, Educational, and Cultural Institutions

Quasi-public and private institutions and organizations such as churches, synagogues, schools, museums, theaters, hospitals, cultural groups, and performance groups possess assets crucial to the quality of life in every community. They offer jobs, education, facilities, services, and attractions that cannot be obtained otherwise. They are staffed by people who often contribute disproportionately to community life. The accomplished, often well-educated professionals attracted to such organizations and institutions possess transferable skills—an asset that any smart growth town must try to obtain and hold.

One of the ways to obtain and retain such people and simultaneously enable the continual upgrading of these institutions is to offer supportive community policies. Readily available strategies are real estate tax abatement, donations of land in expansion areas, and low-cost public financing. There are self-help strategies too. Religious institutions, schools, and colleges possess valuable but underutilized facilities that should be shared. Kitchens, gyms, auditoriums, laboratories, art studios, infirmaries, when made available to others at times not needed by the host organization, will become cherished and supported by growth-town residents. The sharing of facilities will convert residents into advocates of the institution.

Link Business Recruitment to Community Goals

When recruiting new companies and while encouraging the expansion of existing ones, growth towns need to be especially wise about identifying hidden problems and recognizing potential ancillary benefits. Are the inevitable growth and change in the town's best interest socially, physically, and environmentally? Is the town well prepared through sensible advance planning? Some towns, in some periods of their evolution, might be better off not introducing expansion for which they are environmentally unprepared—which they do not have the natural resources to support or to which they do not have the terrain to contribute. Especially with industrial expansions, careful selection is crucial. The industrial operation must be willing to mitigate environmental and social impacts such as noise, traffic, water use, water pollution, air pollution, and school crowding. The kinds of businesses recruited make a long-term difference. New business types targeted should be connected to work with promise in the decades ahead. If the right companies are successfully recruited, latent local talent and entrepreneurial skills will be tapped.

It is also wise to seek out and to nurture businesses that enhance those already in place. In farming areas this might mean farm-equipment suppliers. In a community with a forest or fishing economy, other forms of supply, consulting, and management services would be logical. Sticking with local resources and building on traditional local skills can help to distinguish a place and keep it attached to its roots, while updating and upgrading its workers and industries.

Use Tax Revenue to Acquire Land

In every smart growth town, a portion of local public revenue should be dedicated to the purchase of especially important open space. Public funds can be obtained by setting aside a fraction of the local property tax or by instituting a dedicated sales tax or a 1 to 2 percent surcharge on real estate transfers. Programs should be ongoing and slated to continue over a long period of time. Besides outright purchase, which is the most expensive approach, a smart community will continuously acquire easements, options, leases, or development rights to key lands in town. The land obtained must be historically, environmentally, or strategically important. It should be chosen with care based on sound, long-term reasoning, not selected to benefit politically potent friends.

Control Tourism

Tourism can enhance or wreck a place. A wise tourist growth town must continuously assess how much it can handle. It must acknowledge the fragility of each environmental area and protect it by setting visitation limits. As the years go by and as tourism continues to expand, use limits may have to be increasingly imposed. During periods of exceptional fifth-migration growth, recreational resorts, seaside enclaves, ski communities, and towns that are gateways to national parks must adopt wise land-use controls, population growth limits, and development boundaries to avoid certain deterioration. On the positive side, tourism provides free community advertising. A good impression brings back a fifth-migration visitor in a new frame of mind—as home buyer, investor, business creator. But once the innate character of a place is lost, it risks losing its appeal to in-place residents, tourists, and potential new homeowners.

Encourage the Involvement of Private Citizens and Citizen Organizations

Fifth-migration growth towns are brimming with talented people, many of them with spare time; these towns are negligent if they fail to activate this priceless resource. Appropriate individuals and nonprofit groups should be encouraged to engage in all realms of the community enterprise connected with planning for, developing, and maintaining physical assets. Beyond the institutionalized use of citizens in the planning and development process, other opportunities are available, although often lost. Volunteer help is needed by historical societies, land and nature conservancies, beautification organizations, and the like. Work and money donated by engaged fifth-migration residents can be productively applied all over town.

To achieve communitywide objectives that depend on the skills and financial resources of private citizens, it is essential to create formal, standing public-private or quasi-public partnerships. As with business improvement districts, these meld the professional expertise and management capabilities of the private sector with the financing and regulatory power of government. Through these partnerships a town can set in motion specialized studies, long-term planning, technical contracts (think of cable-franchise negotiations), quality maintenance of open space (as with the New York City Central Park Conservancy), and much else.

Monitor Progress

Any community wise enough to be self-directed toward becoming a smart growth town should want to measure its progress. It should create a community report card at least every five years, starting with preset benchmarks, targets, or thresholds. This report must reiterate objectives and goals and note any changes to them. It must describe what has been achieved and what is now planned, how these activities are consistent with the long-term goals and objectives of the community, and how and when they are to be implemented. Locally conceived indicators can be established to organize the report and to give those who produce it a framework. These indicators should be innovative and specific. They should portray links among the economic, environmental, and social dimensions of community development.

How Can You Evaluate a Community?

If you want to know whether your town or any place you might be interested in is acting wisely, how can you find out? It is a lot easier than you might think and a lot easier than some in town hall might lead you to believe. Here is how to evaluate a particular community. This entire process—if done thoroughly—might take a week. Is this too long if you are considering buying a house, moving a business, changing the place where you live, or investing in a community? With the information contained in this book in mind, at the end of a week's site visit you will know enough to reliably evaluate the people and the policies guiding the destiny of a place. One week is a bargain when you consider the magnitude of the investment in a new home, the upheaval involved in moving, or the implications of relocating your business.

QUESTIONS TO ASK OTHERS

Read and evaluate several reports or pamphlets obtainable at the town hall: the zoning ordinance, subdivision regulations, the comprehensive plan (this may include a land-use plan, a land-classification plan, a policy plan, and a development-management plan), the town code (only chapters relevant to zoning, planning, land use, and development), the capital budget, the highway department five-year plan. This evaluation will require one to two days. How does the content of these documents compare with the strategic initiatives and principles just described? If these or similar documents do not exist, become wary until satisfied by further investigation. If you are considering buying property in a particular location, you must also examine the zoning ordinance and zoning map for that target area. These maps are the blueprint of the future of the town.

The subcomponents of the comprehensive plan should at least cover the following topics. The *land-use plan* indicates the form the community is projected to take in the future. It incorporates zoning, open spaces, special districts, roadways, and other land-use attributes. In the past, this was often the only document that community managers and citizens had to rely on. But now, in an aware community, the three other types of information described below are usually available and crucial.

The *land-classification plan* details wetlands, steep slopes, subsurface areas of significance, watercourses, farmland, and woodlands. Maps should indicate where development should be encouraged and where it should be minimized or forbidden. The land-classification plan is an inventory of resources that must be respected in any future modifications of the land-use plan.

The written *policy plan* reveals community goals and objectives that include but are not exclusively focused on land use. It might indicate population-growth parameters, tourism objectives and controls, means of collaboration between public and private sectors, neighborhood planning initiatives, and attitudes toward regional collaboration. It might also discuss town fiscal policies and parameters.

The written *development-management plan* is the blueprint for projected infrastructure expansions and expenditures. It also indicates the pace and scale of other projected capital improvements as well as property-acquisition goals. As such it portrays the location, type, and pace of growth that will be supported or inhibited by public expenditures. With a horizon of usually three to ten years, this document serves as a means for coordinating the actions and programs of specific agencies of local government. It must be updated at least every five years to be effective.

After you have reviewed these documents, make an appointment to meet personally with the town chief executive, the director of planning, the superintendent of highways, the town attorney, the chief assessor. Have the questions that matter to you ready and write down the answers. Maybe two days are required for these meetings. The director of planning will be able to tell you what you might expect in any particular part of town or the total community. Ask whether the comprehensive plan was ever adopted as official town policy. Find out to what extent it is being followed. What updates are under way? What policies are likely to be changed in the next few years? Is the capital budget being followed and continually updated to finance the comprehensive plan? Make it a point in your investigation to find out how seriously the comprehensive plan is taken in setting the town's future directions and policies and how closely it relates to population growth.

If you are concerned about tax trends and assessments, the assessor will discuss your questions and give you projections. When a rapidly growing town spends much more than its current income, it assumes mounting debt. The town managers are wagering that future growth will pay for current and past expenditures. This happens at home too. Only when family debt is incurred based on a projected income stream that does not materialize, bankruptcy follows. In towns the anticipated income stream is more often than not more paying customers—new residents in new taxable houses and new commercial activity in newly developed, tax-paying business property. Therefore, in debt-driven communities, as public debt rises, so does the likelihood that town officials will support planning, zoning, and legal decisions that stimulate quick growth. The alternative is for them to become captains of a municipal ship foundering on the shoals of insolvency or, almost as dangerous for elected officials, to be forced to advocate property-tax increases coupled with cutbacks in schools, police, public-sector jobs, and other municipal services.

In a growth town—or indeed any community—a warning signal flashes when local real estate taxes rise for several consecutive years at rates that exceed the rate of inflation. Unless the increase is for a special and understandable limited purpose, such as major school or infrastructure expansion, it is time to become vigilant. Are town government and its payroll growing at an unjustifiable rate? Are benefit programs in town expanding while the tax-paying population is evacuating? Is the school system suffering from bloat of one sort or another? Anyone who wants to live in and invest their personal assets in a town should pay attention to these signals.

After assessing the public records and the views of elected officials, meet also with the executive director of any local environmental advocacy group, land trust, conservation organization, historic district, or other not-for-profit group. If the town nonprofit and quasi-public organizational network is active, another one or two days are required here. Take notes. If this network is inactive, be wary.

After completing the steps above, try to meet with several other people in the private sector. The manager of one or two of the major banks in town should be on your list, along with head of the school board. In an informal way, go into local stores and talk with owners about the community, its direction, its attitudes toward the future, its promising and troublesome trends.

Questions to Ask Yourself

Summarize what you have learned through your research by asking yourself questions. Does the community seem to be aware of the benefits of becoming a smart or wise place? What is the dominant local attitude about smart growth? If you find positive projections, judge how the place intends to realize its goals. How practical is its strategy? Here are some of the initiatives to look for in checking out whether what you have heard or read is simply good intention or whether there is real commitment to moving forward wisely.

- Is there a communitywide vision or shared view of a desirable future among citizen leaders, private organizations, planning departments, budget agencies, business circles, civic groups, and cultural institutions? If not, is work ongoing to create one? Is there seeming convergence or increasing divergence?
- How many community goals have distinct steps and a time frame attached? How firm are plans to undertake specific initiatives?
- What signs of success are there? Have guideposts been set up, indicators of success, by which the community can measure its own progress, calibrate its moves, and even reformat its original thinking?
- Are the risks and the barriers to wise growth openly acknowledged and identified so that they may be confronted?
- How committed are the leaders in public, private, and nonprofit entities, including private entrepreneurs, to working together?
- Is there enough courage and commitment in the public sector to follow and perhaps improve the comprehensive plan, zoning ordinances, subdivision regulations, building codes, and the capital budget in order to achieve wise growth?

After this inquiry, it should become obvious whether the community is currently capable of moving toward wise growth. You should be able to decide to what extent any growth town that interests you is coming to grips with its future.

CHAPTER TWELVE

The Benefits of Wise Growth

I N THE 1990s fifth-wave values and priorities began to assert their influence. A few informed public agencies, a handful of private developers, a small group of architects and planners, and a broad segment of enlightened residents began to consider new directions. Environmental and quality-of-life concerns gained prominence; development assumptions were revised.

This shift in emphasis signals the maturing of the nation as it abandons the heady assumption, long held by its top business and political leaders, that nothing will ever give out, that everything will last forever—much the way an adolescent imagines his or her own life. And it also reflects a generational change of leadership in government and in communities; interests awakened in the environmental consciousness-raising years of the 1960s mixed with the newest technology of the 1990s are becoming lodged in the policy initiatives and philosophical underpinnings of land development. The activist pendulum, always swinging, has shifted toward a more comprehensive view of what desirable community growth entails.

As the years go by, fifth-migration growth towns that follow a deliberate policy of wise development will provide unusual and selective advantages to residents. Within them, the quality of life will be more desirable; investment will be more rewarding; and specific benefits of great appeal will be obtained by society as a whole.

The Economic Payoff

With new asset deployment and new investment pouring into growth towns at the rate of $150 billion a year or more, there will be economic payoffs within a wise growth town of many different sorts. Increases in real estate values and job opportunities are but the two most obvious.

A Good Place to Invest in Real Estate

Since the early 1980s, I estimate that housing values in the most sought-out growth towns have soared, often increasing 5 to 10 percent per year, whereas the national average has been closer to 2 percent per year, about in line with the rate of inflation. In certain places and at particular times, these unusually robust value growth rates have even been exceeded. Between 1992 and 1997 in Salt Lake City, for instance, the median price of a single-family house increased by 92 percent, or 15 percent a year. From 1992 to 1997 in Portland, Oregon—where its Urban Growth Boundary is a continuing influence—the advance was 13 percent a year. In declining communities, or those seized by temporary recession, median housing prices have hardly advanced or have even retreated. This disparity will continue, I believe.

As the fifth migration proceeds, this divergence becomes increasingly evident in places as diverse as New York and California. During the much-improved real estate market of 1996–1997 in New York City, for instance, average cooperative and condominium prices rose about 12 percent, while the price of the city's most desirable residential properties escalated by over 30 percent. In Los Angeles during the same period, average properties hardly appreciated in value, and some declined. But the most sought-out fifth-migration locations on the west side of Los Angeles were up over 6 percent.

As fifth-migration participants succeed in the modern global economy, strong demand for quality housing at the top of the market will continue. The divergence in market price between the average and the highest quality real estate will continue to expand. Fifth-migration target areas of proven appeal will be the location of relatively steep price increases compared with urban, suburban, and rural places that do not attract fifth-migration participants.

Viable downtowns, safe neighborhoods, and well-conceived commercial and industrial areas, all set in attractive surroundings, also mean top and sustainable property values. As wise growth towns become lively places in which to live, to shop, to spend leisure time, they become profitable places in which to own a business or commercial property. Through the twenty-first century, I predict that the value of houses, commercial property, and land in smart growth towns will increase at more than twice the national average and will continue to do so reliably through economic cycles. Because smart growth towns are in no danger of becoming ghost towns, they will be relatively immune from the sharpest phases of boom-and-bust real estate fluctuations.

Places with clean air and high-quality drinking water are already sought out as havens and will become increasingly rare. Value is also added by natural beauty, a desirable climate, good access, and fiscally sound community management. Real estate demand escalates wherever institutions and jobs are growing. Whenever conservation, historic preservation, and aesthetic enhancement are demonstrable priorities, values move up. The same goes for public safety, which establishes the confidence necessary for business and residential investment. The inescapable conclusion is that a smart growth town will be a fine place in which to invest.

How will a real estate investment in a smart growth town compare with other typical investments? I will hazard a guess. Consider for a moment that real-property prices are likely to continue to advance sharply in well-managed fifth-migration growth towns. These places will continually attract new residents and jobs, which will provide support on the demand side of the equation. On the supply side, if planning and development constraints are wisely crafted, overbuilding will not occur. In top-quality locations within the most thoughtfully managed communities, I project annual property-value increases of 10 to 15 percent, or an average of 12.5 percent. Stock-market shares, including dividends, have appreciated on average about 10 percent annually since the end of World War II, excluding the dramatic and uncharacteristically high returns of the later 1990s. Over the same time period, corporate and municipal bonds have appreciated at approximately half the rate of stocks, or about 5 percent per year. Thus, I expect a well-located holding in a smart growth town to outperform the average security asset over the next several decades by at least 2.5 percent per year. After ten years, if the effect of compounding is taken into account, the difference will be 65 percent.

Let me hazard one other projected comparison. What about the return on an average real estate investment compared with one in a smart fifth-migration growth town? Over the next ten to twenty years, the value of a typical real estate investment, I believe, will increase somewhere between 2 and 8 percent a year, or an average of 5 percent, compared with 12.5 percent in a smart growth town. As a consequence, property investments in well-located growth towns will advance at more than twice the rate that may be expected from investment in a typical property in a typical town. These projections, if anywhere close to accurate, point up the expected extremely significant positive impact of real estate investment in a smart growth town. Added to this desirable return on investment, of course, is a superior experience of living, a return on life.

The problem of powerful community appeal creating high entry costs for newcomers and housing difficulties for established residents of modest means is a knotty one. As the price of a house and the value of land continue to rise in a smart growth town, the boom drives up real estate costs to a level that bars the entry of many newcomers and that creates difficulties for younger residents who wish to remain in town. At some price point more people will look elsewhere, thereby creating new demand in another part of town—or maybe in another town altogether. As a result, high-quality communities on the periphery of recognized fifth-migration growth towns are surely going to be affected by growth-town policies. And the operation of the marketplace, at some price point, will mitigate value escalations in the growth town itself.

Various artificial ways exist to counter the high-cost problem, none entirely effective, as discussed earlier. A smart growth community will always have to determine how to contain price and value increases to ensure housing access to a broad economic and social cross-section of people. However achieved, the fundamental goal of limiting or controlling the rate of growth must not be abandoned. But excessively stringent regulatory limits and controls will drive up real estate values faster and further because of the created compliance and cost scarcity.

Jobs and Economic Security

Although quality jobs are scarce in many growth towns, the situation will improve over time if job growth and work diversity are achieved. Stability for most residents increases when a community is not dependent upon a single industry or a single employer. Job growth and diversity are enhanced by the availability of vocational training centers, job counseling services, and adult extension courses, to name but a few. Educational opportunities help workers upgrade and retrain to obtain needed skills. Because a skilled, flexible work force allows employers to succeed, a smart growth town can attract new types of economic organizations and nurture those growing in place. Young residents will have job choices and sound economic opportunities right at home. Older residents are able to move up without moving away.

A high concentration of poorly educated, unskilled individuals will remain in the older big cities and in many of their near-in suburbs. As these places struggle, growth will likely be moderate at best, and job-related services are likely to shrink. As a result, work-force skills and educational levels will not be competitive. Children growing up in these places will likely fall even further behind, as adverse social and economic impacts reduce cultural, institutional, and educational options. It is increasingly likely that many aspiring fifth-wave residents will move away.

The Societal Payoff

Where residents believe that a reliable and desirable economic future is likely, a townwide sensation of promise and stability emerges, affecting the mood of people and their tolerance for one another. Among the collective stakeholders, when the pie is growing there is less subversive political and social bickering over the control of power and sources of wealth. When a shrinking resource base is perceived, the mood turns ugly and the grab is on.

If nothing more were achieved, the promotion of social harmony and the diminution of crime would be reason enough to bend all effort toward creating a pattern of smart community evolution. Imagine what it would mean, for instance, if the ever-growing public and private assets devoted to curbing crime could be diverted to more productive communitywide uses. Money used to construct jails, finance social rehabilitation programs, and expand police services could be turned to other uses.

Commitment to Place

Ask any parent about one of the most unfortunate consequences of living in a place perceived to be without a desirable, expanding economic future.

They will tell you about the loss of their young adult children, often the most promising ones, to another place. Listen to the families of New Orleans, St. Louis, or Pittsburgh or of so many other once vibrant places that for generations attracted newcomers and held the best of their own. In our mobile, migrant culture, many young, capable adults seek a place where community fundamentals are aligned with their own wish for a bountiful future. When a large portion of the most promising members of a generation abandon a town as members of the fifth migration, continuity, energy, talent, and community devotion are all drained out, with real consequences.

In a compelling place to live, young people find jobs, establish families, and thereby contribute to long-lasting, in-place networks. Abiding in a particular place for a long time, particularly for generations, creates an identification between individual and place, between family and place, which in turn leads to commitment to a community over the long term and encourages residents to devote time to civic affairs.

Engaged Citizens, Empowered People

A town dedicated to wise growth will continuously engage a large number of citizens in focusing on, debating and negotiating about, and ultimately deciding on a town's future, and then working to realize it. The standard of smart growth, never perfectly achievable, creates a focus for people throughout a town. As long as they keep this goal in mind, the longevity of a growth town will be optimized. Along the way, individuals will endeavor to attain commonly shared goals such as reduction of crime and traffic, mitigation of environmental destruction, preservation of historic remnants, diminished public costs and taxes. By considering the immediate while being mindful of, and committed to, the long term, individuals and groups have a logical basis for conflict resolution.

The local community is the only place where most people have a chance to experience authentic political power and social involvement. When individuals across the social and economic spectrums work toward smart growth, remarkable gains are achieved, not just by the place but by the participants themselves; getting involved is a way for people to enhance their own lives. A sense of accomplishment emerges. A community wider than self and family is joined. Shared learning is inevitable; and the satisfaction of well-intended service is obtained. More often than not, social barriers dissipate, and understanding is promoted among people who might not otherwise encounter one another. In time this positive experience radiates into the family and out to community groups. These personal and free benefits come from the remarkable experience of getting involved in one's own community. They are what a democratic society has to offer at its best, an offer neither recognized nor accepted by most people. Democracy offers so much more than the right to vote. A truly successful civil society emerges when its members get involved.

The Environmental and Aesthetic Payoff

Great gains for all residents follow when worthy buildings and the natural environment are protected. Previously built places worth preserving are less likely to languish. Waste is reduced; the cost of depletion and destruction is avoided. The carefully protected natural environment remains available for all to enjoy. Local history is preserved. Every great space, indoors or out, conveys a feeling of uplift. Conversely, a physically degraded, dilapidated, destroyed part of a town imparts a feeling of despair or perhaps anger.

Part of the personal payoff that comes from living in a well-directed community is the frequent experience of pleasure derived from inhabiting physically appealing surroundings, where attention has been paid to the design and landscaping of all aspects of the public realm. The aesthetic experience is of subtle but substantial significance in assuring residents that they inhabit a desirable community. As long as attention to aesthetics remains a basic part of development decisions, a place will continue to appeal and will do so increasingly as time goes by, as so many other places ignore this dimension of their residents' and visitors' personal experience.

Living in an aesthetically pleasing place translates into a wish among residents to keep the community attractive and indeed to make it even more appealing. A general pride in place occurs, and energy is unleashed to improve physical surroundings. Residents become willing to contribute skills and money and energy to make a place ever more desirable.

The Cultural, Educational, and Recreational Payoff

When smart growth occurs, schools, medical centers, performance institutions, libraries, religious institutions, and sports organizations will improve. Their quality will be upgraded, and they will be able to offer individuals a wide range of programs built on more fully guaranteed institutional finances. Individuals' opportunity for personal and social growth will expand through programs offered by these thriving organizations.

When a town is securely and comfortably located between the fear of collapse and preoccupation with headlong expansion, citizens find time to release athletic, social, and creative impulses. When human beings have space and time and security to follow their own proclivities, community theater, amateur art exhibitions, choral societies, amateur sports leagues, and a variety of other endeavors pursued purely for pleasure flourish. A wise fifth-migration community, in supporting these activities, will nurture the talents of its citizens and strengthen private links among diverse groups.

The quality of public education tends to improve as new business investment occurs and as newcomers with high standards move in. When foreign companies or internationally minded domestic ones come to town, school training in mathematics, science, computers, and technology tends to improve, as does foreign-language instruction, competence in geography, and knowledge of world cultures. Exchange programs and sponsored internships abroad often become available to students, connecting residents to other parts of the world. Foreign children in school create a positive cross-cultural experience for everyone.

The Reduction of Waste in Community Development

Beyond undeniable individual benefits, smart growth will result in enormous savings in the heretofore generally wasteful process of American community development. Leaders are beginning to recognize that, like imperiled natural resources, declining communities set off a gigantic, profoundly harmful chain reaction. Community decay throws away all the time, energy, social networks, and capital expense that add up to a place. That is what settlers in each migration have done persistently since the colonization of North America. This wasteful process has been based on the fundamental assumption in America that there is always another and better place, no end to potential, and limitless resources.

Even if we don't abandon entire towns, we often abandon neighborhoods. We allow adverse social and economic forces to overwhelm them. Sometimes managing authorities, in response, cut off municipal services. Lending institutions become hesitant or even unwilling to offer loans in these neighborhoods. Property owners cut off capital in the form of building maintenance and management. Entire neighborhoods, sometimes large enough to qualify as substantial towns, are then left to their own devices and often decay as abandonment becomes rampant. This disease has been notorious in America, affecting parts of smaller towns, older cities, and inner suburbs—remnants of the second, third, and fourth migrations. By way of contrast, most communities in Europe and Asia have been slowly expanded, upgraded and updated to remain viable, treasured for centuries rather than allowed to become outmoded because of commercial, technological, or transportation shifts, and then abandoned.

Even in declining, older center-city neighborhoods, quality renewal is possible using some of the precepts of smart growth. Locked-in-place, nonprofit medical, academic, and cultural institutions contain thoughtful and energetic leaders who can contribute in persuasive and powerful ways to the future of their institutions' immediate surroundings and thus to their well-being. An instructive example is the effort being led by Trinity College to upgrade its blighted Hartford (Connecticut) neighborhood, known as Frog Hollow. Trinity, like Yale in New Haven, Marquette in Milwaukee, Spelman in Atlanta, and countless other universities, hospitals, and cultural centers, is surrounded by a decaying third-migration neighborhood. At the urging of Trinity's dynamic president, Evan S. Dobelle, Hartford Hospital and its mental health component, the Institute of Living, together with Connecticut Children's Medical Center and Connecticut Public Television, all located in Frog Hollow, joined Trinity College in committing $10 million in seed money. The rest of a $175 million rehabilitation fund comes from city, state, and federal bonds and grants and from local companies. A bus yard at the center of the area is being transformed into a science and technology center for students in kindergarten through high school. A Boys' and Girls' Club will be managed by Trinity students, and within the redevelopment area a job-training center, a family-resource center, and a new police substation will be located. Trinity and the other institutions are buying up fundamentally handsome but now derelict houses, having them renovated by local contractors, and then reselling them at near cost with favorable financing to residents who agree to participate in job training and to others who seek jobs at the college and hospitals. The goal is safe streets, stable homeownership, and state-of-the-art schools and job-training facilities. In speaking of his vision and his aspirations for the Frog Hollow initiative, President Dobelle raises issues pertinent to older places that wish to once again become attractive growth communities. "I've chosen a field that has all the capacity to bring back America," he says, "a field that's a sleeping giant."[1] It is indeed possible in the years ahead that any number of now-languishing neighborhoods and communities managed by alert and courageous leaders and public officials, supported by interested citizens, will be incrementally retrofitted in the same way.

The notions of smart growth, then, need not apply only to fifth-migration growth towns and other places in relatively good condition. Wisely utilized, the principles and initiatives summarized in Chapter 11 will help troubled places find a new life and in doing so will reduce an incredibly expensive form of waste—discarding resources we can no longer afford to replace. As government seeks to become more economical and as so many social, economic, and environmental initiatives focus on conservation and preservation, there is no target more worthy or appropriate than needy communities in America.

On a long-term basis, a wise growth town produces a ripple effect into its region, its state, and the country. Exemplary places protect special local, regional, and nationally significant environments. They stimulate job growth. They are capable of muting the devastating cycle of growth, followed by self-destructive excessive growth, followed by decay. The first generation of successful fifth-migration growth towns will serve as nationwide examples, a positive benefit for many people and many places across the continent.

Diminished Future National Mass Migrations

At the beginning of this book I described the history of settlement in America using the prior four mass migrations as an organizing device. The fifth migration, still gaining steam, has produced a boom in a limited number of growth communities. This current vast relocation has already released a huge amount of energy and caused the redeployment of an immense amount of capital. And much more is still to come, with the direct corollary being great losses in the places abandoned. So the fifth migration is close to a zero-sum game when looked at from the perspective of national resource allocations. The consequence for the nation is at best neutral and probably negative. The consequence for many places, both those growing and those declining, is decidedly negative. The consequence for the boom towns is temporarily exhilarating, but the story is not yet over for them; their future depends on the wise use of the skills of town managers and the committed energy of residents.

What about the consequences of these vast human migrations on the people involved? In the past great hardship was endured, frightening risks were taken, and many families were disrupted. Contained within this experience and memorialized in the literature of prior national migrations is the unending pain to the great majority of people who were driven by need to become participants. With the fifth migration, just the opposite is taking place: the migration is primarily voluntary; assets travel with participants; the loss that occurs is most pronounced in the places being left behind and among their nonparticipant residents.

Wisely growing settlements will not solve many of the economic and social problems that beset America, but they will help. I have argued in admittedly large strokes that local communities need to be much more wisely and coherently managed, in part to provide stability and opportunity for all residents. If these changes are made in enough locales, regional or even national social and economic dislocations are not as likely to threaten to the same degree as in the past. On the local level, the urge among residents to join the fifth migration will be much diminished. As more places become smart settlements, social stability will increase. Local managers will more likely keep the office or the plant where it is. Local workers will not be forced to relocate. New jobs will be attracted increasingly to well-managed towns dedicated to the long-term well-being of their residents and to the maintenance of their quality of life.

The Leap to Wise Growth

The million people a year who relocate as members of the fifth migration would like to live within a smart growth town. But to create one requires good judgment, hard work, and a special vision of what a place can be. One of the root inhibitors of positive change in recently thriving growth towns has been lack of conviction, understanding, vision, and guts on the part of elected town policymakers. Is this an inevitable consequence of democracy? Is the manifest preference by community leaders to follow rather than to lead based on the belief that they have been elected by a complacent majority fearful of initiative and innovation? Is it a reflection of an abhorrence of land-use controls and long-term planning ingrained deeply in the American spirit? Although each of these factors must be reckoned with, I believe sentiment has changed. In fifth-migration growth towns, leaders who guide their communities toward incremental, long-term, wise growth will be all the more popular for doing so. Public leadership, which requires a degree of courage and the ability and patience to communicate, to educate, to explain, to adjudicate, to arbitrate, is still a prerequisite for community change. In most growth towns, private residents fail to lead even when it is in their best interest. Surely, if during each electoral period all concerned recognized that the choice between slow deterioration and prosperous, long-term, wise growth—or even anything approaching these alternatives—hung in the balance, support for the highest quality, most thoughtful, and best-informed local government leadership would be decisive.

And if genuine leaders were sought and respected in town government, communities would attract more of them. Communities must begin to recognize that salaries and benefits commensurate with great responsibility are appropriate. They must understand that the best investment they can make is to attract the right leader. If the compensation of top local-government managers matched that of other respected leaders, such as officers of private corporations, thoughtful, dynamic people would be eager to sign on.

Even though an overwhelming majority of residents in any community would like their town to become a smart, sustainable place, a small but powerful group will predictably resist the policies and programs needed to implement wise growth. This group is not, contrary to popular assumption, the entrepreneurial real estate development community. As long as town policies and procedures are equitable and observant of free-enterprise operations and opportunities, entrepreneurs and developers are likely to cooperate. Rather, objections arise from conservative ideologues who do not wish to acknowledge that modern community life is a collective experience in which all residents' futures are inevitably joined, in which the success of each person's investment in the long run depends on the others' sensible behavior. Those I am characterizing as conservative ideologues still long for the romance of laissez-faire frontier America—a romance that dominated the first four migrations—without noticing the ruined towns and destroyed social structures left in its wake.

These attitudes must change if growth towns are to be successful. Looked at over all, in the coming century of limited natural resources, inevitable national and even international job migrations, and worldwide rivalry for capital, I believe that the competition will be Darwinian. There will be distinct winners and losers. Predators with honed skills will prevail. Others, unable to compete, will be victims. Most states are already out there offering relocation incentives to out-of-state businesses. Many cities and towns are out there with public and private weapons such as actively recruiting Chambers of Commerce, development commissions, tax incentives, and liberal municipal bond and debt programs; they are competing for residents, for jobs, and for intellectual capital residing elsewhere. In this context, making a place smart can be seen as a survival strategy. Towns that win will do so by learning to think and manage in new ways. When it comes to sustaining growth towns in the twenty-first century, boldness and creativity and fresh initiatives will be essential.

Within growth towns that thrive, leaders will become dedicated enough to risk asking new questions, with the sure knowledge that this is the first step toward obtaining fundamentally new answers. The old questions and the traditional answers have gotten us where we are today: diminished quality within even the most vibrant communities compared with what is possible. Some of the new questions will, I hope, be provoked by this book. The questions will be valid for a long time. So it is important to get them right and to target them toward smart growth. The answers, even if at first hesitant and temporary, will be evolutionary and creative compared with town-development initiatives of the past two hundred years.

Making the leap to wise growth requires deciding which values to promote. Is a town willing to live in a way that is compatible with the ecosystem in which it exists and on which it partially depends? Are its inhabitants willing to conduct their lives in a way that is less "now-centered" and more conducive to ensuring a quality future? Once the principles of wise growth are agreed upon, broad-based community teamwork will be effective. Citizens will work more successfully with public and private groups. Departments of government will be able to work in greater harmony with other public and private entities. All through the gritty, slow reality of community evolution, differences will be more easily negotiated and more gracefully resolved.

Fifth-migration growth towns can decide to become attractive, alluring, high-quality places way out into the future by acting wisely now. Any community—growing, static, or shrinking—that embraces the feasible and cost-effective principles I have outlined will be on its way to a physically, socially, and economically healthier future. Before the year 2020, residents of the most prescient fifth-migration growth towns will, I predict, launch broad-based new initiatives. These towns will become smart growth communities, the first wisely evolving settlements in America. And it is equally possible, if wise growth principles are selectively embraced, that some neighborhoods and towns now languishing will also find ways to become more desirable than is currently imagined possible.

NOTES

ABBREVIATIONS

AD	*American Demographics magazine*
JAPA	*Journal of the American Planning Association*
NYT	*New York Times*
PL	*Planning (published monthly by the American Planning Association)*
WSJ	*Wall Street Journal*

THE NEW MIGRATION: PERILS AND PROMISES

1. The term *fifth migration* was coined, as far as I know, by Jack Lessinger in *Regions of Opportunity* (New York: New York Times Books, 1986).
2. The first four migrations are discussed with different emphasis by Lewis Mumford, *The Urban Prospect* (New York: Harcourt, Brace and World, 1956), pp. ix ff.; reprinted from the *Survey Graphic*, May 1925.

CHAPTER 1. THE FIFTH MIGRATION BEGINS

1. Quoted in Steve Madis and James J. Mackenzie, *Car Trouble* (Boston: Beacon Press, 1993), p. 7.
2. *AD*, June 1997; for the year 1997 extrapolated from one month of statistics.
3. Figures are courtesy of Gregory Heym, Real Estate Board of New York. Based on the tentative assessment roll for fiscal year 2000, as of January 15, 1999, the assessed value of New York City is $87.56 billion, and of Manhattan $52.47 billion; the market value of New York City is $330.58 billion, and of Manhattan $126.98 billion.
4. Regional Plan Association and Quinnipiac College Polling Institute, *Regional Quality of Life Poll* (New York and Hamden, Conn., April 1995).

Chapter 2. Forces Driving the Fifth Migration

1. Regional Plan Associates and Quinnipiac College Polling Institute, *Regional Quality of Life Poll.*
2. Jack Milles, a former spacecraft designer and now part of JALA International in Los Angeles, coined the term *telecommuting.*
3. Forecast based on projections in 1998 by Jack Milles of JALA International, Los Angeles, and Ray Boggs of IDC/LINK, a New York market-research concern, and on household growth projections by the Census Bureau.
4. Bill Rogers, "Technology Affects Living Patterns," *WSJ*, November 21, 1994, p. A8.
5. See Taichi Sakaiya, *The Knowledge-Value Revolution* (Tokyo: Kodansha International, 1991).

Chapter 3. Where the Fifth Wave Is Going

1. These lists were derived by Cognetics, Inc., a business-oriented demographic research firm in Cambridge, Massachusetts. The ranking for each place is based on (1) the firms started in the previous ten years that employ at least five people today, as a percent of all firms, and (2) the percent of firms ten years old or less four years ago that had a "growth index" of at least 3 over the past four years; the growth index is a firm's percent employment growth (expressed as a decimal) times its absolute employment growth.
2. Judy S. Davis, Arthur C. Nelson, and Kenneth J. Dueker, "The New 'Burbs': The Exurbs and Their Implications for Planning Policy," *JAPA*, Winter 1994, p. 46.
3. "Small Is Beautiful," *AD*, January 1998, p. 47.
4. Quoted in Mark Potok, "Phoenix," *USA Today*, June 2, 1995, p. 1A.
5. Quoted in Scott Kilman and Robert L. Rose, "Demographics: Population of Rural America Is Swelling," *WSJ*, June 21, 1996, p. B1.
6. Calvin L. Beale and Kenneth M. Johnson, "The Rural Rebound Revisited," *AD*, July 1995, p. 54.
7. Quoted in Steven A. Holmes, "Leaving the Suburbs for Rural Areas," *NYT*, October 19, 1997, p. 34.
8. Beale and Johnson, "The Rural Rebound Revisited," pp. 47ff.
9. The typology for classifying counties by economic function was developed by the Economic Research Service of the U.S. Department of Agriculture. The "recreational" classification was developed by Beale and Johnson.
10. Eric Pooley, "The Great Escape," *Time*, December 8, 1997, pp. 52–64.
11. Potok, "Phoenix," p. 1A.
12. Kevin Helliker, "Guests Pay Better Than Cattle for Many Ranchers," *WSJ*, August 1, 1997, p. B1.

13. Quoted in Lindley H. Clark, Jr., "Some Rocky Mountain States Outpace Rest of U.S. in Economic Expansion," *WSJ*, April 29, 1994, p. A6.

Chapter 4. Causes and Consequences of Community Decay

1. Alexis de Tocqueville, *Democracy in America* (1840), Vol. 1 (New Rochelle, N.Y.: Vintage Books, 1990), p. 134.
2. Frederick Jackson Turner, *The Frontier in American History* (1892) (Albuquerque: University of New Mexico Press, 1993), p. 124.
3. Vincent Scully, *The Architecture of Community* (New York: McGraw-Hill, 1994), p. 223.
4. Jerry Gray, "Tax Judge Lowers Assessment of Undeveloped Wetlands Tract," *NYT*, May 1, 1992, p. B5.
5. Gertrude Stein, *Everybody's Autobiography* (1937) (New York: Cooper Square, 1971), p. 151.
6. Quoted in Timothy Egan, "Urban Sprawl Strains Western States," *NYT*, December 29, 1997, p. 1.
7. Jerry Adler, "Bye-Bye, Suburban Dream," *Newsweek*, May 15, 1995, p. 43.
8. Quoted in Jennifer Preston, "Battling Sprawl, States Buy Land for Open Space," *NYT*, June 9, 1998, p. B5.
9. Quoted in ibid., p. B5.
10. Quoted in Iver Peterson, "Suburban Town Houses Losing Their Welcome," *NYT*, June 1, 1998, pp. B1, B2.
11. Quoted in Marcelle S. Fischler, "Security Is the Draw at Gated Communities," *NYT*, August 16, 1998, sec. 14, p. 6.
12. Quoted in Ron Suskind, "As Urban Woes Grow 'PLUs' Are Seeking Psychological Suburbia," *WSJ*, May 15, 1997, p. 1.
13. Ibid.
14. *Cincinnati Enquirer*, June 11, 1995, p. 3.
15. Charles Lockwood, "Edge Cities on the Brink," *WSJ*, December 21, 1994, p. A14.
16. Joel Garreau, "Edge Cities in Profile," *AD*, February 1994, p. 33.
17. "Rethinking the Suburbs," *Observer*, February 16, 1998, p. 4.
18. William Lucy and David Phillips, "Why Some Suburbs Thrive," *PL*, June 1995, p. 20.
19. Lockwood, "Edge Cities on the Brink," p. A14.

Chapter 5. The Whiff of Self-Destruction in Particular Growth Areas

1. Egan, "Urban Sprawl Strains Western States," p. 1.
2. Terry Goddard, "Making the Valley More Livable; Panel Outlines Problem Areas We Need to Tackle," *Phoenix Gazette*, May 18, 1995, p. 2.

3. Quoted in Nico Calavita, "Value of Tiers," *PL*, March 1997, p. 20.

4. Quoted in Tony Horwitz, "Cultural Mismatch: Californians Flood in and Tension Is Rising in Small Towns in Utah," *WSJ*, April 29, 1994, p. 1.

5. Pooley, "The Great Escape," p. 55.

6. Clarke Canfield, "Dayton: Small Town's 'Been Found,'" *Portland Press Herald*, July 6, 1997, p. 7.

7. Quoted in Michael Janofsky, "Year's End Is No Holiday in Snow-Crazy Aspen," *NYT*, January 3, 1997, p. A8.

8. Jim Howe, Ed McMahon, and Luther Propst, *Balancing Nature and Commerce in Gateway Communities* (Washington, D.C.: Conservation Fund and Sonoran Institute, 1997), p. 6.

CHAPTER 6. WHAT IS WISE GROWTH?

1. Gregg Easterbrook, "Here Comes the Sun," *New Yorker*, April 10, 1995, p. 41.

2. William D. Ruckelshaus, *Scientific American*, September 1989, p. 38.

3. Speech reported by Reuters News Service, June 14, 1993.

4. *Commercial Appeal* (Memphis), January 9, 1995, p. 5B.

5. Timothy Egan, "Boomtown, U.S.A.," *NYT*, November 14, 1993, sec. 3, p. 1.

6. Sam Howe Verkovek, "Austin Rides a Winner: Technology," *NYT*, January 31, 1998, p. A7.

7. Lewis Carroll, *Alice's Adventures in Wonderland* (1865) (New York: Penguin Books, 1960), p. 64.

8. Frank Jossi, "Small Town Survival Strategies," *PL*, October 1997, p. 4.

9. Greg Low, "The Question of Sustainable Development," *Nature Conservancy*, January/February 1995, p. 13.

10. *Time*, December 8, 1997, p. 46.

CHAPTER 7. PLANNING, ZONING, AND LAND USE

1. Reid Ewing, *Best Development Practices* (Chicago: Planners Press, 1996), p. 83.

2. David M. Herszenhorn, "Personal Touch Draws Shoppers to Revitalized Downtowns," *NYT*, December 22, 1997, p. B1.

3. Quoted in Charles Lockwood, "Onward and Upward in Downtown Santa Monica," *PL*, September 1997, p. 16.

4. Quoted in Mary Fitzpatrick, "Conference Highlights Preservation as Economic Development Tool," *Preservation in Print*, April 1998, p. 22.

5. Michael A. Mantell, Stephen F. Harper, and Luther Propst, *Creating Successful Communities* (Washington, D.C.: Island Press, 1990), p. 202.

6. Fredric Howe, "The Garden Cities of England," *Scribner's Magazine*, October 1912, pp. 1–19.

260 *Notes to Pages 87–146*

7. *Regional Plan of New York and Its Environs* (New York: New York Regional Plan Association, 1929).

8. Jane Holtz Kay, *Asphalt Nation: How the Automobile Took Over America and How We Can Take It Back* (New York: Crown Publishers, 1997).

CHAPTER 8. RESOURCE PRESERVATION AND ENHANCEMENT

1. Surface Mining Control and Reclamation Act of 1977 (Public Law 95–87).

2. Chris Maser, *Sustainable Community Development: Principles and Concepts* (Delray Beach, Fla.: St. Lucie Press, 1997), p. 154.

3. Ibid., p. 157.

4. D. J. Chasan, *Up for Grabs, Inquiries into Who Wants What* (Seattle: Madrona, 1977), p. 133.

5. Rutherford H. Platt, "The 2020 Water Supply Study for Metropolitan Boston: The Demise of Diversion," *JAPA*, Spring 1995, p. 196.

6. Lewis Mumford, *The Culture of Cities* (New York: Harcourt, Brace and World, 1938), p. 5.

7. Mantell, Harper, and Propst, *Creating Successful Communities*, p. 86.

8. Quoted in Brenda Scheer and Wolfgang Preisler, *Design Review: Challenging Urban Aesthetic Control* (New York: Chapman & Hall, 1994), p. vii.

9. Robert A.M. Stern, *Houses* (New York: Monticelli Press, 1997), pp. 19, 11.

10. Scheer and Preisler, *Design Review*, p. viii.

11. Tony Hiss, *The Experience of Place* (New York: Knopf, 1990), p. 68.

12. See Donald C. Shoup, "Regulating Land Use at Sale: Public Improvement from Private Investment," *JAPA*, Summer 1996, p. 364.

13. James Brooke, "Rare Alliance in the Rockies Strives to Save Open Spaces," *NYT*, August 14, 1998, p. A18.

14. Quoted in Howe, McMahon, and Propst, *Balancing Nature and Commerce in Gateway Communities*, p. 21.

15. Quoted in Preston, "Battling Sprawl, State Buys Land for Open Space," p. B5.

16. Quoted in Robert Hanley, "A Tax Catches On in New Jersey," *NYT*, May 20, 1998, p. B1.

CHAPTER 9. SMART PUBLIC POLICY

1. For a good discussion of how to prepare a community report card, see Virginia W. Maclaren, "Urban Sustainability Reporting," *JAPA*, Spring 1996, p. 186.

2. Nico Calavita and Roger Caves, "Planners' Attitudes toward Growth: A Comparative Case Study," *JAPA*, Autumn 1994, p. 496.

3. William Reilly, ed., *The Use of Land: A Citizen's Policy Guide to Urban Growth* (New York: Crowell, 1973), p. 33.

4. Calavita and Caves, "Planners' Attitudes toward Growth," p. 491.

5. *A Vision* (Lincoln Center, Mass.: 1000 Friends of Massachusetts, 1990), p. 4.

6. For details, see facts and figures in Donovan D. Rypkema, *The Economics of Historic Preservation: A Community Leaders Guide* (Washington, D.C.: Preservation Press, 1995).

7. E. Lynn Stacy, *The Entrepreneurial Opportunity* (Mobile, Ala.: Institute of the Future South, 1997), p. 6.

8. Michael M. Phillips, "More Suburbs Find City Ills Don't Respect City Limits," *WSJ*, November 13, 1997, p. B1.

9. For a useful summary, see Samuel Nunn and Mark S. Rosentraub, "Dimensions of Interjurisdictional Cooperation," *JAPA*, Spring 1997.

10. *High Country News*, April 5, 1993, p. 3.

Chapter 10. Private and Nonprofit Initiatives

1. Brooke, "Rare Alliance in the Rockies Strives to Save Open Spaces," p. 1.

2. Quoted in ibid., p. A18.

Chapter 12. The Benefits of Wise Growth

1. Jane Gross, "Trinity College Leads Effort to Spark Hartford's Renewal," *NYT*, April 14, 1998, p. 1.

INDEX

Mount Vernon, Wash., 60, 62, 81
MSM Regional Council (N.J.), 226
Mucklow, C. J., 175
Mumford, Lewis, 146, 167
Muskegon, Mich., 54, 79
Myers, Phyllis, 177
Myrtle Beach, S.C., 26, 40

Nantucket, Mass., 177–178, 223
Nantucket Conservation Foundation,
    178
Napa, Calif., 23
Naples, Fla., 26, 40, 48, 49, 76, 80, 111
Nashua, N.H., 23, 55, 77, 79
Nashville, Tenn., 30, 33, 54, 80
National Association of Home
    Builders, 46
National Cattlemen's Beef Association,
    224
National City Lines, 13
National Environmental Policy Act
    (NEPA), 89, 157–158
National Heritage Area, 201
National Historic Preservation Act
    (NHPA), 89, 139
National Park Service, 120, 201, 202
National Parks and Conservation
    Association, 113
National Parks and Recreation Act, 202
National Register of Historic Places,
    139–141
National Trust for Historic
    Preservation, 139, 202
Natural Lands Trust, 144
natural resources, 85, 89; management,
    120–123; preservation and
    enhancement, 159–181, 231–232
Nature Conservancy, 130, 177, 178,
    179, 222
Nebraska, 70, 79, 163
    Lincoln, 55
    Omaha, 79
    York, 81
Needham, Mass., 98

Nevada, 53, 69, 70, 73, 125
    Clark County, 22
    Douglas County, 22, 107
    Elko, 62, 81
    Las Vegas, 25, 25, 26, 28, 29, 38, 39,
        40, 48, 49, 55, 69, 70, 73, 100,
        107, 125, 165, 173
    net population migration to, 18
    Nye County, 22
    Reno, 23
Newark, Del., 77
Newark, N.J., 11, 29, 214
New Hampshire, 80
    Concord, 61, 81
    Dover, 23
    Lebanon, 81
    Littleton, 81
    Manchester, 23, 55, 77, 79
    Nashua, 23, 55, 77, 79
    Plymouth, 81
    Portsmouth, 23, 79
    Rochester, 23
New Haven, Conn., 29, 64, 251
New Jersey, 33, 79, 80, 130, 176–177,
    196–197
    Atlantic City, 40, 151
    Bergen County, 30
    Cape May, 40
    East Rutherford, 91–92
    Fairlawn, 146
    Hunterdon County, 49
    Mercer County, 77, 226
    Middlesex County, 49, 226
    Monmouth County, 79
    Newark, 11, 29, 214
    Ocean County, 21, 79
    outmigrants from, 20
    Passaic County, 30
    Paterson, 194
    Princeton, 226
    Somerset County, 49, 226
    Somerville, 135–136
    Trenton, 77
New Mexico, 53, 55, 68, 73, 115, 165

urbanization, 12
Urban Land Institute (ULI), 184–185
Utah, 53, 55, 70, 71, 73, 115, 165
  Bluff, 70
  Ogden, 72, 79, 80
  Orem, 24, 26, 48, 49, 60, 78
  Park City, 68, 125
  Provo, 24, 26, 48, 49, 50, 60, 72, 78, 200
  St. George, 60, 62, 109–110
  Salt Lake City, 28, 29, 54, 60, 69, 70, 72, 73, 79, 80, 107, 125, 174, 200, 245
  Summit County, 19
  Washington County, 19, 22

Vail, Colo., 149
Vallejo, Calif., 23
Vancouver, British Columbia, 80
Vancouver, Wash., 79
Vaux, Calvert, 193
Ventura, Calif., 49
Venturi, Robert, 123
Vermont, 223
  Brattleboro, 81
  Rutland, 81
Vermont Land Trust, 223, 226
Vieux Carré (New Orleans, La.), 137, 167, 168
Virginia, 10, 47, 53, 56, 66, 79, 171
  Blacksburg, 174
  Charlottesville, 52, 77
  Culpeper, 81, 91
  Fredericksburg, 199
  Hampton, 194
  Harrisonburg, 81
  Loudoun County, 91
  Lynchburg, 77
  net population migration to, 18
  Newport News, 77
  Norfolk, 30, 77
  Petersburg, 77, 80
  Portsmith, 54
  Prince George County, 155

Prince William County, 155
Richmond, 39, 54, 77, 80
Roanoke, 77
Virginia Beach, 30, 54, 77
Winchester, 81
Virginia Beach, Va., 30, 54, 77
virtual firm, 41
Visions 2000 (Chattanooga, Tenn.), 124
Voith, Richard, 99

Waco, Tex., 217
Wall Street Journal, 46, 71, 98, 102
Wal-Mart, 65
Walt Disney Company, 169, 220
Walton County, Fla., 148
Warner Brothers, 66
Warren, Ohio, 24
Washington, 18, 73, 177
  Anacortes, 81
  Bellevue, 77, 79
  Bremerton, 80
  Everett, 77, 79
  King County, 162
  Longview, 61, 81
  Mount Vernon, 60, 62, 81
  Olympia, 49, 77
  Port Angeles, 61, 81
  Seattle, 11, 23, 29, 33, 36, 39, 50, 60, 69, 73, 74, 75, 76, 77, 79, 80, 95, 125, 132, 152, 166, 171, 180
  Tacoma, 26, 49, 77, 80, 156
  Vancouver, 79
  Wenatchee, 61, 81
Washington, D.C., 29, 47, 52, 54, 66, 77, 79, 99, 125, 135, 146, 155, 166, 167, 181, 197
Washington County, Utah, 19, 22
Waterbury, Conn., 64
water conservation, 163–166
Waterford, N.Y., 201
Waterloo, Iowa, 49
Watson, Kirk, 126
Waukesha, Wis., 80
wealth transfer, 31–32, 32, 33

About the Author

PETER WOLF is a nationally recognized authority on land planning, asset management, and urban policy. He manages his own investment advisory firm and is chairman of the Board of Trustees of the Van Alen Institute.

Wolf's award-winning books, *The Future of the City* (1974) and *Land in America* (1981), explain dynamic forces that have shaped the contemporary settlement pattern of the United States. Over the last two decades, he has observed, researched, and analyzed new trends that he predicts will have a dramatic impact on the most desirable communities, and investment within them, deep into the twenty-first century. His observations, suggestions, and predictions are reported in *Hot Towns*.

Born in New Orleans, he was educated at Yale, Tulane, and the Institute of Fine Arts, New York University, and resides in New York City. Distinguished as a Fulbright Fellow and winner of the Charles B. Shattuck Memorial Award of the National Research and Education Trust Fund, Dr. Wolf has been singled out as a scholar and author for individual honors by the Graham Foundation, the Ford Foundation, the American Federation of Arts, and the National Endowment for the Arts. The initial research for *Hot Towns* was funded by a fellowship awarded by the Graham Foundation for Advanced Studies in the Fine Arts.

Concurrent with other professional activities, Dr. Wolf has taught at Pratt Institute and New York University and as adjunct professor at Cooper Union. He also served for a decade as chairman of the Board of Fellows of the Institute for Architecture and Urban Studies.